SALVAGING SPENSER

Salvaging Spenser

Colonialism, Culture and Identity

Willy Maley
Lecturer in English
University of Glasgow

First published in Great Britain 1997 by
MACMILLAN PRESS LTD
Houndmills, Basingstoke, Hampshire RG21 6XS and London
Companies and representatives throughout the world

> This book is published in Macmillan's *Language, Discourse, Society* series
> Editors: Stephen Heath, Colin MacCabe and Denise Riley

A catalogue record for this book is available from the British Library.

ISBN 0–333–62942–6

First published in the United States of America 1997 by
ST. MARTIN'S PRESS, INC.,
Scholarly and Reference Division,
175 Fifth Avenue, New York, N.Y. 10010

ISBN 0–312–17234–6

Library of Congress Cataloging-in-Publication Data
Maley, Willy.
Salvaging Spenser : colonialism, culture, and identity / Willy
Maley.
p. cm. — (Language, discourse, society)
Includes bibliographical references and index.
ISBN 0–312–17234–6 (cloth)
1. Spenser, Edmund, 1552?–1599—Knowledge—Ireland. 2. National
characteristics, Irish, in literature. 3. Ireland–
–History—1558–1603—Historiography. 4. British—Ireland–
–History—16th century. 5. Language and culture—Ireland. 6. Group
identity in literature. 7. Colonies in literature. 8. Ireland—In
literature. 9. Renaissance—Ireland. I. Title. II. Series.
PR2367.I67M35 1997
821'.3—dc21   97–12088
                                                          CIP

This book is printed on paper suitable for recycling and made from fully managed and
sustained forest sources.

10   9   8   7   6   5   4   3   2   1
06   05   04   03   02   01   00   99   98   97

Printed in Great Britain by
The Ipswich Book Company Ltd
Ipswich, Suffolk

Contents

Acknowledgements

Every monograph is a polygraph. It must to some degree be co-authored, ghost-written, the work of many hands. Leaving aside the host of scholars whose work I have read and drawn on, and which no amount of bibliography, citing and footnoting can fully acknowledge, there are the major individual and institutional debts. I wish to thank my supervisor, Lisa Jardine, who started me on Spenser and Ireland at Cambridge in 1985. Andrew Hadfield, with whom I have collaborated in the past, has been an invaluable friend and guide. Thanks are due to the staff of Cambridge University Library, the British Library, and Glasgow University Library. I wish to thank my external and internal examiners – Richard Axton, Richard McCabe and Ciarán Brady – for constructive criticism at an early stage. My editor at Macmillan, Charmian Hearne, has shown great patience and understanding as deadlines were stockpiled. Some of this material has already appeared in print. Chapter 2 was published previously as 'Spenser's Irish English: Language and Identity in Early Modern Ireland', in *Studies in Philology* 91, 4 (1994), pp. 417–31; Chapter 6 appeared as 'How Milton and some contemporaries read Spenser's *View*', in Brendan Bradshaw *et al* (eds), *Representing Ireland: Literature and the Origins of Conflict, 1534–1660* (Cambridge: Cambridge University Press, 1993), pp. 191–208; and a version of Chapter 7 will appear in *Prose Studies* 19, 1 (1996), pp. 1–18. All of these essays appear here in a revised form.

Abbreviations

AHR	*American Historical Review*
ANQ	*American Notes and Queries*
BIHR	*Bulletin of the Institute of Historical Research*
BL	British Library, London
BN	*A Briefe Note of Ireland*
Cal. S. P. Ire.	*Calendar of State Papers, Ireland*
Cal. S. P. Scot.	*Calendar of State Papers, Scotland*
DNB	*Dictionary of National Biography*
EHR	*English Historical Review*
ELH	*English Literary History*
ELR	*English Literary Renaissance*
Eng. Misc.	*English Miscellany*
EUQ	*Emory University Quarterly*
FQ	*The Faerie Queene*
HJ	*Historical Journal*
HLQ	*Huntington Library Quarterly*
IER	*Irish Ecclesiastical Record*
IHR	*International History Review*
IHS	*Irish Historical Studies*
IMC	*Irish Manuscripts Commission, Dublin*
JBS	*Journal of British Studies*
JCHAS	*Journal of the Cork Historical and Archaeological Society*
JEGP	*Journal of English and Germanic Philology*
JEH	*Journal of Ecclesiastical History*
JGAHS	*Journal of the Galway Archaeological and Historical Society*
JHI	*Journal of the History of Ideas*
JKAHS	*Journal of the Kerry Archaeological and Historical Society*
JWCI	*Journal of the Warburg and Courtauld Institutes*
MLN	*Modern Language Notes*
MLQ	*Modern Language Quarterly*
MP	*Modern Philology*
NCWJ	*North Cork Writers Journal*
NM	*Neuphilologische Mitteilungen*
NMAJ	*North Munster Antiquarian Journal*
N&Q	*Notes and Queries*

OED	*Oxford English Dictionary*
PMLA	*Publications of the Modern Language Association of America*
PNR	*Poetry Nation Review*
P&P	*Past and Present*
PQ	*Philological Quarterly*
PRO	Public Record Office, London
Ren. Q.	*Renaissance Quarterly*
RES	*Review of English Studies*
RSAI	*Journal of the Royal Society of Antiquaries of Ireland*
RIA Proc.	*Proceedings of the Royal Irish Academy*
SAQ	*South Atlantic Quarterly*
SC	*The Shepheardes Calender*
SEL	*Studies in English Literature*
SHR	*Scottish History Review*
SP	*Studies in Philology*
TCBS	*Transactions of the Cambridge Bibliographical Society*
TCD	Trinity College, Dublin
TLS	*Times Literary Supplement*
TRHS	*Transactions of the Royal Historical Society*
TSLL	*Texas Studies in Language and Literature*
TWASAL	*Transactions of the Wisconsin Academy of Sciences, Arts, and Letters*
UCD	University College, Dublin
UJA	*Ulster Journal of Archaeology*
Variorum	*The Works of Edmund Spenser: A Variorum Edition*, eds Greenlaw *et al*, 10 vols, Baltimore, 1932–49
View	*A View of the Present State of Ireland*

Introduction:
We 'Other' Elizabethans

In volume one of *The History of Sexuality*, in the first chapter entitled 'We "Other" Victorians', Foucault reminds us of the ways in which we can retrospectively impose our own values on an earlier period, through an act of backward projection. Foucault speaks of a traditional view of Victorian sexuality which he designates 'the repressive hypothesis'.[1] Foucault opposes, or juxtaposes, another way of seeing things, which he calls an 'incitement to discourse'. Thus what we have inherited as prudery and denial is transformed into a compulsion to speak, an obligation to explain oneself with regard to one's sexuality. Part of Foucault's project here is to argue that, far from being a time of sexual repression, the Victorian period witnessed an intense interest in sexuality, an obsession that filled every available discursive space. Thus Foucault can conclude that something more than sexual liberation is at stake in sexual politics. Indeed, it is almost as though the emphasis on sexuality was a displacement of other kinds of politics, including class. The Victorian sexual warded off in some way the awesome materiality of the Victorian social.

Something similar could be said of the investment in Ireland in contemporary cultural studies and in the periods within which a specifically Irish focus is visible. In *Inventing Ireland*, Declan Kiberd writes of the suppression of Irish material around 1600, and remarks that 'already Ireland was turning into the official English Unconscious'.[2] This should be read against the well-known remark by James on visiting Whitehall shortly after his accession: 'We had more ado with Ireland than all the world besides.'[3] The risk implicit in holding to the repressive hypothesis is that the desire to speak of the unspeakable, to represent the unrepresentable, becomes an incitement to discourse that may ultimately serve the same purpose as the original act of censorship upon which the repressive hypothesis depends. There is a certain undeniable *frisson* in approaches to Spenser that take Ireland seriously as source and context. Censorship only serves to enhance this charge. In the *View*, Spenser derives Ireland's name 'Sacra Insula' from 'sacra' for 'accursed', rather than 'sacred'.

But in Spenser criticism the dual meaning has dominated criticism, the sacred and accursed.

There is a double jeopardy here. On the one hand, there is the risk that Spenser is made the sole scapegoat for all of the negative stereotypes of the Irish in the Renaissance, and, on the other, that he is exonerated due to aspersions being cast on his authorship of the treatise most likely to damn him. Between too much weight and no weight at all there is some careful negotiating to be done. Not least of the problems with seeing Spenser as anti-Irish in any simple sense is the fact that this perception ignores the Scottish and Old English contexts of the *View*. 'Spenser and Ireland' can act as a decoy, taking us off the scent of something larger, a Blatant Beast that remains at large, in the form of an inclusive British identity that has its roots in Spenser's day and is foreshadowed in his work. Seamus Deane speaks of Spenser as an exponent of 'British nationalism' in the same breath as 'Sir John Davies, Sir William Temple, Coleridge, Carlyle, Arnold, Enoch Powell, Ian Paisley'.[4] But surely the views of these authors cannot be subsumed under such a heading? To do so is to gloss over the historical discontinuities that are exposed in Spenser's texts. Despite all of the essays on Spenser and Elizabethan Ireland, and my own insistence that, within the British state and its dominions, we are Elizabethans still, I shall argue that Spenser's greatest impact was on Caroline and Cromwellian Ireland, and that the boundaries of 'Spenser and Ireland' have to be extended *chronologically*, to include, at one end, the 1570s and *The Shepheardes Calender*, and, at the other, the post-1633 impact of the *View*; and *geographically*, to incorporate Scotland.

'Spenser and Ireland' is a topic that elicits personal responses, as well as political ones. Just as the country is held to have had an adverse effect on Spenser, so critical biography becomes a dominant mode in responding to the poet's Irish experiences. Thus Colin MacCabe expresses the predicament of the Irish reader faced with an epic whose author is deeply implicated in colonial violence: 'I find it difficult to read *The Faerie Queene* without remembering that Spenser urged the most brutal policies in Grey's administration and wrote of his delight in seeing the Irish starve.'[5] Thus Tom Healy tells of a seminar that reached a similar conclusion: 'A student of mine in a Spenser class which read *A Present View* suggested it seemed peculiar to be reading a piece by an author commonly hailed as one of the great writers of the English Renaissance putting forward views which makes him a type of war criminal within a twentieth-century perspective.'[6] But war criminals are only tried on the losing side.

Andrew Hadfield recounts an incident that can be juxtaposed with the responses of MacCabe and Healy: 'At a conference I attended in 1985, entitled "Spenser and Ireland", a student stood up at the end and thanked the speakers for helping her to appreciate that there may well have been some interest in studying a figure she had previously regarded only as the brutal butcher of her ancestors.'[7] The interpretations are no more sophisticated than the conclusions.

Spenser has long functioned as a 'take-the-blame', a scapegoat, onto whom all of the anxieties and tensions around the representation of Ireland and the Irish have been projected. Edward Said, for example, has asserted that 'it is generally true that literary historians who study the great sixteenth-century poet Edmund Spenser, for example, do not connect his bloodthirsty plans for Ireland, where he imagined a British army virtually exterminating the native inhabitants, with his poetic achievement or with the history of British rule over Ireland, which continues today'.[8] Said says 'for example', but Spenser is much more than an example, he is *the* example, an exemplary figure, and he is constantly made an example of.

Pace Said, I shall argue that literary historians have been only too eager to connect Spenser's Irish vocation with his poetic career, and in ways that are often hackneyed, stereotyped or dogmatic. Later, Said, speaking of the 'high age of imperialism', refers to 'an amazingly persistent cultural attitude toward Ireland as a place whose inhabitants were a barbarian and degenerate race ... to whose formation such impressive figures as Edmund Spenser and David Hume contributed in very large measure'.[9] Now, such figures, for example, have to be distinguished, just as imperialism and colonialism have to be separated. Spenser attacks the English for degenerating. He calls the Irish barbarous through analogy with the Scots, and the Scot David Hume is a bird of a different feather.

Elsewhere, Said observes: 'The idea of English racial superiority became ingrained; so humane a poet and gentleman as Edmund Spenser in his *View of the Present State of Ireland* (1596) was boldly proposing that since the Irish were barbarian Scythians, most of them should be exterminated.'[10] The move is a familiar one. Spenser is gentle and humane, so why was he saying such terrible things about the Irish? The same strategy was employed by Christopher Hill in speaking of Milton's views of Ireland.[11] Ireland diseases the mind of the humane and gentle poet. This sets up a division between poetry – as the site of the humane – and Ireland, as the site of a process of dehumanization that affects native and colonizer alike. Ireland becomes the take-the-blame of the take-the-blame.

How do we reconcile the 'gentle' poet with the man accused of beating Lord Roche's servants and making corrupt bargains in order to force the Old English noble from his land?[12] Simple. We only have to recognize gentility as a social drive rather than a connoter of sensitivity. As Ray Heffner comments: 'Spenser as clerk of the Council of Munster, the governing body of that Province, was in a good position to beat out Lord Roche in the courts and to hold the land against him.'[13]

Spenser's *View* remains one of the most controversial documents in the corpus of a major canonical figure, arguably the most cited and least read text in a certain strand of English literary history. According to Said: 'Since Spenser's tract on Ireland, a whole tradition of British and European thought has considered the Irish to be a separate and inferior race, usually unregenerately barbarian, often delinquent and primitive.'[14] In fact, Spenser's tract drew on all of the 'British and European' thought that considered the Irish to be a separate and inferior race. Said's efforts to distinguish between Spenser as British imperialist and Yeats as nationalist require deconstruction. Joyce would have seen the complicity between the two.

In 1580 Sir Henry Sidney wrote to Lord Grey: 'if you will this year go about the extirping of those cannibals in Goulranell'.[15] From the famous passage on the Munster famine to the recollection of the actions of a foster mother at the execution of her foster child, cannibalism lurks at the edges of Spenser's conception of the Irish. In May 1583 Sir William Stanley wrote to Ormond: 'The poorest sort hath been driven to eat the dead men's bodies which was cast away in shipwreck.'[16] These stories for the consumption of an English readership point to a profound cultural cannibalism.

The word 'salvage', used by Spenser in *The Faerie Queene* and the *View*, has connotations of law and land, being both littoral and literary. The *OED* defines 'salvage' as property retrieved from shipwreck or recycled material, from the medieval Latin *salvagium*, anchored in the Latin verb *salvare*, to save. 'Selvage' is defined as an 'edge of cloth so woven that it cannot unravel; border of different material or finish along edge of cloth intended to be removed or hidden; edgeplate of lock with opening for the bolt', derived from Middle English 'self' and 'edge'. Salvaging is thus a process of self-fashioning. Immerito, Colin Clout, hobgoblin run away with the garland from Apollo, Peregrine and Sylvanus – the personae of Spenser are strange, alien, foreign.

Selfhood in Ireland was a borderline guise, always in danger of being dismantled. As David Baker contends: 'Selves slipped in and out of categories which should fix them, and the declarations of these shifting selves took on different meanings within the conventions of different legal codes simultaneously.'[17] Spenser played with the several senses of the word, producing finally a myth of an Irish land and nation, bordering and barbaric, originally belonging to England, and now awaiting recovery. The modern view of early modern Ireland as a 'Tudor borderland' owes much to Spenser's linguistic colonialism.[18]

Andrew Hadfield has dryly alluded to Spenser's Irish estate as 'an ivy covered ruin surrounded by an electric fence which the irate owner turns up to full strength to repel Spenser groupies'.[19] However, in a recent issue of the *Spenser Newsletter*, there was the following report:

Kilcolman Project. Sponsored by EarthCorps, Dr. Eric Klingelholfer. Mercer U, will direct three 'teams' in a project at Kilcolman Castle between 4 July and 14 August 1993. Based at a rented house with a cook 30 kilometers from Cork, teams will split their time between surveying and mapping Kilcolman's castle grounds; using magnetic resistivity to detect buried features; and clearing the castle tower of ivy, sampling masonry and mortar, and conserving it. Team I: 4–17 July; Team II: 18–31 July; Team III: 1–14 August.[20]

What were they looking for? Spenser's reputation? The lost manuscripts of *The Faerie Queene*? The charred bones of the child who allegedly perished in the fire? A scorched manuscript decomposing in a foxhole? And can't they cook? What if Team I had found something? Would they have informed Team II, thus rendering their efforts redundant?

The search for literary remains is by no means an eccentric occupation. That salvage soil can still bear fruit. Jean Brink, in one of a number of valuable articles on Spenser, has drawn on 'salved Chancery proceedings'.[21] Patricia Coughlan observes that the *View* posits 'an assumption that the Irish are a "salvage" nation, who represent an irredeemable otherness and are impermeable to authority', and that Ireland is a country 'whose inhabitants are "Scythian" in their propensity to wander with their cattle-herds from place to place and thus defy the imposition of civil order'.[22] But of course the relationship between 'salvage' and 'Scythian' is rather more complex than Coughlan and others would have us believe. The

Scythians are Scots, the Scots are savages, and the Scots are in Ulster. Savagery and Scottishness are one and the same thing. Moreover 'salvage', in its punning sense, can mean recoverable or 'redeemable'. Coughlan does go on to note that there are in *The Faerie Queene* 'some "salvage" characters about whose development to fully human status he can express a possibility, and who are basically benign in spite of living outside the bounds of normal society'.[23] 'Savage', no less than 'gentle', is a complex term, one whose connotations change depending on the cultural and historical context. Tom Healy observes that: 'In both *A View of the Present State of Ireland* and *The Faerie Queene* Spenser reveals his anxieties about the resilience of the savage, the apparent inability of England to deal effectively with it.'[24] Part of the problem is that, as Irenius notes in the *View*, it is but the other day since England grew civil, and so savagery is never far away. Spenser is the Salvage Man in this double sense, the salvageable and the compulsively barbarous. But where Artegall, in disguise at Satyrane's tournament in Book IV, has his shield emblazoned with the legend 'Salvagesse sans finesse' (wildness without art), Spenser's wildness is his art, the fruit of savage soil, a record of a barbarism that is, finally, the poet's own. The 'studied barbarity' of *The Shepheardes Calender*, mocked by Samuel Johnson, is Spenser's art. He studied barbarity and his art is barbaric, from the Greek 'barbarismos', meaning 'speak like a foreigner', or 'barbaros' for 'foreign'.

Kenneth Borris underlines the ambivalence of the Salvage Man: 'Ultimately ... the Salvage's significance may be compared to that of Una's lion, her satyrs, and Satyrane: he embodies fundamental human strengths, while also indicating their limits.'[25] According to Andrew Hadfield: '"Savage" and "sacred" are perhaps the foundational puns which link Spenser's poetry and prose, simultaneously expressing the hope of salvation and religious purity, and the fear of disintegration and damnation. Whilst Spenser's work deals with the question of transformation – salvaging what has been lost – such puns point in two directions at once, articulating the horror that what has to be transformed might well be precisely that which resists transformation.'[26]

In the dedicatory sonnets to *The Faerie Queene* Spenser speaks of his poem as the fruit of 'salvage soyle'. Something can always be salvaged. Savage and salvage, like culture and colonialism, share the same roots. Salvage comes from medieval Latin *salvagium*, from Latin *salvare*, to save. But what is saved from a shipwreck? Why, the timber of which the ship is made, hence 'silvage', in some renderings. Save and continue. To salvage is to salve, to save wood, from which paper is made. A salvable vessel is one which is still usable. In the early modern period 'Salvage' is an archaic form of savage, from French *sauvage*, in Old French *salvage*, from Latin *salvaticus*, woodland, wild, from silva, wood, forest, as in Sylvanus. There are those who cannot see the wood for the trees. Spenser's work is the fruit of savage soil. To say to Spenser: 'Come down off that cross. We need the wood in order to save and print.'[27] I would like to invoke another early modern term – 'selvage', or 'selvedge'. 'Selvedge', an amalgam of 'self' and 'edge', is the 'edge of a piece of woven material finished in such a manner as to prevent the ravelling out of the weft. Also, a narrow strip or list at the edge of a web of cloth, which is not finished like the rest of the cloth, being intended to be cut off or covered by the seam when the material is made up.' The 'selvedge' is the margin between Self and Other, somewhere between salvage and savage. Perhaps we have the chance of salving something more than desiderata.

Roland Smith has shown Spenser's debt to Irish sources in his tale of the two sons of Milesio in Book V, the brothers who argue over a treasure chest salvaged from the sea.[28] How is this salvage to be divided? Whose claim to ownership is to be upheld? Artegall decides in favour of salvage rather than original ownership:

> For what the mighty Sea hath once possest,
> And plucked quite from all possessors hand,
> Whether by rage of waves, that never rest,
> Or else by wracke, that wretches hath distrest,
> He may dispose by his imperiall might ... (V.19.2–6)

Salvaging Spenser does not mean going back to some original source, but rather entails sifting laboriously through the items of wreckage washed ashore.

'Spenser and Ireland' is such an easy coupling. The same small pool of incriminating quotations circulates among critics, drawn chiefly from Renwick's accessible edition of 1970, complete with modernized spelling and spellbinding moralizing. There is a glibness employed by critics on the topic of 'Spenser and Ireland'. There is also a tendency in recent approaches to the subject to dismiss too readily the efforts of earlier critics. This is then a general rehearsal of fierce wars of interpretation, and a salvaging of Spenserian criticism as well as Spenser's corpus. Those notes and queries, reviews and rejoinders, observations and comments tucked away in obscure corners are here brought to book. This is an act of salvaging. I come not to bludgeon Spenser, but to appraise him.

The early modern period in England witnessed a cultural revolution in English society which had as its concomitant a colonial revolution in Ireland. Ireland's original English ruling class was supplanted by a new generation of English settlers. The Irish experience had a singular impact on English culture and society, an impact seldom registered either in modern English histories or in Renaissance literary theory. The work of Edmund Spenser is intimately bound up with the English experience in early modern Ireland. Critics continue to limit coverage of that experience to questions of biographical and geographical detail, ignoring the wider implications of the Irish colonial struggle for English Renaissance culture.

The only published book-length study on the subject of Spenser and Ireland to date is Pauline Henley's *Spenser in Ireland*.[29] One anonymous reviewer of the day was in no doubt as to the worth of Henley's historiography: 'she must sharpen her pen again if she is to give us that interpretation of Ireland's Spenser and Spenser's Ireland which we need'.[30] The reviewer's assertion that the *View* ought to be read, not for its political relevance to the present, but for its prosaic relation to the past, its 'antiquarian value', is the predictable response of someone for whom history and literature are separate spheres of study which do not admit of anything as obtrusive and divisive as politics.

The argument of this book is fairly simple. Broadly, my contention is that Spenser's texts were produced within the context of a peculiar colonial struggle in Ireland between, not just two English communities, but two concepts of Englishness, two kinds of English culture, and that this conflict has to be viewed within a wider British context, in relation to what historians have come to call the 'British Problem'. The intractability of Spenser's texts is due, at least in part, to the complexity of the Irish colonial situation.

I offer new textual analyses of Spenser's three major works, and seek to establish, for the first time, an intimate association between *The Shepheardes Calender* (1579) and contemporary Irish politics. Sandwiched between two strangely similar texts – the Irish section of Holinshed's *Chronicles* (1577), and John Derricke's *Image of Irelande* (1581) – the *Calender* has an extremely problematic relation to New English colonial history. This innovative pastoral poem is conventionally considered to be engaged in promoting Protestantism, but has not hitherto been regarded as adverting to the quandary of

Elizabethan planters as they encountered, in Ireland, an older generation of predominantly Catholic English settlers. Exploring issues of language, genre and community, the chapter indicates that the February Eclogue, which deals most immediately with the generational struggle here adumbrated, can be taken as a literary analogue for the contemporary historical configuration of forces in Elizabethan Ireland.

I then try to present new insights on *The Faerie Queene*. The focus here is on the question of English sovereignty in Ireland as it manifests itself in Spenser's epic poem. On the one hand, the physical division of the English throne implicit in the Irish viceroyalty is adverted to. On the other hand, Ireland's ambiguous status, being neither kingdom nor colony but both at once, is outlined. These separations and contradictions, it is argued, suggest further permutations to be derived from recent excellent work on the Elizabethan subject and the Spenserian text.

There follows a series of essays on Spenser's Irish dialogue, beginning with the reception of the *View* following its publication in 1633, with specific reference to its status as a point of reference for authors of opposing views in the pamphlet controversies of the 1640s and beyond. The next chapter is an attempt to unravel a Scottish strand in Spenser's work, centring on his prose treatise, while maintaining that England's northern neighbour exerts a powerful influence on Spenser throughout his career. The final chapter, by way of a conclusion, rehearses the recent debate on censorship of the *View*, an issue that threatens to enact another form of suppression. Once more we are back with the aporia opened up by Foucault.

Spenser has suffered perhaps more than any other figure in the canon of English literature from 'history', and in particular, from 'Irish history'. My own feeling is that it has been a glaring present rather than a guilty past which has exerted the greatest pressure on perceptions of the poet, popular and professional. Readers all too aware of Ireland's troubles immediately link Spenser's Ireland with all that is dark and negative in his work. The spectre of Ireland haunts the texts of Edmund Spenser. The Irish legacy continues to determine the readership of the *View* and Book V of *The Faerie Queene*. We know that Irish historians will come to Spenser for evidence of his role in the Elizabethan plantation process. We know that English literary critics will in the main judiciously avoid these texts, preferring to draw a discrete veil over Ireland's Spenser, and over experiences which, I have argued, shaped all of his major compositions from *The Shepheardes Calender* to the *Briefe Note*.

Those still scouring the bog around Spenser's Kilcolman estate for traces of Spenser may never find what they are looking for. My aim in this book is to salvage something. Richard Rambuss has argued that Spenser's life and career are characterized by secrecy: 'Secrecy circulates through and traverses nearly all of Spenser's texts, and it provides the deep structure of those texts.'[31] The secret of Spenser and Ireland is arguably secreted within the double bind of an insidious and self-perpetuating censorship and an insatiable desire to know the colonial space inside out. The *View* speaks of Ireland in terms of 'some secret scourge which shall by her come unto England'.[32] This has to be balanced by a secret advantage, in the shape of cultural capital. Salvaging Spenser means attending to, and trying to negotiate, the deep complicity that exists between the repressive hypothesis and the incitement to discourse. It also means 'surveying and mapping', in order to 'detect buried features'. It is, finally, an exercise in 'clearing' and 'conserving'.

1

'Who knowes not Colin Clout?': *The Shepheardes Calender* as Colonial Text

I THE GENERALL ARGUMENT OF THE WHOLE BOOKE

In this chapter – and the one that follows – I want to argue for an Irish context for the earliest of Spenser's major works, one which allows it to be seen within a broad colonial milieu. Readers of *The Shepheardes Calender* are rarely asked to consider the poem in relation to Ireland. This is to be expected, since it predates in the minds of most critics any serious implication of the poet in Irish affairs. A minority of specialists have insisted on an earlier date, accepting as autobiographical Spenser's recollection in the *View* of the execution of Murrogh O'Brien in Limerick on 1 July 1577.[1] Other critics doubt the verity of this anecdote in the absence of corroborating evidence.[2]

In 1933, Raymond Jenkins, in the light of manuscript proof of Spenser's presence at Smerwick at the time of Grey's Massacre, asked if we need any longer doubt the historicity of the experiences recounted by Spenser in the *View*.[3] Paul McLane has proposed that Spenser was a possible courier in November 1579, carrying letters from London to Limerick for the Lord Justice, Sir William Pelham, and this proposition is made all the more credible when placed alongside W. H. Welply's observation that a relative of the poet's was apparently installed as constable of Limerick at this time.[4] There is a further piece of tantalizing circumstantial evidence. Leicester's inclusion, on 23 November 1579, in a Privy Council select committee 'appointed by her majesty's special commandment to consult of the affairs of Ireland', suggests that the Earl was actively involved in the government of that country at a time when Spenser was enjoying his patronage.[5]

Critics have variously underlined the visual, vocative and vocational aspects of *The Shepheardes Calender*. Richard Helgerson has viewed the *Calender* as a supreme instance of literary self-promotion. Ruth Samson Luborsky has maintained that the eclogues, complete with woodcuts, create a collage effect. Michael McCanles has pointed to the poem's editorial effacement in literary history: 'It is part of the fiction of *The Shepheardes Calender* that E. K.'s glosses are not part of the fiction.' Richard Mallette has compared the *Calender* to Joyce's *A Portrait of the Artist as a Young Man*. David L. Miller has argued that Spenser was intent upon 'the making of a community'. Roscoe Parker found Spenser's 'specialized diction' less remarkable than the 'studied barbarity' of the Johnsonian tradition would have it. Marie-Sofie Røstvig contends that the poem's topical allusions have dated it for the modern reader. Bruce Smith has drawn our attention to Spenser's complex confusion of genres.[6]

Paul Alpers has written of a 'domain of lyric', a metaphor of literary independence, related to the legal concept of *demesne*. Alpers is concerned primarily with 'aesthetic' or 'imaginary space'. He adverts to the *OED* definition of *demesne*, as land held 'mediately or immediately from the king'.[7] Extending the emphases on career and domain, I wish to argue for a more historically concrete manifestation of the vocational and territorial motifs foregrounded by such recent work.

My own method of exposition corresponds closely to Spenser's preferred mode of historical inquiry – anachronistic, probabilistic, positioned. I will cite, and often, from contemporary works:

> but unto them besides I adde mine owne readinge and out of the[m] both together, with comparison of times, likewise of manners & customes, affinity of words and names, properties of natures, & uses, resemblances of rites & ceremonies, monuments of Churches and Tombes, and many other like circumstances, I doe gather a likelyhood of truth, not certainly affirming anything, but by conferring of times, language, monuments, and such like, I doe hunt out a probability of things, which I leave to your judgement to believe or refuse.[8]

This eclecticism allows new insights to coexist peaceably with established scholarship, without that reductive one-sidedness which disfigures much academic debate.

II FROM GENERATION TO GENERATION

Insofar as it centres on the issue of generational conflict as a major motif in *The Shepheardes Calender*, the present critique is in line with recent writings on the poem.[9] Social historians have posited the issue of generation as a social division comparable to the more traditional differences of class and gender.[10] Keith Thomas warns against the decontextualization of age, its dilution as a universal, unchanging social factor:

> Of all divisions in human society, those based on age appear the most natural and the least subject to historical change ... Yet there is nothing constant about the social meaning of age.[11]

The emphasis on degeneration and regeneration is familiar to readers as a stock Renaissance theme threaded through each quarter of the *Calender*.[12] The attention to competition for favour at court is equally familiar.[13]

Where, however, traditional readings confine those generational tensions to the perennial debate between Youth and Age, historicizing it as generally symptomatic of a growing rift between the Elizabethan younger generation and its conservative peers, or as an account of the Reformation which cautions against throwing out the spiritual baby with the bath water of superstition, my reading takes up the issue of generation in colonial Elizabethan Ireland. Still turning upon issues of placement and patronage, and retaining the useful insights into a religious allegory which stresses continuity as well as change, my reading points to a specific political dimension to the poem which has hitherto been underdeveloped.

Louis Montrose has argued that:

> Tensions between generations and between cultural values that are observable in later Elizabethan society are mirrored in the uneasy mixture of two currents within the *Calender*.[14]

Nicholas Dawtrey is attributed in Bryskett's *Discourse of Civill Life* with this speech:

> I have knowne, and know at this day some young men, who at 18.yeeres of age are of sounder judgement and more setled behaviour, then many, not of 25.yeeres old onely, but of many moe, yea then some that are greyheaded with age.[15]

If there was 'no room at the top' in England for the younger generation of Elizabethans, then Ireland permitted such 'disdainfull younkers' to make space for themselves abroad.[16] It displaced social and generational tensions.

The publication of Holinshed's *Chronicles* in 1577 broadcast to England's 'learned throng' what had hitherto been a commonplace confined to court circles:

> Againe, the verie English of birth, conversant with the savage sort of that people become degenerat, and as though they had tasted of Circes poysoned cup, are quite altered. Such force hath education to make or marre.[17]

Stanyhurst's obsession with the purity of the pale is not the first printed protest against 'degeneration'. Five years earlier, a New English text harped on the same potential disincentive to prospective planters: 'This degenerating and daily decay of the English manners by little and little in the countrey, discorageth those that have not perfectly wayed all that is aforesaid, to attempt any new enterprise.'[18] The author of this piece of planter propaganda refers to 'reform' in a very specific context, meaning 'the whole countrey to be replenished with Englishe men'.

What Sir Thomas Smith, a prominent patron of the New English, and Stanyhurst, a principal proprietor of the Pale, share is a common commitment to reforming, educating and modernizing the English colonial system in Ireland. Like the anonymous Old English author of the 1550s, they ask: 'How can Ireland prosper that is thus divided?'[19] The answers they arrived at were very different. Stanyhurst advocated education and the extension of the Pale via a peaceful process of Anglicization, whilst Smith favoured a programme of plantation. None among the English doubted that the lordship was in dire need of reforming. The question was, whether the regeneration of the English presence in Ireland should depend upon the injection of fresh blood or the revival of the old strain.

III THE CAMBRIDGE CONNECTION

Spenser spent some seven years in Cambridge, from his admission as a sizar, or poor scholar, on 20 May 1569, to his graduation in 1576. As a young MA, it would have been difficult to predict the future elevation to gentry status afforded him just over a decade later by the acquisition of a considerable estate in Ireland. How did a young man of humble origins and modest means come to secure the appointment of Clerk of the Council of Munster, the linchpin of the germinal provincial presidencies which were the legacy of Sidney's second term of office as viceroy? The conventional dismissal of this post as a sinecure, or as a part-time preferment which allowed Spenser time to write, does not quite square with what we know of the office.[20] The modern idea of a clerk as an insignificant pen pusher is responsible for the popular misconception that Spenser was frustrated in his ambitions and aspirations in Ireland.[21]

How did Spenser achieve what was, by contemporary standards, an enviable position within the New English colonial hierarchy, only five years after graduating from Pembroke Hall? To answer this question, it is necessary to take a brief detour through a parallel career, that of Barnaby Googe (1540–1594), a fellow graduate of Cambridge who came to hold a similarly high office in the Ireland of the 1580s. Googe was educated at New College Oxford and Christ's College, Cambridge. He appears to have taken a degree at neither institution. He was patronized by his kinsman, William Cecil, later Lord Burghley, and owes his incorporation into the English literary canon to a short volume of pastoral pieces published in 1563.

Googe's Irish experiences have received scant attention.[22] He went to Ireland in 1572, and was appointed Provost Marshal of Connaught in 1582, the year that Spenser became Clerk of the Council of Munster. Googe served in this post for three years. Ireland offered valuable career opportunities to men of his class and education. As one critic observes, for 'Googe and young men of his type in Elizabethan England, literary men, soldier-poets, pamphleteers, most of them, Ireland was a veritable Eldorado'.[23] Paul Parnell, in an article suggestively entitled 'Barnabe Googe: A Puritan in Arcadia', underlines his 'attempt to make the pastoral English and Protestant'.[24] More recently, Mark Eccles has plotted out Googe's life in fine detail, referring to Googe's compliment to 'learned Master Bale'.[25] Like his predecessors, though, Eccles refuses to relate his subject's work – reform treatises, pastoral eclogues, a farming manual – to the Irish colonial situation. This stems from the fact that Googe's departure for Ireland comes after the *Eglogues, Epytaphes, and Sonnettes* (1563) for which he is best known to literary critics. Interest in him often stops at the agreed opinion that his 'Cupido Conquered', a long, awkward

poem placed at the end of his pastoral collection, directly influenced
Spenser's 'Court of Cupid' in Book VI of *The Faerie Queene*.

I want to suggest that the Protestant reform treatises, the pastoral
poems and the books on husbandry are all part of the same colonial
genre. Their conjunction was achieved in a unique way by Spenser in
The Shepheardes Calender. There is no doubt about *The Foure Bookes of
Husbandry* (1577) dedicated to the late Lord Deputy of Ireland, Sir
William Fitzwilliam, Sidney's predecessor, then in semi-retirement
at his country house in Milton, Northamptonshire being a colonial
tract, taking the term 'colonial' in its widest application. Specific
references to arable and pastoral innovation include praise of Nicholas
Malby, then military governor of Connaught, who 'published a cure
for a foundered horse in 1576', and Richard Bingham, Malby's
successor.[26]

Since Bale, the English radical reform treatise occupied a special
position in relation to Ireland, as did the English radical reformer. As
Barnaby Rich put it in 1615, after forty years of service in Ireland, 'thos
wordes that in Englande would be brought wythin the compasse of
treason, they are accounted wyth us in Ireland for ordynary table
taulke'.[27] Rich had in mind the seditious statements of Irish Catholics,
but the same freedom of speech applied to English *arcana imperii*.

The Popish Kingdome (1570) is Googe's most decisive instance of
pronounced Protestant propaganda. He appended to it another work
of its original author, Thomas Kirchmeyer, *The Spiritual husbandrie*,
'which I long before translated'. He justified the rudeness of his
translation in the dedication to Elizabeth on the grounds that it was
'chiefely made for the benefite of the common, simpler sorte'.[28] It is
significant that Googe's 'puritan' compositions cease when he is
transported to Ireland in 1574, as part of the doomed effort of the first
Earl of Essex to plant Antrim.

Googe's *Foure Bookes of Husbandry* (1577) was a translation of Conrad
Heresbach's *Rei rusticae libri quatuor* (Cologne, 1570), a major manifesto
for the agrarian revolution which transformed the landscapes of early
modern Europe.[29] Far from Church and Court, Cono, the retired civil
servant, contemplates the country life as an ideal alternative to the
life of institutions, regal and religious. His staged withdrawal is of
course a stock Renaissance trope. First for the court:

Surely I must confesse I have taken a happy way, yf these goddes
of the Earth would suffer me to enjoy suche happinesse, that have

bequeathed the troublesome and ambitious life of the Court to the bottome of the Sea.

Then for the Church:

> For my part (without vaunt be it spoken,) I have service every day at certaine appointed houres, where preacheth to me dayly the Prophetes, the Apostles, Basil, Christostome, Nazianzen, Cyril, Ciprian, Ambrose, Austen, and other excellent preachers, whom I am sure I heare with greater profite, then yf I shoulde heare your sir John lacklatines and foolishe felowes in your Churches.

Cono goes on to suggest that nature is itself a library, and he and his servants enjoy daily opportunities to 'read the woonderfull woorkmanship of God'.[30] We recognize here the familiar classical and medieval motif of the good life of rural retreat as a covert critique of court culture, adumbrated in *Piers Plowman* and, most famously, in Virgil's Eclogue I.[31]

If one can press for a reading of Googe's various translations of continental Protestant literature, alongside his preoccupation with the modernization of the countryside, which highlights their strategic intervention in Irish colonial politics, what of the *Eglogues*? Aside from the allusion to Bale, is there any basis for arguing that their composition, all of twelve years prior to Googe's known connection with Ireland, was connected with events in the Irish colony? I shall argue that there is, and that their implication in the Irish colonial milieu surfaces in 'Cupido Conquered', the poem which has been handed down to us as a recognized Spenserian source.

'Cupido Conquered' is an allegory of rural rebellion suppressed by royal power. The narrator succumbs to sleep in a tranquil rural spot, where the sounds of the countryside appeal to him more than music:

> I rather judge the thracian wold,
> His Harpe wherewith he played,
> Have erst a way as one whom Ire,
> Had utterly dismayed.[32]

Note the symbol of the 'Harpe', and the play on the proper name of 'Ire'. Presently, the narrator has a dream in the tradition of the medieval vision. The dreamer is transported by a ghostly guide to an inhospitable region, and he complains thus of his new situation:

Unhappy Wretche, I wolde I hadde,
his Person heare in hand,
Then shuld I wreak mine Ire of him,
that brought me to this Land.

This pun on Ireland, as a 'Land of Ire', is a familiar feature of
contemporary English colonial discourse. John Derricke refers to
Ireland's troubles as 'her exceadyng Ire'. Punning on the name of Rory
Og O'More, 'a wretched Roge', he has him apologize to his own
country thus: 'Wo maie I be, for moving her to Ire.'[33] Sir John Davies,
in his *Discovery*, uses it to distinguish the New English colony from
its Old English predecessor:

> So as we may well conceive a hope, that Ireland (which heerto fore
> might properly be called the Land of Ire, because the Irascible
> power was predominant there, for the space of 400. yeares together)
> will from henceforth prove a Land of Peace and Concorde.[34]

The anonymous author of the 'Dialogue of Sylvanus and Peregrine'
(1599) opens with the same play on words:

> Sylvan: In Ireland man? Oh what a Country of wrath is that, It hath
> not the addicon of the syllable Ire in vayne.[35]

As far as I know, no other critic has placed 'Cupido Conquered' in
its proper Irish context. Its use of the Diana and Orpheus myths
assumes greater significance in the light of this contextualization.

I think that the Googe poem, with its untidy allegorical
representation of the subjection of Shane O'Neill, brought to the
Elizabethan court as part of a major publicity coup by Robert Dudley,
later Earl of Leicester, against his rival Sussex, the Hipolitus of the
piece, suggests that Ireland constituted a pastoral location par
excellence for the projection of the radical reforming impulse of
'puritan' planters.[36]

Sir Thomas Smith (1513–1577) is mentioned by name in E. K.'s
gloss on the January Eclogue for the word 'couthe':

> [couthe] commeth of the verbe Conne, that is, to know or to have
> skill. As well interpreteth the same the worthy Sir Tho. Smith in
> his booke of goverment: wherof I have a perfect copie in wryting,
> lent me by his kinseman, and my verye singular good freend, M.

Gabriel Harvey: as also of some other his most grave and excellent wrytings.

This is a 'conne'-text, a gloss that offers a pretext for the acknowledgement of clientage. The 'booke of goverment' to which E. K. refers is Smith's *De Republica Anglorum*, written before 1565, but not published until 1581. The 'other his most grave and excellent wrytings' indubitably includes the promotional pamphlet commissioned by Smith in support of the colonial venture he undertook early in the 1570s with his son of the same name.[37] Smith's pamphlet was published in 1572 by Henry Bynneman, the same publisher who had produced *A Theatre for Worldlings* (1569), as well as Geoffrey Fenton's *Discourse of the civile warres in Fraunce* (1570) and *Actes of conference in religion* (1571), and who later published Harvey and Spenser's *Three proper, wittie and familiar letters* (1580), and, in 1583, the English edition of Richard Stanyhurst's *Translation of the first four books* of the Aeneis.[38] Smith argues for a regeneration of the Irish colony: 'This degenerating and daily decay of the English manners by little and little in the countrey, discorageth ... any new enterprise.' Smith singles out 'younger brothers' as ideal colonists on two grounds. Firstly, he attributes to the dissolution of the monasteries a twofold increase in the incidence of 'gentlemen and marriages'. Secondly, he cites 'our lawe, which giveth all to the elder brother'.[39]

In June 1565, Smith had written to Cecil on the question of Ireland, complaining that: 'For this two hundred years not one hath taken the right way to make that country either subject or profitable.'[40] Smith was one of those privy councillors petitioned by William Piers (d.1603) that same year. Piers, constable of Carrickfergus, was actively promoting a plan for the settlement of the north parts of Ireland, known as 'The Ulster Project'. This was a scheme backed in May of that year by Sidney, who was installed as Lord Deputy on 13 October 1565.[41] Smith, then, was not the architect but the artisan of the affair. An idea originating among officers in the field, almost certainly with Sidney's involvement, was organized from Whitehall by Smith, whose elegant marketing of the whole operation, amply evident in the promotional pamphlet of 1572, gave it the official stamp of approval.

D. B. Quinn has insisted that Smith was above all a theoretician, 'happiest as an armchair empire builder':

What is clearest about Sir Thomas Smith's views on colonization is that they are strongly influenced by classical precedent. Indeed, it might be argued that it was his knowledge of ancient, especially Roman, history which most strongly turned his attention to the possibility of developing new English settlements on Irish land, if it were not that on his re-admission to the Privy Council in 1571 Smith could scarcely have avoided the debates on Irish colonization which he found going on there.[42]

It is to one such debate that we now turn.

Gabriel Harvey (1550–1631) was undoubtedly Spenser's closest personal mentor during his most mature years at Cambridge. Harvey's own academic aspirations suffered a series of setbacks which culminated in his retirement to his home town of Saffron Walden, near Cambridge, where he ended his days as a respectable citizen, relinquishing his earlier ambitions of high office in the Elizabethan government. At one point he looked a likely candidate for a key secretaryship under the Earl of Leicester. Sympathetic scholars have cautioned against the risk of taking Thomas Nashe's biting satire, *Have with you to Saffron-walden* (1596), too seriously, and assuming that Harvey was, like that other arch opportunist and Cambridge product, Richard Boyle, an upstart whose motives were as transparent as his missives. Whereas Boyle rose to be the richest landowner in Ireland, Harvey lapsed into local anonymity, a sign, we are led to believe, of his insipid intellect and literary mediocrity.[43]

As Gabriel Harvey's patron, Sir Thomas Smith exercised a decisive influence on his intellectual development. His death in 1577, followed by Sidney's final departure from Ireland in 1578, and Leicester's fall from favour soon after, left Harvey in a far less secure position than he had enjoyed in the mid-1570s. What of Harvey's connection with Ireland? Lisa Jardine has uncovered a series of Latin marginal notes by Gabriel Harvey in his copy of Livy's *Decades* which show that Harvey was acquainted with the ideological justifications for the Smith enterprise in the Ards.[44] She has dated these notes to 1572, the year of the publication of the Smith promotional pamphlet. Spenser was then under Harvey's tutelage at Pembroke Hall in Cambridge. This is the time of his closest involvement with Harvey.

These marginal notes record a debate held at Hill Hall, Theydon Mount, centre of the Smith family estate, sometime between 1570 and 1571, and show that the use of classical precedents for colonial projects stretched to set-piece intellectual skirmishes intended to stimulate discussion, and to offer fresh solutions to anticipated obstacles:

Thomas Smith junior and Sir Humphrey Gilbert [debated] for Marcellus, Thomas Smith senior and Doctor Walter Haddon for Fabius Maximus, before an audience at Hill Hall consisting at that very time of myself, John Wood, and several others of gentle birth. At length the son and Sir Humphrey yielded to the distinguished Secretary: perhaps Marcellus yielded to Fabius. Both of them worthy men, and judicious. Marcellus the more powerful; Fabius the more cunning. Neither was the latter unprepared [weak], nor the former imprudent: each as indispensable as the other in his place. There are times when I would rather be Marcellus, times when Fabius.[45]

Like the suburban setting of Bryskett's *Discourse,* or the Kilcolman context of the Spenser–Raleigh encounter in *Colin Clouts Come Home Againe,* the Hill Hall debate illustrates the way in which the humanist pursuit of 'civil conversation' could be both a means of securing civility against a barbarous other, and of devising ways of subduing that other. The juxtaposition of English Renaissance civility with Irish colonial incivility was exploited in the interests of the New English.

Sir Humphrey Gilbert, appointed Colonel of Munster in October 1569, was the author of *Queene Elizabethes Achademy* (c.1570), in which he advocated the establishment of a school to train young men for government service:

As, also, for that the greatest number of younge men within this realme are most Conversant aboute London, where your majesties Cowrte hath most ordinarie residence ... the apliaunce to use is principally in the vulgare speach, as in preaching, in parliament, in Cownsell, in Commyssion, and other offices of Common Weale.[46]

Compare this passage from Sir Thomas Smith:

England was never that can be heard of, fuller of people than it is at this day, and the dissolution of Abbayes hath done two things of importance heerin. It hath doubled the number of gentlemen and marriages, whereby commeth daily more increase of people, and suche younger brothers as were wonte to be thruste into Abbayes, there to live (an idle life), sith that is taken from them must nowe seeke some other place to live in. By this meanes there are many lacke abode, and few dwellings emptie. With that our lawe, which giveth all to the elder brother, furthereth much my purpose. And the excessive expence, both in diet and apparell, maketh that men

which have but small portions, can not maintaine them selves in
the emulation of this world with like countenaunce as the grounded
riche can do thus stand we at home.[47]

Gilbert desires a 'trained Company' for war, and recommends Law,
Politics, and Mathematics:

> ffor not without Cawse is Epaminondas commended, who, riding
> or Journeying in time of peace, used oftentymes sodenly to appose
> his company upon the oportunity of any place, saying, 'What yf
> our enemies were here or there, what were best to doe?'[48]

Harvey's preoccupation with colonial theory suggests that there was
a high cultural context for discussion of such practical governmental
problems in Renaissance England. In short, there was a platform for
'policy'.[49]

IV THE SIDNEY CIRCLE

Sir Henry Sidney (1529–1586) served a staggering seven terms in
high office in Ireland, from his first stint there as undertreasurer,
starting in the spring of 1556, to his final spell as Lord Deputy from
5 August 1575 to 12 September 1578.[50] His last three periods of office,
as Elizabeth's viceroy, from 1565–7, 1568–71 and 1575–8, saw a
significant realignment in Anglo-Irish politics.[51] Sidney's initial
posting to Ireland followed on from the marriage, in the spring of 1555,
of his youngest sister, Frances, to Thomas Radcliffe, third Earl of
Sussex. In the light of Sidney's marriage on 21 March 1551, to Mary
Dudley, daughter of John Dudley, Earl of Warwick, and later Duke
of Northumberland, the Sidney–Sussex match assumed great
significance. The likelihood of an end to the traditional hostilities
between the viceroys of Ireland materialized. These two marriages
moderated the rivalry between the Sussex and Dudley factions.
Sidney was prompted by his brother-in-law, Robert Dudley, Earl of
Leicester, to assume the role of deputy in Ireland on 13 October 1565,
enjoying the broad support of both factions.[52]

Edmund Campion served Sidney during his penultimate
viceroyalty. He portrayed his mentor in glowing terms:

statelie withowte disdaine, familiar withowte contempte, verie continente and chaste of bodie, no more then enoughe liberall, learned in manie languages, and a great lover of learninge, perfitt in blasinge armes, scilfull of antiquities, of witt freshe and livelie, in consultations very temperate, in utterance happie which his experience and wisedome hath made artificiall, a preferrer of many, a father to his servantes, bothe in warre and peace of commendable courage.[53]

Since their early careers are bound up with Spenser's own vocation, and because his literary reputation owes an outstanding debt to them, Campion and Stanyhurst's relations with the Irish arc of the so-called Sidney circle have to be registered.

Born in London on 25 January 1540, Edmund Campion (1540–1581) entered St John's College, Oxford, on its foundation in 1557. He was junior proctor of that institution from April 1568 to April 1569. By August 1570, he had departed for Dublin amid an atmosphere of growing suspicion and religious persecution. At this time he conformed publicly to Anglicanism, though most of his biographers explain his Irish excursion as the flight of a conscience in crisis. During his stay in Dublin, Campion resided with the Stanyhursts. He was interested in a scheme then being put forward by Henry Sidney to establish a university in Dublin. From Ireland, Campion moved to the English college at Douay, where he renounced Protestantism. He returned to England in 1580, and was arrested at Dover on 25 June. Released after a brief period of detention, he made his way to London to preach counter-reformation Catholicism. Betrayed by one of his company, he died a Jesuit martyr at Tyburn on 1 December 1581.[54]

Campion's *Two Bokes of the Histories of Ireland* was composed in Dublin between 1570 and 1571. The dedication, to Robert Dudley, then Chancellor of the University of which Campion was still a registered fellow, dated from Dublin 27 May 1571, is justified on two grounds:

First, that by your patronage of this boke yow may be induced to way the state, and become a patrone to this noble realme, which claymeth kynred of your eldest ancestours and loveth entierly your noble vertues, the fame wherof is now caried by those straungers that have felt them into many far contries that never saw your person. Secondly, because their is none that knoweth me familiarly but he knoweth withall how many wayes I am beholden to your Lordship.[55]

Its most eloquent section is the closing speech attributed to Sir Henry
Sidney, delivered in March 1571, in the light of which one critic has
suggested that 'Campion surely merits recognition as the father of Irish
parliamentary reporting'.[56] Campion's report of Sidney's oration
deserves to be quoted in full. After a brief prefatorial disclaimer – 'I
canne no skill of written tales' – Sidney proceeds thus:

Manie a good fellowe talkes of Robbin Hood that never drewe his
bowe, and manie an idle head is full of proclamacions and
conceiveth certaine farr fetches, hable in his weninge to welde a
realme. But lett me see whiche of them all can justefie that Ireland
maye spare the armie they kicke so muche against? Are your
enemies more tractable then they have been? Are they fewer? Are
you by yourselves of force to matche them? If you be, then weare
Englande starke madd to disbusse twentie or thirtie thousande
poundes a yeare for none other purpose but to vexe and greve you.
That weare like the husband whoe gealded himself to anger his wife.
You muste not thinke we love you so evill. Naye, rather thinke
truelie we tender your quietnes and preservacion as a nation
derived from our ancetors, engraffed and incorporate into one
bodye with us, disturbed by a sorte of barbarous odious to God and
man that lapp your blood as gredelie as ours ...

Touchinge Scotlande it is well knowen they weare never the
men whome England neded to feare. They are but a corner cutt oute,
and easelie tamed when they waxe owtragious. Your foes lie in the
bosome of your cuntries, more in number, ritcher of grownd,
desperate theves, ever at an inche, unpossible to be severed from
yowe, withowte anye fence beside your owne valiantnes and the
help of our souldiers. England is quiet within itself, thoroughlie
peopled, one that side of Scotland which most requires it, guarded
with an armie; otherwise the lordes and gentlemen and lustie
yoemen that dwell on a rowe are readie to mayster their private
vagaries; from all forrein invasions walled with the wide ocean.
Weare theare suche a sea betwene you and the Irish, or weare they
shutt up into an odd ende of the land, or had they no suche
oportunities of bogges and woodes as they have, or weare they
lordes of the lesser parte of Irelande, or weare they scattered into
small handfulles, not hable to annoie whole townshippes and
baronies as they doe, the comparison weare sumwhat alike. But
alack, it fareth not so with you. You are besett rownde, your townes
are feble, the lande emptie, the commons bare; everie country by

itself cannot save itselfe ... Therefore, to conclude wheare I beganne, way well the sicke and wounded partes of your common wealth, cure the roote, regarde the foundacion, the principall pillers, the sommer postes, the stone walles; as for the roof and the tiles, if ye repaier them onelye and suffer the growndeworke to perishe, a tempeste of weather, a flawe will shake your building.[57]

Sidney's description of the Old English as 'a nation derived from our ancetors, engraffed and incorporate into one bodye with us', indicates the conciliatory nature of the speech. A generation later, with the Old English and the Gaelic Irish united in a war of attrition, one New English planter would describe their alliance as 'uniformity in difformitye'.[58] Campion was one of those writers included in Geoffrey Keating's list of calumniators of the Irish nation in his seventeenth-century *History of Ireland*.[59] With the rise of Catholic nationalism in Ireland in the nineteenth century Campion was recuperated and the burden of historical reproach was laid increasingly on Protestant calumniators like Spenser.[60]

Little is known of John Derricke (fl. 1578). He may have been a customs officer at Drogheda, or the Master Derrick, a surgeon, who served Sir Robert Sidney in the Low Countries from 1597–1601.[61] Devised in 1578, Derricke's *Image of Irelande* (1581) was one of the most influential Elizabethan books on Ireland. The dedication to Sir Philip Sidney is dated from Dublin 16 June 1578. One group of woodcuts are in the form of a 'strip cartoon', recording the downfall of Rory Og O'More at the hands of Sir Henry Sidney.[62]

Derricke treats the Old English generously, as one would expect of a follower of Sidney at this juncture:

it is not our English Pale, whiche in any respecte I have touched, nor yet those of the Southe, whom I have impeched, nor yet of the Weste, whom I have nipped, but a people out of the Northe, whose usages I behelde after the fashon there sette doune, and those are thei whom I have detected, shadowing notwithstandyng parte of their maners with flowres of that Countrey ... it is not againste any one good member of this Common wealthe of Irelande, that I have made my discoverie, but onely against the pernicious vipers of the saied lande.[63]

The book begins with 'Marses Knight, that mightie man of warre', offering the reader images of 'a society of hibernian nymphs and fauns'. There is a panegyric on English sovereignty from Arthur to Elizabeth, and a sideswipe at the Pope. The second part records a battle between Sidney's English army and a disordered Irish opposition, in which the Lord Deputy's forces are victorious.[64] With its twelve intricate woodcuts, its attacks on Catholicism, its dedication to Philip Sidney, its blend of classical mythology and contemporary satire, its exultation of militant Protestantism, and its ambiguous attitude to Ireland and the Irish, *The Image of Irelande* suggests itself as a text to be read alongside *The Shepheardes Calender*.[65]

Philip Sidney (1554–1586) was born at Penshurst on 30 November 1554. He entered Christchurch, Oxford in 1568, where fellow students included Richard Carew, William Camden and Richard Hakluyt. He left Oxford early in 1571 to escape the plague. In the early 1570s he toured the continent, travelling to Italy in the company of Lodowick Bryskett, who had served as secretary to his father in Ireland. On 5 August 1575, Sidney's father was reappointed viceroy of Ireland, and the following summer saw Philip join him in Connaught. At Galway he was introduced to the notorious Mayo pirate, Grace O'Malley, and we have a report from Sidney senior to Sir Francis Walsingham of the main events of his son's Irish sojourn, the meeting with 'Granauile' and the death of Walter Devereux:

> There came to me also a most famous femynyne sea captain, called Grany I'Malley, and offred her services unto me, whersoever I would command her, with three galleys and two hundred fyghting men, either in Ireland or Scotland. She brought with her her husband, for she was as well by sea as by land more than master's mate with him. He was one of the nether Burkes, and now as I hear Mack William Euter, and called by nickname, Richard in Iron. This was a notorious woman in all the coast of Ireland: this woman did Sir Philip Sydney see, and speak with: he can more at large inform you of her. Here heard we first of the extreame and hopelesse sickness of the Earl of Essex, by whom Sir Philip being often most lovingly and earnestly wished and written for, he with all the speed he could make went to him, but found him dead before his coming, in the castle at Dublin.[66]

Sidney's Irish experiences are not generally acknowledged as a component part of his cultural formation, more emphasis being placed upon his continental contacts.

In 1577, Philip composed a short 'Discourse of Irish Affairs' in defence of his father's policies, of which only a fragment survives, in response to a deputation of Old English lawyers who had presented a petition against the imposition of the land tax known as the 'cess' to the Queen in January 1577. Sidney expresses outrage at the way in which his father's reputation was tarnished by reports which reached the Queen before they reached the viceroy: 'A strange and unused course in all provincial causes, that it should thus sooner be known here than to the governor.'[67]

Philip's brief treatise was intended to supply the Irish Lord Chancellor, William Gerrard, with arguments when he came over to answer the charges of the Palesmen before the Privy Council in October of that year. Gerrard's 'Notes' submitted to Leicester in May 1578 contain the Lord Chancellor's own justification of the cess. Gerrard, no doubt mindful of Sidney's speech to the Irish parliament in 1571, argued that the principal purpose of the levy was the defence of the Pale 'agaynst the force of the Irisherie'.[68] Young Sidney, who had evidently witnessed enough of the Irish during his visit there the previous year to form an opinion on the subject, observed that there was 'not a nation which live more tyrannously than they do one over the other'. By emphasizing the Irish propensity for rebellion, Sidney justified the imposition of the cess:

> For little is lenity to prevail in minds so possessed with a natural inconstancy ever to go to a new fortune, with a revengeful hate to all English as to their only conquerors, and that which is most of all, with so ignorant obstinacy in papistry, that they do in their souls detest the present government.[69]

The 'Discourse' displays all the familiar New English contradictions. The Irish, despite being tyrannous over one another, can still direct all their animosity towards the English, and the Old English, despite being besieged by the wild Irish, have time to appeal to the crown for redress of grievances against the viceroyalty.

Philip sees three possible solutions to Elizabeth's Irish problem:

> Either by direct conquest to make the country hers, and so by one great heap of charges to purchase that which indeed afterwards would well countervail the principal; or else by diminishing that she doth send thither; or, lastly, with force and gentleness, to raise at least so much rents, as may serve to quit the same charges.[70]

Sidney favours the first option, and he sees the third as a necessary
prelude to a direct conquest. Spenser makes precisely the same point
about defraying the charges once and for all.[71] Sidney ends his brief
treatise by declaring that 'there is no so great injustice, as that which
puts on the colour of demanding justice'. His contribution to the
acrimonious colonial debates of the decade ought not to be seen
simply as the act of a loyal son. Under different circumstances, Philip
may have assumed the deputyship instead of Grey. Fenton later
urged Leicester to confer upon his nephew the title of Baron of Kerry.[72]

Maureen Quilligan has noted that Sidney's Sonnet 30 includes a
reference to his father's recent suppression of the Irish in its recital
of contemporary political problems facing the Elizabethan regime,
confirming the young courtier's concern with the outcome of Sir
Henry's campaigns.[73] Arthur Kinney maintains that Sidney's unique
contribution to English historiography was his poetic juxtaposition
of past and present in order to suggest solutions to contemporary
problems.[74] Edward Berry claims that:

> Sidney's desire for military action ... may be said to shape in subtle
> ways the argument of the *Defence*, transforming a treatise on poetry
> into a call to arms.[75]

The call to arms urged by Barnaby Rich was taken up in Sidney's
celebration of poetry.[76] Berry argues that in the *Defence* (composed
around 1579/80), there is an 'underlying commitment to heroic action',
and an implicit urge to 'abandon poetry for the battlefield': 'His
greatest ambition lay in war.'[77] Sidney chose not to pursue that
ambition in Ireland after his father's fruitless efforts there. How
different would the history of Elizabethan culture be had Sidney
died, like Thomas Smith junior, a victim of Elizabeth's Irish wars.

V COLIN AND ROSALINDE

I want to tentatively suggest a possible solution to the identity of the
one figure in *The Shepheardes Calender* who has been most famously
the subject of critical inquiry, Rosalinde, Colin Clout's unrequited
love.[78] I want to propose, not a 'lasse', but a location. I intend to place
Colin's object of desire in Ireland, subverting the critical history that
would see Spenser's colonial career in Ireland as a consolation prize.

My contention is that Spenser's acquisition of an Irish estate represents the fulfilment of his youthful passion, not its displacement.

Who is Rosalind? The January gloss tells us it 'is a feigned name, which being wel ordered, wil bewray the very name of hys love and mistresse, whom by that name he coloureth'. He colours her rose, of course, looking at her through rosy-coloured glasses. Or perhaps she is a red herring? We know that she is 'a countrie lasse' who dwells in a 'neighbour towne' (*SC, Jan* Arg, 50), but what is a nice girl like her doing in a place like the April Eclogue, the month most immediately associated with the founding of the imperial myth of Gloriana? A 'feigned name' might suggest that it is a name, but not that of a woman. The phrase, 'which being wel ordered' implies an anagram of sorts. We know that in the Renaissance the figure of woman and the trope of unrequitedness denoted social rather than sexual desire.[79] Colin's unrequited love is therefore a vehicle that gets him to Ireland, but it is also, I am suggesting – and this is Spenser's ironic genius at work – the destination of his true love, his life's ambition, his colonial desire. Andrew Hadfield is, I believe, right when he remarks of *Colin Clouts Come Home Againe*: 'Pastoral, as a genre of protest literature, is located quite clearly within the community of the "New" English in Ireland and the poem serves to define their identity and speak with their voice.'[80] Hadfield maintains that the 'shepherdes nation' are the New English.[81] I would want to project this critical observation back onto *The Shepheardes Calender* and claim that there too we have a hybrid genre – colonial pastoral. Rosalind is Ireland. Hobbinol advises Colin to 'Forsake the soyle that so doth thee bewitch.' E. K.'s gloss elaborates on this bewitchment: '"Come down", they say, "from your bleak North country hills where she dwells who binds you with her spell, and be at peace far away from her in the genial South land."' It is a question here of a geography of desire.

Rosalind is alluded to as 'the Widdowes daughter of the glenne' (*Apr* 26), and Roland Smith has indicated that 'glenne' is one of several Irish words used in the text, others being 'kernes' (*Jul* 199), wrongly glossed as 'Churle' by E. K.[82] According to Barbara Bono:

> In *The Shepheardes Calender*, Rosalind, the Elisa of *Aprill*, and the Dido of *November* variously represent the Virgilian problem of desire, which remains unresolved in the *Calender* but is further explored in *The Faerie Queene*.[83]

Also in the April Eclogue we find a reference to a 'Bagpype' and a 'Wolfe' (*Apr* 2, 3). Through her rejection of Colin 'his frend is chaunged for a frenne'. In pursuit of Rosalinde, Colin is leaving Hobbinol behind. 'Frenne' is glossed as:

> a straunger. The word I thinke was first poetically put, and afterwarde used in commen custome of speach for forenne. (*Apr* gloss)

Between Cambridge and Cork lies Kent, but even while serving under John Young, the Bishop of Rochester, Spenser may have been steeped in Irish politics. If we leave aside the unresolved question of whether or not Spenser was present at the execution of Murrogh O'Brien at Limerick on 1 July 1577, there is other evidence that points to a cultural cross-fertilization. As I have pointed out, Paul McLane has conjectured that Spenser was in Ireland in November 1579.[84] Lisa Jardine has pointed to the extent to which Spenser's cultural formation was bound up, from the early 1570s, with an Irish milieu.[85] Roland Smith has pointed to the use of Irish words in *The Shepheardes Calender*.[86] Mary Parmenter has noted the reference to wolves in the September Eclogue, a creature at large in Ireland but not in England in Spenser's day.[87] There are other possible Irish elements. One candidate for 'E. K.' is the Earl of Kildare, an Old English noble with close links to the Leicester–Sidney circle.[88]

Rosalind scorns Colin's 'rurall musick', and 'Shepheards devise she hateth as the snake' (*Jan* 65). One could deduce from this merely that Rosalinde dislikes Colin's poetry. Alternatively, one could posit Ireland as the country from which St Patrick banished all serpents. The gloss on 'the Widdowes daughter of the glenne' is intriguing:

> He calleth Rosalind the Widowes daughter of the glenne, that is, of a country Hamlet or borough, which I thinke is rather sayde to coloure and concele the person, then simply spoken. For it is well knowen, even in spighte of Colin and Hobbinol, that she is a Gentle woman of no mean house, nor endewed with anye vulgare and common gifts both of nature and manners. (*Apr* gloss)

Now, consider one of Richard Stanyhurst's most striking anecdotes in his *Description of Ireland* in Holinshed's *Chronicles* (1577).[89] Describing Cork, Stanyhurst interrupts his narrative in order to tell the story of the walling of New Ross.[90] Stanyhurst rewrites this event in order to represent it as an act of defence undertaken by the Old English against the Gaelic Irish, rather than the by-product of a feud between two Old English factions.[91] In Stanyhurst's version, Ross is constantly subject to molestation by 'Irish enemies', a theme he illustrates with the tale of an Irishman who rides into the town and tricks a merchant out of a piece of cloth by pretending to haggle and then suddenly making off with the item.

The townspeople consult 'a famous Dido, a politike dame, a bountifull gentlewoman, called Rose', who devises a plan to prevent further intrusions and offers to fund the enterprise, 'two good properties in a councellor'. Rose's solution to the problem entails the construction of fortifications around the town, resulting in such scenes of industry that it seemed 'Carthage were afresh in building'. Stanyhurst cites the contemporary translation of Virgil by 'master doctor Phaer' on the construction of Carthage, then returns 'from Dido of Carthage, to Rose of Rosse'. Ross enjoys security until the wife of one of Rose's three sons commits adultery. Rumours of this indiscretion reach the husband, whose 'pangs of gelousie' provoke pity in one faction of the town, who then murder the adulterer and his kin. The adulterer is a friar, and by turning a 'privat injurie into a publike quarrell' the townsfolk are able to justify the slaughter of the occupants of an abbey. Things were 'turned arsie versie, topside the otherwaie'. Excommunicated, the town goes into decline.

The alleged infidelity of Rose's daughter might have some bearing on 'the Widdowes daughter of the glenne' who betrays Colin Clout. In a list of 'The names or surnames of the learned men and authours of Ireland' in Chapter 7 of his *Description*, Stanyhurst mentions one 'Dormer, a lawyer borne in Rosse, scholler of Oxford. He wrote in ballade royall *The decay of Rosse*.'[92] As well as Rose of Rosse, there is another clue to the identity of Rosalind, no less tenuous. Barnaby Scurlock, a committed Catholic, was one of three Old English lawyers – the others being Richard Netterville and Henry Burnell – who came over to England early in 1577 to petition the Privy Council about what they saw as the excessive costs of Sir Henry Sidney's government. It was to Scurlock and his cohorts that Philip Sidney was responding in the surviving fragment of text known as the 'Discourse of Irish Affairs' (1578). Scurlock is described in a contemporary text as being 'of Roselande'.[93] There was also, it should be noted, a Barry Rowe of Buttevant, abutting Spenser's estate, another possible rival for Rosalind (Rowe's land). Barry Rowe, or Roe, was the Red Barry, head of the sept of the Barrys.[94] Then again, Rosalind may stand for 'Roche's land',

the domain of Lord Roche, with whom Spenser was in constant
litigation. One thinks here immediately of the reference in Book IV
of *The Faerie Queene* to 'Rosseponte boord' (IV.xi.43.4). In short,
Rosalind, far from being a person left behind in England, may
represent the land upon which Spenser eventually settled through the
Munster plantation, land which reverted to the crown with the
Desmond Rebellion of 1579, the year of the publication of *The
Shepheardes Calender*, a watershed year in Anglo-Irish relations.[95]
Could it be that Rosalinde is a precursor of Irena, signifying not a
person, but a place?

So much for Rosalind, what of Colin Clout? Is there an Irish 'context'
for his name? In his *Description*, Stanyhurst notes that the inhabitants
of the English Pale in Ireland, 'named Fingall', are called 'Collonnes':

> But Fingall especially from tyme to tyme hath bene so addicted to
> all the poyntes of Husbandry, as that they are nicknamed by their
> neighbours, for their continual drudgery, Collonnes of the Latin
> word *Coloni*, wherunto the clipt English worde, Clowne, seemeth
> to be aunswerable.[96]

Readers will recall that Redcrosse, in the 'Letter to Raleigh', is
described as a '*clownishe* younge man' (my emphasis).

In the dedicatory epistle to Sidney, Stanyhurst first chastises
Edmund Campion on the grounds that 'it was greatly to be lamented,
that eyther hys theame had not beene shorter, or else his leasure had
not beene longer ... it twitled more tales out of schoole, and drowned
weightyer matters in silence, then the Auctor upon better view and
longer searche would have permitted'.[97] Stanyhurst then speaks of
his debt to Campion in these terms:

> But weighting on the other side, that my course pack threede coulde
> not have beene suteably knit with his fine silcke, & what a disgrace
> it were, bungerly to botch up a riche garment by clowting it with
> patches of sundrye colours, I was forthwyth reclaymed from my
> former resolution, reckening it for better that my penne should
> walke in such wyse in that craggie and balkishe way, as the truth
> of the matter being fore-priced, I would neyther openly borrow, nor
> privily imbezill, ought to any great purpose from his historie.[98]

Stanyhurst dresses in borrowed clothes, borrowed from Campion, and
Spenser dresses in Stanyhurst's clothes. Having read Stanyhurst,

Spenser may have cloudily enwrapped his book in the colonial cloth of an Irish mantle.

If Colin echoes *Coloni* and Clout resonates with 'clowte', or cloth, which is also the very fabric of the text, then one rendering of 'Colin Clout' would be 'colonial text'. After all, it was the theft of 'a piece of cloth' that, in Stanyhurst's tale in the *Description*, led Rose of Rosse to her 'devise, that the towne shoulde incontinently be inclosed with walles'.[99]

My reading of Spenser alongside Stanyhurst suggests that Spenser may have composed his pastoral, with its Old English diction, its planting metaphors, its allegory of frustrated courtship, and its reforming rhetoric, within a broad colonial milieu. *The Shepheardes Calender* evolved out of a tradition of English reforming literature which had an urgent application in Ireland, and with which Spenser was familiar. Stanyhurst's Irish discourse offered an exemplary instance of the genre. If the *Chronicles* provided the immediate stimulus for the *Calender*, Stanyhurst's subsequent sortie into poetic composition, under the influence of Harvey, gives us a glimpse of what might have become of Spenser had he remained loyal to his tutor's metrical system.

We might pursue Stanyhurst's compelling fiction, with its classical allusions and allegory of religious reform, as a central motif in *The Shepheardes Calender*. This text, I suggest, is a colonial one, and not simply at the level of *genre*. With Spenser, the vocations of poet and planter dovetail. Written on the cusp of his colonial adventure, *The Shepheardes Calender* may bear the marks of an Irish future as well as an English past. The possible incorporation of an Old English historian's digression in the interests of one of the most complex texts in the English literary canon perhaps reveals the extent to which that culture is enmeshed in colonial history. It would be ironic were the object of Colin's desire to be, not an unrequited love he left behind in England, but his colonial destination in Ireland.

2

Spenser's Irish English: Language and Identity in Early Modern Ireland*

In this chapter I shall suggest that Spenser's choice of 'Chaucer's English', based upon a nationalistic literary revivalism, was also influenced by a variety of English which survived as a spoken language beyond the pale of the cultural metropolis, in the colonial margins. (Perhaps I should say at the outset that I am approaching this, not as a linguist, nor as a medievalist, but as a 'cultural historian'.) Spenser's Irish English, or Hiberno-English, was most certainly influenced by Chaucer, but it was also inspired by the survival of an ancient dialect of English in Elizabethan Ireland. Sixteenth-century Munster, the southern province of Ireland, was a multilingual environment, with Latin as the language of learning, Gaelic Irish as the language of the bards and the peasantry, Middle English as the language of the Catholic descendants of the twelfth-century colonists, known as the 'Old English', and early modern English as the language of the post-Reformation Protestant planters, known as the 'New English'.

Richard Stanyhurst (1547–1618), a Dubliner by birth, was an Old English contemporary of Spenser, and principal author of the Irish section of Holinshed's *Chronicles*. Educated at Kilkenny in Ireland and at Oxford in England, Stanyhurst went from Waterford, where he studied under Peter White, to University College, Oxford, in 1563. He was admitted BA five years later. During his undergraduate days at Oxford, he made the acquaintance of Edmund Campion.[1] On graduating from Oxford, Stanyhurst studied law in London, initially at Furnivall's Inn, then at Lincoln's Inn. He returned to Dublin in the company of Campion. It was during this stay in Dublin that the Stanyhursts, Campion, and Sidney were acquainted.

34

When Holinshed commissioned him to work on the Irish section of his projected *Chronicles*, Stanyhurst submitted the revised and enlarged version of Campion's history in partial fulfilment of his contract. He dedicated his work to Lord Deputy Sidney, who had close connections with both his tutor, Campion, and his father, James, through the parliamentary sessions of 1569–71. Sir Henry Sidney was, of course, the father of Philip, to whom *The Shepheardes Calender* was addressed. Stanyhurst's contribution to Holinshed is a peculiar piece of 'English' literature, particularly in its considerations of language. The English Pale, he writes,

> especiallie from time to time hath bin so addicted to all the points of husbandrie, as that they are nickenamed by their neighbours, for their continuall drudgerie, Collonnes, of the Latine word Coloni, whereunto the clipt English word clowne seemeth to be answerable.[2]

Stanyhurst argues, *contra* Spenser – who favoured integration and assimilation – for partition and proscription as a solution to degeneration:

> The inhabitants of the English pale have been in olde time so much addicted to their civilitie, and so farre sequestered from barbarous savageness, as their onelie mother toong was English. And trulie, so long as these impaled dwellers did sunder themselves as well in land as in language from the Irish: rudenesse was dale by dale in the countrie supplanted, civilitie ingraffed, good lawes established, loialtie observed, rebellion suppressed, and in fine the coine of a yoong England was like to shoot in Ireland.[3]

Stanyhurst remembers the southern pocket of the Pale, the county of Wexford, as a stronghold of Englishness:

> But of all other places, Weisford with the territorie baied and perclosed within the river called the Pill, was so quite estranged from Irishrie, as if a traveller of the Irish, (which was rare in those daies) had pitcht his foot within the Pill and spoken Irish, the Weisfordians would command him foorthwith to turne the other end of his toong and speaks English, or els bring his trouchman with him. But in our daies they have so acquainted themselves with the Irish, as they have made a mingle mangle or gallimaufreie of both

languages, and have in suche medleie or checkerwise so crabbedlie
jumbled them both together, as commonlie the inhabitants of the
meaner sorte speaks neither good English nor good Irish.[4]

Elsewhere, Stanyhurst rails against what he sees as the excessive
pride and impropriety of the Gaelic Irish:

> For the Irish man standeth so much upon his gentilitie, that he
> termeth anie one of the English sept, and planted in Ireland,
> Bobdeagh Galteagh, that is, English churle: but if he be an
> Englishman born, then he nameth him, Bobdeagh Saxonnegh, that
> is, a Saxon churle: so that both are churles, and he the onelie
> gentleman. And thereupon if the basest pezzant of them name
> himselfe first, as I and Oneile, I and you, I and he, I and my master,
> whereas the courtesie of the English language is clean contrarie.[5]

Stanyhurst shared Campion's perception of 'the course of
interchanging and blending of speeches togither, not by invention of
art, but by use of talk'.[6] Spenser is also convinced that social intercourse
rather than literary invention determines speech, and on the subject
of Old English 'degeneration' he holds 'that the Chief Cause of
bringinge in the Irish language amongest them was speciallye theire
fosteringe and marryinge with the Irishe'.[7]

By drawing on contemporary 'Irish' expressions, Spenser was not
polluting his English, but purifying it, by tracing a pure British source
in Tudor Ireland. A close comparison of the life and work of Spenser
and Stanyhurst could prove fruitful. Both authors were beneficiaries
of the same literary patron; each had direct experience of the colonial
situation in Ireland; their respect for Harvey, their association with
Sidney, and their protection under Leicester bound them together.

Stanyhurst has a comic writer's eye for a good anecdote, as this
example of a New English cultural *faux pas* shows:

> There was of late daies one of the peeres of England sent to Weisford
> as commissioner, to decide the controversies of that countrie; and
> hearing in affable wise the rude complaints of the countrie clowns,
> he conceived here & there some time a word, other whiles a
> sentence. The noble man being verie glad, that upon his first
> comming to Ireland, he understood so manie words, told one of
> his familiar friends, that he stood in verie great hope to become
> shortlie a well spoken man in the Irish, supposing that the blunt

people had pratled Irish, all the while they jangled English. Howbeit to this daie, the dregs of the old ancient Chaucer English are kept as well there as in Fingall, as they terme a spider, an attercop, a wisp, a wad, a lumpe of bread, a pocket, or a pucket, a sillibucke, a copprous, a faggot, a blease, or a blaze, for the short burning of it (as I judge) a physician, a leach, a gap, a shard, a base court or quadrangle, a bawen, or rather (as I doo suppose) a barton, the houshold or folks, meanie, sharpe, keene, estrange, uncouth, easie, eeth or eefe, a dunghill, a mizen; as for the worde bater, that in English purporteth a lane, bearing to an high way, I take it for a meere Irish worde, that crepte unawares into the English, through the daily entercourse of the English and Irish inhabitants. And where as commonly in all countreys, the women speake most neately and pertely, whiche *Tully* in hys thirde booke *de Orators,* speakyng in the person of *Crassus,* seemed to have observed, yet not withstandyng in Ireland it falleth out contrary. For the women have in theyr English tongue an harrish and broade kynd of pronunciation, with utteryng their wordes of two sillables, they give the last accent. As they say, Markmeate, Baskeate, Gossoupe, Pussoate, Robart, Niclase, &c. which doubtlesse doth disbeautifie their English above measure. And if they could be weaned from that corrupt custom, there is none that could dislyke of their English.[8]

The tendency to stress the second syllable of disyllabic words, singled out by Stanyhurst as one of the most remarkable features of Irish English, appears to have had no contemporary analogue in early modern English. Its existence in English Ireland is attributable to the influence of Norman French, in which the final syllable was regularly stressed. The Irish language itself was affected by Norman French in much the same way.[9]

Stanyhurst's list of 'Chaucerisms' in current usage in the Pale includes 'uncouth.' 'Uncouth' is the first word of E. K.'s dedicatory epistle to Gabriel Harvey, and 'couthe' is the term which calls forth the gloss to the January Eclogue alluding to Sir Thomas Smith as a kinsman and friend of Harvey: 'Uncouthe unkiste, Sayde the olde famous Poete Chaucer.'[10]

Stanyhurst's attitude to the Irish language, and his own cultural identity, is ambiguous. At Oxford University Stanyhurst's speech was ridiculed by fellow students who considered him to have 'bought at Chester a grotes worth of English'.[11] After his flight to the continent in the early 1580s as a Catholic recusant, he was often asked why an 'Irishman' like himself could not speak Irish. In his spirited defence of the vernacular, Stanyhurst anticipates E. K., Spenser's editorial persona in *The Shepheardes Calendar*:

> And first of the wordes to speake, I graunt they be something hard, and of most men unused, yet both English, and also used of most excellent Authors and most famous Poetes. In whom whenas this our Poet hath bene much traveiled and throughly redd, how could it be, (as that worthy Oratour sayde) but that walking in the sonne although for other cause he walked, yet needes he mought be sunburnt; and having the sound of those auncient Poetes still ringing in his eares, he mought needes in singing hit out some of theyr tunes. But whether he useth them by such casualtye and custome, or of set purpose and choyse, as thinking them fittest for such rusticall rudenesse of shepheards, eyther for that theyr rough sounde would make his rymes more ragged and rustical, or els because such olde and obsolete wordes are most used of country folke, sure I think, and think I think not amisse, that they bring great grace and, as one would say, auctoritie to the verse.[12]

Spenserians have assumed that it was text – his reading of Chaucer – rather than context – his stay in Ireland – which brought Spenser into contact with a language 'of most men unused', or 'used most of country folke', but Spenser had encountered Stanyhurst and heard 'Hiberno-English' before he composed *The Shepheardes Calender*. According to a reference in the Spenser–Harvey correspondence, he had certainly read Holinshed by April 1580.[13] The Irish section of the *Chronicles* and *The Shepheardes Calender* are of course very different kinds of texts, but the same nostalgic longing for an undiluted English identity governs both discourses. Until 1579, the year *The Shepheardes Calender* was published and the year that Spenser finally took up permanent residence in Ireland, the Old and New English retained an uneasy alliance. In the 1570s, Spenser and Stanyhurst both enjoyed the patronage of the Leicester–Sidney circle and were influenced by Gabriel Harvey's poetic theory. Spenser was 'much travailed and throughly redd', and it was his travels as much as his reading that inspired his literary and linguistic choice.

The Old English peasantry in Ireland spoke Chaucer's English in the sixteenth century and an early variety of English survived well into the nineteenth century. In 1682 an English army officer described the dialect of Wexford in these terms:

> Its idiom of speech, tho its not Irish, nor seems English as English is now refined, yett is it more easy to be understood by an Englishman that never heard Irish spoken than by any Irishman that now lives remote. Itt's notorious that itt's the very language brought over by Fitzstephen, and retained by them to this day. Whoever hath read old Chaucer, and is at all acquainted therewith, will better understand the Barony of Forth dialect than either an Englishman or an Irishman, that never read him, though otherwise a good linguist.[14]

In 1780 an observer noted that in Wexford 'they all speak a broken Saxon language, and not one in an hundred knows any thing of Irish'.[15] Around 1800, another commentator noted,

> It may be related, as a singular fact, that the Rev. William Eastwood, rector of Tacumshane, barony of Forth, while amusing himself one day in his field with a volume of Chaucer, fancied some of the obsolete words which met his eye resembled those which also met his ear, as his workmen conversed together; he accordingly called them around him, and commenced reading a page or two of old Geoffrey aloud, to their great delight, as they well understood the most obscure expressions, and often explained them better than the glossarial aids of Dryden and Johnson.[16]

A variety of English considered literary in a metropolitan context by the sixteenth century was a familiar dialect form in Ireland until the time of the Gaelic Revival. This distinctly archaic variety of English survived almost intact in the remains of the original English Pale. The English language developed unevenly in England and Ireland, and the 'dregs' of Chaucerian English lingered on in Ireland while the language of the metropolis was modernized and renovated. There is a compelling modern instance of this tendency for Ireland to retain an English dialect that lends itself to literary production in the Irish dramatic movement at the turn of the century with playwrights like Synge claiming for contemporary Irish English an 'Elizabethan richness'.

Piecing together the linguistic map of early modern Ireland, Alan Bliss has argued that two varieties of English were spoken in Ireland:

one, readily intelligible to Englishmen, spoken in the towns; the other, nearly incomprehensible to outsiders, spoken in the rural districts where English still survived.[17]

Both of these varieties were compounded by the impact of early modern English spoken by the post-Reformation colonists. In *The Shepheardes Calendar* E. K. upbraids those who 'have made our English tongue, a gallimaufray or hodgepodge of al other speches', who,

> if they happen to heare an olde word albeit very naturall and significant, crye out streight way, that we speak no English, but gibbrish, or rather such, as in old time Evanders mother spake. Whose first shame is, that they are not ashamed, in their own mother tonge straungers to be counted and alienes.[18]

Where Stanyhurst claimed that the pure English of the Pale had been defiled by the 'tettar or ringworme' of the Irish language, and asked rhetorically if 'we must gag our jawes in gibbrishing Irish', E. K., calling for a return to the ancient English of Chaucer, upbraids those courtiers 'that of their owne country and natural speach ... have so base regard and bastard judgment'.[19] Critics have found it hard to reconcile the vigorous champion of the vernacular with the archaist who wrote, as E. K. informs us in the dedicatory epistle to *The Shepheardes Calender*, in a language 'of most men unused'. My suggestion is that Spenser's archaisms were not simply gleaned from the Middle English of Chaucer, but were garnered also from the marginal variety of English spoken in Elizabethan Ireland.

Spenser's poetry in 'archaic' English earned mixed reviews from contemporaries and near contemporaries. Sidney's *Apology for Poetry* (1595) praised Spenser's literary achievement in *The Shepheardes Calender* but voiced reservations about the author's language:

> That same framing of his style to an old rustic language I dare not allow, since neither Theocritus in Greek, Virgil in Latin, nor Sanazzaro in Italian did affect it.[20]

Sidney here anticipated Ben Jonson, who thought that Chaucerisms 'were better expunged and banished', and declared that 'in affecting the ancients, Spenser writ no language'. Later, Samuel Johnson would mock the poem's 'studied barbarity', and it was not until the Romantic reification of rural speech in the nineteenth century that *The Shepheardes Calendar* was recuperated by poets like John Clare.

Philip O'Sullivan-Beare, a Gaelic Irish author who wrote in Latin, claimed of the Old English that they spoke the 'English language, albeit in a crude and archaic form'. In the *View*, Spenser notes that there are 'in the Irish language manye wordes of *Galles* remayninge and yeat dailye used in Comon speache'. He further observes:

> *The Gallish speech is the verye Brittish* the which was generallye used heare in all Britany before the Comminge of the Saxons and yeat is retained of the welchemen the Cornishemen and the *Britones* of ffraunce, thoughe time workinge alteracion of all thinges and the tradinge and enterdeale with other nacions rounde aboute have Chaunged and greatlye altered the dialect theareof, but yeat the originall wordes appears to be the same.[21]

An early seventeenth-century commentator echoed Spenser's view of the origins of the English language in Ireland:

> it is certain that the old English Saxons learned their alphabet letters from the Irish as may appear at this instant by comparing both characters together.[22]

In his encounters with the Old English in Ireland, Spenser discovered a community who were drinking from the 'well of English undefyled' (*FQ*.IV.ii.32.8).

Of course, the claim that Spenser's English was enriched by the Irish milieu in which he wrote is not new. In 1958 Roland Smith asserted:

> the only significant changes in Spenser's spelling are not so much individual or personal as social, and reflect the poet's increasing familiarity with his Irish background. They concern not English but Irish words, such as *kerne* and *Aherloa*.[23]

Smith refers to Spenser's use of the words 'glenne' (*SC, Apr* 26), and 'kernes' (*SC, Jul* 199), both badly glossed by E. K., as 'evidence ... that Spenser was in Ireland in the summer of 1577'. He adds 'Churle', E. K.'s erroneous translation of 'kernes', to the list of Irish words known to Spenser in 1579, and notes that Philip Sidney had used it in his contemporary *Discourse on Irish Affairs*.[24] Did Spenser have to go to Ireland to be aware of the currency of these words? The Sir Thomas Smith Irish colonial promotional pamphlet of 1571 includes an allusion to 'the Husbandmen which they call Churles'.[25] Professor Smith is surely too presumptuous in his claim that Spenser's use of 'glenne', 'kerne' and 'Churle' in *The Shepheardes Calendar* constitutes 'evidence' of the poet's presence in Ireland two years earlier. By his own admission, the word was common in official treatises of the time, treatises to which Spenser most probably had access. His reading of Holinshed would have furnished him with all the Irish words present in the poem.

Why did E. K. gloss 'kerne', a foot soldier, as 'Churle', a farmer? Twice in the *View* Spenser alludes to 'Churle' as a peculiarly Irish expression, and gives it the more general meaning of peasant or 'base sort'.[26] Stanyhurst provides a detailed description of all the social classes in Ireland including the kern:

> an ordinarie souldier, using for weapon his sword and target, and sometimes his peece, being commonlie so good marksmen as they will come within a score of a great castell. Kerne signifieth (as noble men of deepe judgement informed me) a shower of hell, because they are taken for no better than for rakehels, or the divels blacke gard, by reason of the stinking sturre they keepe, wheresoever they be.[27]

It is perhaps understandable that an English author-editor should gloss one 'Irish' term with another, 'kerne' with 'Churle', particularly if the trades of farmer and soldier were amalgamated in his own text.

It should be clear by now that my own argument does not depend upon Spenser having been in Ireland before 1579, although, as I have suggested in the previous chapter, there is some evidence to support this claim, even if we do not accept as autobiographical the recollection by Irenius in the *View* of the execution of Murrogh O'Brien in Limerick on 1 July 1577.[28] My argument does depend upon Spenser having had contact with the Irish colonial milieu – through Stanyhurst, specifically his reading of Holinshed, and through his acquaintance, via Gabriel Harvey, with the Smith colonial venture of 1571.[29]

Charles Barber's thorough investigation of the expanding English vocabulary in the early modern period uncovered a single Celtic loan word:

> *bawn* 'a fortified enclosure' (1537), from Irish *babhun*; it was used only in Irish contexts, and was obviously picked up by soldiers and administrators engaged in England's colonial wars against Ireland.[30]

Francis Bacon was equally convinced that it was an Irish term. His Irish treatise alludes to 'bawnes as they call them'.[31] Yet according to Stanyhurst, 'a bawen, or rather (as I doe suppose) a barton', is drawn from 'the dregs of the old ancient Chaucer English'.

There is an illuminating literary analogue which highlights the Anglo-Irish linguistic chicken-and-egg problem in James Joyce's *A Portrait of the Artist as a Young Man*. Stephen Dedalus, in conversation with his dean of studies, an English convert and thus 'a countryman of Ben Jonson', refers to a funnel as a 'tundish'. The dean is rather perplexed:

> – Is that called a tundish in Ireland? asked the dean. I never heard the word in my life.
> – It is called a tundish in Lower Drumcondra, said Stephen, laughing, where they speak the best English.
> – A tundish, said the dean reflectively. That is a most interesting word. I must look that word up. Upon my word I must.[32]

It is Stephen who finally looks up 'tundish':

> That tundish has been on my mind for a long time. I looked it up and find it English and good old blunt English too. Damn the dean of studies and his funnel! What did he come here for to teach us his own language or to learn it from us. Damn him one way or the other![33]

One might ask whether Spenser, one of the most famous English canonical authors to have settled in Ireland, learned his English there. Ironically, one critic has recently compared *The Shepheardes Calendar* to Joyce's *Portrait*.[34]

If *The Faerie Queene*, to pursue the Joycean analogy, can be compared to *Ulysses*, then there is another Stanyhurst text that could, stylistically, be likened to *Finnegans Wake*. If Stanyhurst's contribution to Holinshed's *Chronicles* offers one point of comparison with Spenser, then Stanyhurst's subsequent sortie into poetic composition offers another. Stanyhurst's *Translation of The first Four Books of P. Virgilius Maro* (1582), dedicated to Patrick Plunket, Lord Baron of Dunsany, has had so much calumny heaped upon it that its generic relation to Spenser's own 'hobgoblin' style has largely passed unnoticed. An eighteenth-century critic observed wryly that since 'Chaucer has been called the well of English undefiled, so might Stanihurst be denominated the common sewer of the language'.[35]

Whatever adverse reviews it attracted, Stanyhurst's translation was praised in 1592 by Gabriel Harvey:

> If I never deserve anye better remembraunce, let mee rather be epitaphed, The Inventour of the English Hexameter – whome learned M. *Stanihurst* imitated in his Virgin, and excellent Sir *Phillip Sidney* disdained not to follow in his *Arcadia* & elsewhere.[36]

Harvey was returning the compliment paid him by Stanyhurst in the preface to the *Four Books*. Writing in June 1582, Stanyhurst makes a direct reference to Harvey's metrical theories in 'one of his familiar letters'. Thomas Nashe observed that the clownish Stanyhurst rather than the courtly Spenser followed Harvey's method of versifying:

> Master *Stanyhurst* (though otherwise learned) trod a foule, lumbring, boystrous, wallowing, measure in his translation of *Virgil*. He had never been praisd by *Gabriel* for his labour, if therein hee had not bin so famously absurd.[37]

In 1598, Francis Meres could 'name but two Iambical Poets, Gabriel Harvey and Richard Stanyhurst'.[38] Barnaby Rich derided Stanyhurst's translation, saying he had taken Virgil and 'stript him out of a Velvet gowne, into a Fooles coate, out of a Latin Heroicall verse, into an English riffe raffe'.[39]

One decisive example of Stanyhurst's 'kitchen rhetoric' will suffice to convey the tenor of the whole translation:

> I that in old season wyth reeds often harmonye whistled
> My rural sonnet; from forrest flitted (I) forced Thee sulcking
> swincker thee soyle, thoghe craggie, to sunder.
> A labor and a travaile too plowswayns hertelye welcoom.
> Now manhood and garbroyls I chaunt, and martial horror.[40]

Compare Spenser's rendition of the same passage in the first stanza of Book I of *The Faerie Queene*:

> Lo I the man, whose Muse whilome did maske,
> As time her taught, in lowly Shepheards weeds,
> Am now enforst a far unfitter taske,
> For trumpets sterne to chaunge mine Oaten reeds,

And sing of Knights and Ladies gentle deeds;
Me, all too meane, the sacred Muse areeds
To blazon broad emongst her learned throng:
Fierce warres and faithfull loves shall moralize my song.
*(FQ.*1.1)

Spenser purified the dialect of the tribe, whereas Stanyhurst stuck to
his source, finally abandoning it in favour, not of a modernized
version, but of Latin, which he had referred to in Holinshed as 'the
language that is universallie spoken, throughout the greater part of
the world'. Gillian Brennan, writing on sixteenth-century English
culture, has pointed to 'a split in the intellectual elite between the
conservatives who wanted to preserve their monopoly of access to
knowledge through the use of classical languages, and the progressive
thinkers who realized that it would be easier to control the ideas of
the masses by using the vernacular'.[41] Spenser was one of those
'progressive thinkers' who privileged his native tongue over Latin,
the universal language of learning, but he was acquainted with
varieties of English both of the centre and the periphery, and his
movement between court and colony arguably allowed him greater
flexibility of expression than contemporaries who confined themselves
to London or Oxbridge.

N. F. Blake has contended that there is a

difficulty in distinguishing between Spenser's archaic and dialect
forms ... because he did not draw his examples from living dialect
speakers; he took them from earlier writers, particularly Chaucer.[42]

Pace Barber and Blake, I am suggesting that Spenser found a ready-
made store of 'archaic' forms in the English dialect spoken in
Elizabethan Ireland, 'the dregs of the old ancient Chaucer English'.
Linguistic borrowing in early modern Ireland meant more than the
occasional 'Celtic loan word' being imbibed by English soldiers. Old
and Middle English lexical items could be borrowed freely from an
environment in which a marginal and marginalized English colonial
community jealously guarded its identity by preserving earlier forms
of the metropolitan dialect. This has implications for our
understanding of Spenser's language, placing his 'highly composite
archaic medium' in an Irish colonial context.[43] To cite one example
from *The Faerie Queene*, there is a close verbal echo in 'Whylome when

IRELAND florished in fame' (*FQ*.VII.vi.37.1) and Stanyhurst's remark in Holinshed: 'It is knowen, and by the historie you may in part perceive, how bravelie Ulster whilom florished.'[44] 'Whilom', and also 'eftsoones', often taken as examples of archaisms, crop up in the Irish state papers and in Holinshed's *Chronicles*. Indeed, 'eft-sones' appears in the *View*.

It remains normal practice in studies of Spenser to modernize all other quotations from Renaissance authors, while leaving the poet's own allegedly archaic language intact:

> Given Spenser's attempt to cast the glow of antiquity upon his work, it seeme perverse to rob it of that genuine antiquity that time has conferred upon it.[45]

Thus Stephen Greenblatt defends his retention of the old usage for Spenser, and thus is the myth of Spenser's archaic language perpetuated. Again, John Hollander has written of

> the distribution of archaisms, coinages and unstable spellings in the interest of multiple readings that make it impractical to modernise the text of *The Faerie Queene*.[46]

By endowing Spenser's poetic discourse with 'the glow of antiquity' critics elide both the politics of the poet's literary language and its cultural context. Surely the Englishness of Chaucer's English is thrown into doubt by its use within an Irish milieu? Although they may see themselves as preserving Spenser's undeniable linguistic resourcefulness, those critics who confine Spenser's linguistic sources to the nascent canonical status of Chaucer are also conserving him from the literature and the history which inspired his work. Ben Jonson's claim that 'Spenser writ no language' is not readily relinquished, but further research on Spenser's Irish English might open up his texts to a wider readership.

Spenser need not have plucked from his library the apparently archaic language which litters *The Shepheardes Calendar*. Indeed, such an artificial resuscitation of a dead language does not quite square with our knowledge of Spenser's self-presentation as a 'poet historicall' in the 'Letter to Raleigh' (1589), where he explicitly describes himself as an author who 'thrusteth into the middest'. What Spenser may have done, in the wake of his Irish sojourn, with Holinshed fresh in his mind, with Stanyhurst a key figure in the cultural matrix of the

Leicester–Sidney circle, is appropriate a variety of English dormant in England but very much alive in Ireland.

What is of interest here is not individual correspondences but the accumulating sense of an Irish milieu as the centre which this earliest of Spenser's works already addresses. *The Shepheardes Calendar* can be seen to owe some of its complexity to its successful absorption and assimilation of an obsolete English literary dialect which was also, significantly, one of the current languages of early modern Ireland. The nature of the Irish colonial *ambience* rendered it, in a succession of ways, an intellectual crux, and a crux of pastoral identity, for key categories of metropolitan English aspirants to office. This complicated Anglo-Irish cultural milieu was one to which Spenser crucially belonged.

Spenser's language was dialectal as well as archaic, synchronic as well as diachronic. He was not simply 'affecting the ancients', but imitating Irish English. This sheds light on the 'imaginative refeudalization ... of Elizabethan culture', the appropriation of antiquity in the interests of a patriotic yearning for a lost nationhood.[47] It also reminds us that Ireland was not simply an arena of confrontation between ready-made English and Irish nations, but, paradoxically, a site of struggle between competing forms of Englishness. Metropolitan identity could be both questioned and constructed in the colonial margins. Spenser 'knew little Irish', but he had a good grasp of English in all its multiplicity, and he wanted to see its sovereignty firmly established.[48] Patricia Ingham has written of Spenser's English: 'The kingdom about which and in which this strange and exotic language is used is ambiguously located.' For Ingham, Faeryland has its own way of speaking: 'This is England and not-England, and it needs a language which cumulatively is English and not-English. Jonson was perhaps paying the poet an unwitting compliment when he said that Spenser "writ no language". In *The Faerie Queene*, we have a new language for a new kingdom – standard and non-standard – and the incorporation of dialect into such a medium suggests that it is felt to possess the necessary exotic quality.'[49] Ingham does not directly link Faeryland to Ireland, as others have, and as I do here. Spenser once asked Harvey in a letter why they could not 'have the kingdom of our own language?'[50] In Ireland he found a colony of it.

3

Varieties of Englishness: Planting a New Culture Beyond the Pale

I MUTABILITY IN MUNSTER

Nicholas Canny has reminded us that 'Spenser's Irish experience was essentially a Munster or even a Cork one.'[1] Rudolf Gottfried writes: 'Of the four provinces ... Munster seems to be that with which the *View* shows the greatest direct familiarity.'[2] Ciarán Brady has drawn our attention to the fact that two other major treatises of the period were composed 'by the Munster planter Sir William Herbert ... and the Munster civil administrator Richard Beacon'.[3] Roland M. Smith extends Spenser's knowledge to the eastern province of Ireland, but plays down the possibility that Spenser was sufficiently widely travelled for his knowledge to encompass the whole country:

> Investigation makes it more and more evident that Spenser's was something more than an Undertaker's knowledge of Ireland, but that his first-hand familiarity was limited to those portions of Leinster and Munster he was closely connected with. For the rest of Ireland he relied upon his reading and maps and hearsay.[4]

Thus Munster was the site of an exemplary personal experience and investment for Spenser. Moreover, it represented a unique political juncture in Anglo-Irish history:

> Munster thus epitomized the general Tudor failure in Ireland; and it was, I suspect, its peculiarly representative character that underlay the remarkable outpouring of political thought which arose among the Englishmen of the province.[5]

Munster thus stands as a centre of cultural creativity and the scene of violence, corruption, and colonial excess.

This chapter is not intended as a history of the Munster plantation. That history has been fully and excellently narrated in a recent book-length study.[6] Some key questions remain unanswered, though. One is the religious dimension to the plantation, which was clearly a predominantly Protestant, and radical Protestant, affair. There is a need for proper attention to be given to the reforming impulse as an ideological lever in the schemes for settlement, not to mention the appropriation of monastic lands. If Spenser is at all representative of the type, then the Protestant planters appear to have been more intent upon confiscation of property than condemnation of popery. One example from the *View* will suffice to throw into doubt the conventional image of Spenser as a radical reformer. Having lamented the decay of churches and advocated their repair and construction on an imposing scale, Irenius berates those who argue for simplicity of form in church buildings, invoking the Orpheus principle in support of his contention that the simpler sort of people are impressed by pomp and circumstance:

> for the outwarde shewe (assure your selfe) doth greatly drawe the rude people to the reverencing and frequenting thereof. What ever some of our late too nice fooles say, there is nothing in the seemely forme, and comely order of the Church.[7]

What Spenser seems to be saying here is that the undergraduate puritanism of the type he was imbued with at Cambridge is fine in that theorizing context. In the much more secular and vexed world of colonial Munster such idealist nonsense is wholly inappropriate.

Leaving aside the question of religious motives for plantation, then, there are four other areas in which MacCarthy-Morrogh's otherwise exhaustive study might be said to be deficient. Firstly, in the author's preface, he admits to 'an inadequate investigation into the settlers' English background'. Nevertheless, his thesis included an appendix which provided brief biographies of the original undertakers, and the published work includes much invaluable biographical material.[8]

I have tried to provide background information on most of the planters and pamphleteers mentioned in the *DNB*, secondary articles, works published and so on, and in this enterprise I sought to combine the best aspects of the new trend towards cultural biography, or 'prosopography', with a thoroughly contextual approach to individual authors. Prosopography is a Renaissance term denoting a branch of biography defined by Professor Lawrence Stone as 'the analysis of the social and economic affiliations of political groupings, the exposure of the workings of a political machine and the identification of those who pull the levers'.[9] There is a real need for a group biography on Spenser's Irish circle, a prosopographic enterprise which would trace the interconnections between the various planters, and examine in greater depth their social origins and previous careers in England.[10]

Broadly, I have attempted to look at the literary evidence for colonization, and to point out some common links between the more prominent settlers in terms of education, employment and patronage. More importantly, I have attended in greater detail to the circumstances surrounding the founding of the Munster plantation, the second area which MacCarthy-Morrogh was unable properly to pursue. Where his book begins with the death of Desmond, my summary starts with New English representations of the Old English rebellion which preceded the plantation scheme.

Histories of the rebellion are invariably presented separately from histories of the plantation. MacCarthy-Morrogh elects to focus on the 'rebellions' which destroyed the two plantations in the 1590s and 1640s, rather than the destruction which made them possible. My own feeling is that the violent introduction of both schemes cannot be dissociated from their violent endings. Accordingly, I concentrate on the distribution of the spoils of war as the most immediate product of the war itself. This method has the advantage of showing the extent to which the eventual undertakers were implicated in the devastation of Munster which was the necessary prelude to its 'repeopling'. Again, Anthony Sheehan has written a series of scholarly essays on the later stages of the plantation, including three studies of the conflicts which caused the ultimate overthrow of the settlement, but this work still stands apart from the accounts of the war of 1579–83. Finally, MacCarthy-Morrogh implies that the Munster plantation played little part in the colonial crisis of the 1640s, having receded in the 'popular memory' to become 'no more than one of many ancient injustices inflicted by the English', a statement which completely ignores the fact that the publication in 1633 of Spenser's *View* and Stafford's *Pacata Hibernica*, two texts concerned primarily with activities in that province in the 1590s, contributed significantly to the heightening of tension in the region forty years later.[11]

This brings me to the third area in which MacCarthy-Morrogh's painstaking study might be supplemented. He claims that:

the question of moral legitimacy for the plantation and the general thrust of government policy much worried over by historians today did not preoccupy those planning the Munster venture.[12]

This is not entirely true. Patrick O'Connor has suggested that: 'Depopulation of the Munster countryside in the course of the rebellion provided the government with one of the ostensible reasons for the plantation that followed in its wake.'[13] If the government needed the excuse of 'depopulation', a process for which crown forces themselves were largely responsible, then there must have been a pressing moral imperative from the very outset, a need to justify the settlement in terms of a 'repeopling' rather than an extirpation. Robert Dunlop similarly refers to the 'utter depopulation of the province, emphatically recorded by Spenser and other contemporary English writers'.[14] He fails to record the fact that Spenser and 'other contemporary English writers' were also contemporary soldiers and secretaries, and that Spenser was a beneficiary of that 'utter depopulation' well before the official plantation got under way.

The 'repeopling' of Munster so generously undertaken by those responsible for depopulating the province was not a by-product of the Desmond Rebellion, but its predictable outcome. The literary adventurers who accompanied Grey in his campaign against Desmond did not do so in order simply to be able to write vivid reports of the scenes of desolation they encountered. Walter Raleigh, the principal executor of the Smerwick Massacre, an event which most certainly concerned the government as a crucial moral issue with disturbing consequences for England's international relations and reputation, was a captain rather than a courtier at the time, and became a major landowner by virtue of his Irish activities.[15]

Furthermore, if the moral side of settlement was not foremost in the minds of the government, then why did Elizabeth find it necessary in her 'Instructions for the Lord Grey, in July 1580' to allay the fears of her subjects in Munster that a general displacement of the Old English and Gaelic Irish was intended by the English army in Ireland? The choice of the expression 'repeopling' in the orders drawn up for his successor, Sir John Perrot, suggests a convenient conservative cover for a truly revolutionary project.[16]

The fourth area in which MacCarthy-Morrogh's research seems to require supplementary investigation is that of political geography, and this is the subject of the first of my two sorties into the question of mutability in Munster. The author's overall thesis is that Munster's proximity and 'special relationship to the south-west of England' determined that it would become an appendix thereof. The same arguments were doubtless deployed to support the retention of the English Pale around Calais until its loss in 1558. Just as history has disposed of the myth of England's geographical claim to France, so it has dispelled the fiction of a 'special relationship' with Munster. If, in a period of modern communications, the province can exist as a separate political entity, then why, in an era of relatively primitive transport, did it constitute a natural 'borderland'? Ireland represented both an outpost of barbarity and a backdoor to invasion from Spain, and it did so by virtue of some fairly deft literary manoeuvring by Old and New English observers alike. One man's 'West England' was another's 'Eutopia', and yet another's 'Canaan'.[17] Modern Spenserians tend to see Spenser's Ireland as a dystopia, the antithesis of the poet's Faeryland.[18]

How did Ireland manage to be in two places at one time, simultaneously situated on England's border and at the uttermost extremities of civilization? How did sixteenth-century English writers discover in it both exotic excess and domestic disorder? The answer is that the geography and ideology of colonization are much more complex questions than MacCarthy-Morrogh's narrow determinism will allow. A nineteenth-century commentator gave little credence to the geographical imperative, pointing out that the protracted length of the struggle to assimilate the natives, and its apparent abject failure after seven centuries of sustained effort, suggested that 'all the geographical pretexts in the world are not enough to prove that it is England's mission to conquer Ireland'.[19]

II PALE, PROVINCE AND PARTITION

English and Irish, natives and newcomers, kingdom and colony; such simplistic divisions, I am arguing, do not do justice to the complexities of the political situation in early modern Ireland. The presence of a third force, in the form of the Old English, radically undermines our conventional two-tier conceptual framework. Neither English nor Irish, neither natives nor newcomers, neither metropolitan nor marginal, this intermediate community, this 'middle nation', marked the boundary, in their own minds, and in the eyes of their would-be supplanters, between English court civility, or culture, and Irish colonial rudeness, or barbarity. Impaled, problematically, within a politics of entrenchment no longer suited to the needs of an expanding English nation state, these intervening subjects occupy, as a distinctive English society in their own right, a position which is shifting gradually from feudal fiefdom to colonial staging post in the sixteenth century.[20]

It is 'new Inglishemens intrudinge', and the attendant alteration in the status of the Pale, from final frontier to fighting frontline, which disrupts the delicate equilibrium established between the Gaelic Irish and their long-term English neighbours.[21] The Pale was always as much a concept of civility-under-siege as an actual administrative region. From Reformation to Restoration, the fundamental change in English policy on Ireland was from the medieval compromise of Pale politics to the darker vision of Renaissance Protestantism, from a scenario wherein Ireland housed an outpost of Englishness, to early modern colonization and control, whereby Ireland played host to some of the most radical elements in native English society.

Spenser was in no doubt as to the limitations and litigations arising from the defensive politics of the Pale. Among many mischiefs inadvertently engineered by previous English monarchs, Irenius lists:

> the grauntes of Counties palatines in *Ireland*, which though at first were graunted upon good consideracion when they were first Conquered, for that those landes lay then as a very border to the wild *Irish*, subject to continuall invacion, so it was needfull to give them great priviledges for the defence of the Inhabitants thereof: yet now that it is no more a border, nor frontiered with enemies why should suche priviledges bee any more continued?[22]

Note Spenser's almost casual dismissal of the pale's *raison d'être*: 'yet now that it is no more a border'. Spenser wishes the Tudor *raison d'état* to discard such a defensive and defeatist policy. Note Spenser's obvious resentment, as a New English planter ostensibly 'beyond the Pale', toward the heirs of an earlier, geographically, and, as he and his New English associates would have it, culturally less advanced colony, who still enjoyed special favours from the crown associated with that initial, incomplete conquest. As ever, Irenius is prompt in replying to the predictable request made by Eudoxus, 'I would gladly know what you call a County palatine and whence it so called':

Iren: It was (I suppose) firste named palatine of a pale, as it were a pale and defense to their inward lands, so as it is called the *English Pale*, and therefore is a Palsgrave, named an Earle Palatine. Others thinke of the Latine, *palare*, that is to forrage or out-run, because those marchers and borderers use commonly so to doe. So as to have a county palatine is, in effect, to have a priviledge to spoyle the enemies borders adjoyning. And surely so it is used at this day, as a priviledged place of spoiles and stealthes, for the Countye of *Tipperary*, which is now the onely county palatine in *Ireland*, is by abuse of some bad ones, made a receptacle to rob the rest of the Counties about it, by meanes of whose priviledges none will followe their stealthes, so as it being situate in the very lap of all the land, is made now a border, which howe inconvenient it is, let every man judge.[23]

What Spenser is objecting to is the existence of 'no-go' areas dominated by Old English magnates, operating regional restrictions which reinforce the New English sense of confinement in their scattered pockets of settlement in Munster. It was this same jurisdiction, so jealously guarded by Lord Roche, Spenser's Old English neighbour, which saw the confiscation of cattle from one of Spenser's Irish tenants follow on from his allowing a New English landlord to lodge with him on his way home from the sessions of the presidency court of Munster in Limerick, the provincial capital.[24]

If Spenser is sure of the limitations placed upon English governance by the existence of the Pale, he is considerably less sure of the exact parameters of the Pale itself. In recounting to Eudoxus the machinations of the Scots in Ulster during the reign of Edward II, Irenius points out the contraction since suffered by English authority in Ireland. The Scots and 'degenerate' English:

marched foorth into the *English* pale, which then was chiefly in the North from the pointe of *Donluce* and beyond unto *Dublin*: Having in the middest of her *Knockfergus*, *Belfast*, *Armagh*, and *Carlingford*, which are now the most out-bounds and abandoned places in the *English* Pale, and indeede not counted of the *English* Pale at all: for it stretcheth now no further then *Dundalke* towardes the North.[25]

In 'Spenser's Linguistics in *A View of the Present State of Ireland*', John Draper investigated the depth of definition usually deployed by Spenser, citing 'Pale' as a prime example of a word which prompts an elaborate exhibition of lexical learning apparently uncalled for by the immediate context of its first occurrence, and one, moreover, which seems to rely upon a somewhat dubious 'popular etymology'. In my judgement Spenser's etymology is astutely political rather than merely popular, that is, he chooses his linguistic fictions as carefully as his historical fictions.[26]

William Camden entertained a vision of the Pale which appears to have anticipated the modern phrase 'beyond the Pale', meaning 'outside the bounds of civil behaviour', insofar as it conceives of the Pale in terms of a fluid notion of Englishness rather than a rigidly structured juridical border:

> Ireland, according to the *Manners* and *Customs* of the Inhabitants, is divided into two parts: They who [would] reject all Laws, and live after a barbarous manner, are called the *Irishry*; but the civiliz'd part, who submit themselves [willingly] to the laws, are term'd the English-Irish, and their Country the English Pale: for the first English that came hither, mark'd out their bounds in the more easterly and the richest part of the island; Within which compass, even at this day [Anno. 1607], some remain uncivilized, and pay little obedience to the laws; whereas some without, are as courteous and genteel as one would desire.[27]

Camden's division of Ireland takes the same dialectical view of the Pale as that suggested by the American scholar D. G. White, who has argued for a much less pedantically geographical comprehension of the politics of the Pale than that which presently prevails in Irish historiography. White overturns the traditional assumption of integrity and impenetrability by displacing the Pale from the realm of geography and empiricism to the domain of politics and ideology. Beginning with the early application of the expression in Poyning's parliament of 1495, where it was decreed that there be constructed a 'doubleditch of six foot of earth above the ground', White proceeds to pin down, one by one, the territorial and psychological meanings of the Pale to a general conception of cultural control. Ultimately, White insists, the Pale was as much a concept of English cultural identity as it was a question of Irish colonial indentation.[28] Not that the pale itself was other than a late medieval notion, as one view of Spenser's Irish geography makes abundantly clear.[29]

It is possible to detect in the Anglo-Irish literature of the sixteenth century a decisive linguistic shift from Pale to province. Nicholas

Browne, the second son of Sir Valentine Browne, one of Spenser's fellow undertakers, predictably felt more comfortable discoursing of the 'Provynce' of Munster, the extensive plantation of which had effectively put paid, much more than any act of kingly title, to the myth of the Pale as a last resort rather than a staging post.[30] A preference for the language of province over the language of Pale represents a calculated effort to overthrow the old colonial strategy and create a modern myth of integration.

One can see why the temporary, tenuous undertones of the latter render it an inferior term, from the perspective of the English crown, to the more domestic, naturalizing propensity of the former expression. With the loss of Calais in 1558, what self-respecting English monarch would want to be constantly reminded of the transient status of English dominions overseas? This change at the level of language was accompanied, of course, by a policy of provincial settlement which went 'beyond the Pale' inasmuch as it was implemented in areas generally thought to be tangential to the traditional English sphere of influence. Plantation schemes in Munster and Ulster circumvented the mid-eastern stronghold of the Old English and threatened to short-circuit the power of the Pale.

What of the Old English position on the Pale, that 'warme neste' to which Stanyhurst alluded in Holinshed's *Chronicles*? One articulate Palesman, writing in the 1550s, attributed, provocatively, the divisiveness arising from the policy of having a Pale of Englishness distinct from the rest of the country to parliamentary legislation implemented against the interests of the Old English. That is, while the Old English themselves were, through fosterage and intermarriage, conducting an assimilatory strategy of their own with the Gaelic Irish, the crown was constantly cutting back on that initiative, fearing 'Hibernicization' rather than encouraging 'Anglicization':

> Whereof followed that the one part called the English Pale was cast under the yoke of continual bearing of soldiers and men of war. Whereof proceeded the mighty murders, ravishing of wives and young women, the daily depredations and burnings, as well between the English and the Irish pales. What kind of godly [purpose?] is this to kindle so great a fire in so narrow a [conduit?] ... by reason of this exempting of the Irishry from the English they have conceived such a terror of banishment that they think England means nothing else thereby but as it were to save only booty and destroy the residue with the sword.[31]

This astute observer correctly identified a central strand of English colonial policy, the persistence of a 'divide and rule' mentality. To play an English Pale off against an Irish Pale was the preferred tactic of the metropolis.

In Munster, by breaking down the forts and fenced Pales of Old English reason, the New English achieved a virtual revolution: in the course of little over a century from the 1580s the political, cultural and economic complexion of the region was drastically altered, on the one hand by an almost complete transfer of property and social control from the Anglo-Norman and Gaelic families to New English and Protestant grantees, and on the other by immigration of 'common English' to a number of districts within the region where the policy of plantation and colonization was actually implemented by the new proprietors.[32]

This unparalleled substitution of one English society for another was accompanied by a series of violent confrontations in which the Gaelic Irish acted as brokers. The bulk of 'rebellions' in this period, from the so-called 'Silken Thomas' revolt of 1534 to the much more protracted Desmond uprising of 1579–83, were led by Old English nobles with the provisional support of the Irish peasantry. Had these recusant aristocrats had the full backing, at an earlier stage, of their native neighbours, events may have taken a different turn. As it was, the New English seem to have succeeded in playing one section of the indigenous community off against another.[33]

The Old English, in the years immediately following the Henrican Reformation, concurred with the English crown in its reforming principles. Indeed, the zealousness evident in their professed desire to civilize the 'mere Irish', and the constant frustrations they faced at the hands of an initially cautious London government, bring to mind the conscientious objections of the royal gardener's assistant in *Richard II*:

> Why should we, in the compass of a pale,
> Keep law and form and due proportion,
> Showing as in a model our firm estate,
> When our seawalled garden, the whole land,
> Is full of weeds, her fairest flowers choked up,
> Her fruit trees all unpruned, her hedges ruined,
> Her knots disordered, and her wholesome herbs
> Swarming with caterpillars? (III 4.407)

Horticultural metaphors abound in the early modern English discourse of plantation, as one would expect, and it is no surprise to discover Shakespeare picking up on the common cultural practice of referring to the English Pale as a plot set apart from the landscape as a whole, a scene of order in a disorderly landscape.

Pale, province and partition: these politico-ideological divisions do not designate distinct phases of an ongoing colonial process, but, crucially, signify constituent parts of a coherent cultural practice. In implementing the Munster plantation, the English government was, superficially, extending the Pale well beyond the narrow coastal strip surrounding Dublin. By setting up a provincial presidency, it was trying to plant, precipitately, what Steve Ellis maintains always already existed, a Tudor 'borderland', administered in the same way as other provinces of England.[34] Through the partial nature of the plantation, in the sense both of piecemeal and partisan, the crown constructed, inadvertently, an alternative Pale, answerable, ultimately, to neither court nor colony, and accepted, finally, by neither native community.

III THE POLITICS OF PLANTATION

'The planting of Ireland', wrote Vincent Gookin (c.1616–1659), Munster settler, Surveyor General, and Member of Parliament for Kinsale, 'is the subject of many men's Desires, most mens Discourse, of few mens Endeavours'.[35] The profusion of ink spilled on the subject in the Elizabethan period earned Ireland the name of 'the paper state'.[36] In the case of late sixteenth-century Munster, desire, discourse, and endeavour were the common dominion of a few uncommon men.

The idea of a large-scale recolonization of Munster had been mooted, seriously, as early as 1568–9. Sir Henry Sidney wrote to Elizabeth in 1567 on the desolation in Munster and concluded: 'Yea, the view of the bones and skulls of dead subjects, who, partly by murder, partly by famine, have died in the field, as in truth hardly any Christian with dry eye could behold.'[37] Sir Warham St Leger (c.1525–1597), a supporter of the Lord Deputy, Sir Henry Sidney, then in his second term of office as viceroy, from 28 October 1568 to 1 April 1571, put forward a plan, in partnership with Sir Richard Grenville, to cultivate lands in Kerrycurrihy which St Leger had purchased from the debt-ridden Earl of Desmond. St Leger, who mortgaged his own lands in Kent to obtain the Desmond property, had served a short-lived period of office in 1566 as President of Munster, before Elizabeth decided that, with Sidney as chief governor of Ireland, the Dudley faction would have too much power concentrated in too few hands, and, accordingly, countermanded Sidney's appointment of St Leger. Now, as a chief commissioner, with the help of his new in-law, Grenville, whom Sidney promptly installed as Sheriff of Cork – a post for which Spenser was shortlisted three decades later – St Leger hoped to insinuate himself into a position of unassailable strength in the province, such as that secured by Richard Boyle (1566–1643), first Earl of Cork, a generation later. Due to a lack of support from central government, and the outbreak of a rebellion which was not wholly unrelated to the colonial scheming of St Leger, and, before him, Sir Peter Carew (1514–1575), the proposed plantation fell through.[38]

St Leger later wrote with revulsion at the ruin of Munster, informing Elizabeth on 12 March 1582 that 'starving numbers of poor innocent people, being already dead by famine in this province not so few as 30,000 at the least within less than this half-year'.[39] According to Richard McCabe: 'Far from recoiling from the experience of the 1580s Spenser demands that it be repeated in the 1590s.'[40] In advocating a scorched earth policy for Ulster, Ireland's most contrary province, Spenser is deliberately contemplating an intensification of the Munster model of famine and sword: 'Moreover, as Ulster is by nature less fertile than Munster, the results of a Northern famine would be proportionately worse ... Spenser is planning not merely to repeat, but to outdo, the horrors of recent history.'[41]

This unrealized venture is best known for the later careers of the adventurers behind it. Sir Richard Grenville and Sir Humphrey Gilbert were subsequently engaged in colonizing schemes in North America. Gilbert, appointed 'Colonel' of Munster in 1569, the first use, as far as I know, of such a title in an Irish context, or in any other English colonial environment, delivered a petition to the Privy Council in March of that year, detailing the intentions of the group of gentlemen, himself included, who wished 'to plant & inhabit certen landes and possessions in that provynce with naturall Englishe men, or at the least with sutche of Ireland birth as are discended of Inglish nacion'. There is no inkling as yet here of a deliberate policy of discrimination against the Old English.[42]

According to Michael MacCarthy-Morrogh, the key ministerial figure behind the second Elizabethan proposal to plant Munster was William Cecil, Lord Burghley. He was aided in this formidable task by Sir Francis Walsingham. Between them, Burghley and Walsingham handled the vast body of paperwork triggered by news of Desmond's attainder on 2 November 1579. From that historical juncture until the final allocation, in 1589, of the letters patent legally conferring the scattered seignories upon the selected undertakers, those two senior civil servants and linchpins of the Privy Council were immersed in the politics of plantation in Munster.[43]

Robert Dunlop has remarked that the letter of intent which heralded the Smith colonial venture in Ulster in the early 1570s was a serious indiscretion on the part of its planners. One can envisage here the contradiction between the need to publicize a scheme for settlement, and the need to maintain some level of secrecy regarding the details of such a scheme, in order to conceal its implications from the native populace which is to be dispossessed thereby. When does an advertisement become an alarm? Dunlop harbours no illusions as to the ill timing of the Smith pamphlet, the first piece of promotional literature of its kind to be published.[44]

No such necessity for prudence prevailed in the formative stages of the Munster plantation. The hard core of its eventual settlers, known, ironically in retrospect, as undertakers, were actively engaged in the process of clearing the lands of rebels whilst the project itself was in its germinal phase. Looking down the list of original grantees compiled by MacCarthy-Morrogh, and, usefully, incorporated as an appendix to his published study, one is immediately struck, not simply by the elevated rank of a sizeable proportion of the individuals involved – the complete list of forty-one planters includes nine knights – nor merely by the financial clout wielded by its mercantile members – wealthy businessmen such as Henry Oughtred and Henry Billingsley feature prominently among the successful nominees – but, more pertinently, in light of the Cromwellian strategy of the 1650s, by the presence of a phalanx of military men. Figures such as captains Edward Denny and Walter Raleigh, for example, had already received, as early as January 1582, lands bestowed, controversially, it transpired, by Lord Deputy Grey, who had also seen fit to confer upon a certain Edmund Spenser proprietorship of the Dublin residence of James Eustace, Viscount Baltinglas. Grey was brought to book by the Queen, as Essex would be later, for his liberal distribution of viceregal favours. Thus, even before the official cessation of hostilities, signalled by the death of Desmond near Tralee on 11 November 1583, and prior to the survey of forfeited territories carried out between September and November of the following year, a provisional plantation of sorts had already taken place.[45]

What separates the Leix–Offaly, Munster and Ulster schemes of the 1550s, 1560s and 1570s, from the Munster operation of the 1580s, is the extent to which the terrain to be planted was the site of what one can only refer to, in the interests of historical accuracy, as the genocidal actions of English forces in that province between 1580 and 1583. I comment elsewhere on Spenser's notorious, and notoriously misread, report on this episode in the *View*.[46] Of course, one can construct all sorts of sophisticated theoretical justifications and elaborate excuses for the horrific events of those years, particularly if one accepts as I do not that the Desmond war was an unprovoked rebellion against a moderate regime.[47] What one cannot do, without an act of wilful suppression, is deny that the eradication of some thirty thousand persons prepared the ground for some four thousand English settlers. I use the most up-to-date approximation provided by MacCarthy-Morrogh, which supersedes the earlier estimates of Dunlop, Quinn and Sheehan. The English euphemism for the settlement which followed in the wake of this act of genocide, 'repeopling', hardly begins to tell the story of that horrific depopulation.[48]

Any study of the Munster plantation has to take as its starting point the reality of its violent induction. Only by acknowledging the extreme violence which brought it into being can one account for its brief and bloody history, or even begin to explain the atrocities which attended its premature demise in 1598. Edmund Spenser's place in that plantation was largely determined by the part he played in its inception. One important reason why it has taken so long for an extensive study of the plantation to materialize, apart from the fact that it was, in the short term, a failure, that is, aside from the ignominy which accompanied its death, is exactly the historical resentment smouldering over the circumstances surrounding its birth. Here, too, we have one of the most decisive indices of Spenser's unpopularity amongst Irish scholars, who, understandably, see beneath the exquisite allegorical veil of *The Faerie Queene* the 'Anotomies of deathe' described in such graphic detail in the *View*, especially when, as I shall argue, the context of that description is, disturbingly, an advocacy of its repetition.

Ciarán Brady contends that Spencer:

coldly recommended a policy of general starvation, widespread confiscation of native lands, ruthless transportation of the innocent populace, and the establishment of military rule over the entire country.[49]

My own feeling is that Spenser is quite heated and passionate in his recounting of the Munster famine, and that this is part of the problem with the passage. There is evidence in contemporary Gaelic poetry to suggest that the 'innocent populace' thought God had punished them for past sins.[50]

The Munster plantation (1584–98) was, from its very inception, a troubled affair, conceived of in the midst of a violent rising led by the Old English magnate, Gerald FitzJames Fitzgerald (c.1533–1583), fourteenth Earl of Desmond (1559–83), one of the Geraldines who had hitherto been closely connected by the politics of Anglo-Irish patronage to the late Lord Deputy Sir Henry Sidney, and, by extension, to the Leicester interest, the so-called 'enchanted earl' of Marianne Moore's sentimental poem.[51] The nostalgia and idealism attached to the whole episode is not restricted to poetic representations alone.[52]

A key element in romantic interpretations of the rebellion is the role of the eccentric Old English aristocrat who led it. After long periods of imprisonment in London, the Earl is reputed to have returned to Munster towards the end of the 1570s an altered man, unwilling or unable to countenance the increasingly high profile of the New English in his traditional domain. With Sidney gone, and a caretaker viceregal administration under first Sir William Drury, then Sir William Pelham, the region was ripe for conflict. The Spanish intervention at Smerwick and the merciless action of the newly appointed Lord Grey on the surrender of the garrison on 10 November 1580 signalled an irreversible turn in Anglo-Irish politics. Desmond's leadership, whatever his supposed personality disorder, was strong enough for the insurgents to withstand four years of fighting. His violent death at the hands of a mixed party of New English and Gaelic Irish mercenaries on 11 November 1583 in a glen in County Kerry – the event which opens MacCarthy-Morrogh's study of the Munster plantation – effectively ended Old English power in the province and cleared the way for the major plantation which ensued. The 'head money' for the assassination of Desmond amounted to £1000, dispensed by Lord Deputy Perrot on 10 March 1585. It was a small price to pay for half a million acres of land in Ireland's richest region. The thirty thousand lives lost in order to make way for a few thousand settlers is a much more difficult exchange to come to terms with.[53]

Moore's metaphor for mental deficiency, albeit a not unkind one, is given little historical credence by Ciarán Brady in his incisive study of the Desmond Rebellion (1579–83). Brady runs through the conventional slurs against the Earl, and proceeds to demolish the arguments, contemporary and modern, which seek to place sole responsibility for Desmond's behaviour on his own allegedly erratic personality, a reductive criticism which:

> By emphasising the simple, reactionary elements in the earl's conduct – his defence of the old feudal ways and of the old religion – it discounted the role which the vicissitudes of factional politics played in his downfall and so exonerated English officials from any part in the tragedy.[54]

The critical 'amnesia' which Brady exposes in relation to the events leading up to the decisive conflagration which ushered in a new era of English occupation, the anaesthetization, as it were, of the injuries sustained by the Earl and his followers in the 1570s, was inaugurated even as the conflict was in progress. Before I focus on one spectacular instance of New English cultural mythology, I want to cite some descriptions and conclusions drawn from the historiography of the rebellion, and the circumstances surrounding it.

On the subject of the order within disorder in the Desmond Rebellion, Patrick O'Connor has observed:

> Depopulation of the Munster countryside in the course of the rebellion provided the government with one of the ostensible reasons for the plantation that followed in its wake.[55]

Another historian has pointed to Sir Henry Sidney's description of the desolation and waste in Munster in 1567, on the eve of the earlier, aborted scheme for settlement of 1568–9, as a reminder that such evocations of disorder and decay were predictable in pre-plantation discourses.[56] This is not to imply that Munster was not the site of supreme desolation following the wars of 1569–73 and 1579–83, but, rather, to insist that colonization was the cause rather than the consequence of such devastation. Steve Ellis has referred to Desmond as 'dim-witted, barely literate, more a captain than a courtier', but he was not so short-sighted as to misread the clear signs of impending colonization. Sir Peter Carew's claim to some two million acres of southern Ireland early in the 1570s did nothing to reassure the Old English that their estates were secure.[57]

The destruction visited upon Munster by Grey's army was a necessary prelude to the already intended New English settlement.

It would be naive to think that the quick-witted and highly literate English captains and courtiers who were risking their own lives and ruining others were doing so in the name of honour, or simply for the love of country. Even as the war was in progress, Grey was redistributing the lands and goods of the enemy to his soldiers and secretaries. Before he was ever an undertaker in the official plantation, Spenser was acquiring properties in Dublin and County Kildare, and Raleigh was receiving Barry's Island. The Queen objected to Grey's excessive generosity just as much as she complained of his alleged extreme cruelty. The two were not unrelated.[58]

It is not simply, as Dunlop would have it, that 'the utter depopulation of the province, emphatically recorded by Spenser and other contemporary English writers' was an act of God which 'providentially' (to use his disturbing phraseology) removed the threat of native resistance to plantation to the tune of 30,000 persons.[59] Providence had very little to do with it. What such a position ignores is that the selfsame individuals who were busily and eloquently describing the aftermath of the Desmond 'rebellion' were themselves in large part responsible for that carnage. Nor should one forget that Spenser's notorious description in the *View* of the famine in Munster occurs in the midst of an argument he is making for the reintroduction of what one Irish historian described as 'a policy of general starvation'.[60]

Spenser's much quoted description of the famine in Munster is usually considered in complete isolation from other contemporary accounts of Grey's government. I want now to set out some of these reports, beginning, crucially, with a rarely cited example from Bryskett's *Discourse*:

> We have (said Sir *Robert Dillon*) great cause indeed to thanke God of the present state of our country, and that the course houlden now by our present Lord Deputie, doth promise us a continuance, if not a bettering, of this our peace and quietnesse. My Lord *Grey* hath plowed and harrowed the rough ground to his hand: but you know that he that soweth the seede, whereby we hope for harvest according to the goodnesse of that which is cast into the earth, and the seasonablenesse of times, deserveth no lesse praise then he that manureth the land.[61]

This speech, with its euphemistic allusion to the 'utter depopulation' of Munster in which most of the men present had participated, is recorded against the backdrop of Dublin's suburbs, in the course of a walk 'in the greene way'. No finer example of the assumed innocence of English colonial discourse in this period exists.

The best known published contemporary report of the Smerwick Massacre must surely be that composed by John Hooker, the editor of the second edition of the Irish section of Holinshed's *Chronicles*, in 1587. Hooker, significantly, dedicated his work to Sir Walter Raleigh. I say significantly because, although Grey is generally held responsible for the bloody episode on 10 November 1580, it is my contention that the principal purpose of Spenser's revision of that event is aimed, not simply at erasing a stain on a past patron, but, importantly, removing a blot from a present patron. Grey died in 1593, and while his honour was no doubt part of the issue, not to mention Spenser's own reputation, the good name of Sir Walter Raleigh was, I would argue, uppermost in Spenser's mind at the time of his recitation. Hooker is, ironically, in light of the glowing dedication to one of Elizabeth's most famous courtiers, the historian who advertised Raleigh's implication in the massacre:

> When the capteine had yeelded himselfe, and the fort appointed to be surrendered, capteine Raleigh together with capteine Macworth, who had the ward of that daie, entered into the castell, & made a great slaughter, manie or the moste part of them being put to the sworde. And when all things were cleere, the lord deputie came to the fort, and having doone what pleased him, his lordship returned, and manie of the capteins he saved.[62]

The two most remarkable things about this version of events are, firstly, Grey's apparent absence from the actual scene of the atrocity and, secondly, and much more disturbingly, the fact that the cruel despatch of the garrison is not excused or explained in any way. We are simply told that, on its surrender, Raleigh and another officer 'entered into the castell, & made a great slaughter'. Interestingly, the entry for Raleigh in the *DNB* suggests that he was acting strictly under orders from Grey in executing the massacre of the garrison, but the evidence of Hooker, who enjoyed Raleigh's patronage, and, one might presume, his confidence, suggests otherwise. Youth and inexperience arguably compounded the problem of extreme political violence in the desperate pursuit of material advantages.[63]

Spenser's recollection of the state of the victims of Grey's scorched earth policy taxed his descriptive powers almost to the limit:

Out of every corner of the woods and glynnes they came creeping forth upon their hands, for their legges could not beare them, they looked like anatomies of death, they spake like Ghostes crying out of their graves, they did eate the dead Carrions, happy were they could finde them, yea, and one another soone after, insomuch as the verye carcasses they spared not to scrape out of their graves, and if they found a plot of water-cresses or Shamrocks, there they flocked as to a feast for the time, yet not able long to continue thearewithall, that in short space there were none almost left, and a most populous and plentifull countrey suddainely left voyde of man and beast, yet sure in all that warre, there perished not manie by the Sword, but all by the extremitie of famine, which they themselves had wrought.[64]

These graphic images of suffering have to be set in the immediate context of the Irenius–Eudoxus 'interview', where they are evoked by Irenius, the interviewee, in order to prove his point that a strategy of total war will break the Irish sooner than any pacifist prevarication. Eudoxus anticipates the modern response to this vision of despair, and proposes, tentatively, that such a policy could be counter-productive:

But now when all things are brought to this passe, and all filled with these ruefull spectacles of so many wretched Carcases starving, goodly Countreyes wasted, so huge a desolation and confusion, that even I that doe but heare it from you, and doe picture it in my minde, doe greatly pittie and commiserate it. If it shall happen that the state of this miserie and lamentable image of things shall bee tolde, and feelingly presented to her sacred Majestie, being by nature full of mercy and clemency, who is moste inclinable to such pittifull complaints, and will not endure to heare such Tragedies made of her poore people and subjects, as some about her may insinuate. Then shee perhappes for very compassion of such calamities, will not onely stoppe the streame of such violence, and returne to her wonted mildenesse, but also conne them little thankes which have beene the authours and Councellours of such bloodie platformes.[65]

It is here that Eudoxus digresses on the subject of Grey's reputation as 'a bloodie man', before being assured by Irenius that the late Lord Deputy had been, slander aside, a 'most just and honourable personage'.[66]

One would not have to look very far to find a modern analogy for this ideological tendency to blame the victims of colonialism for whatever pains they suffer in resisting that process. 'Intransigence' is the most anodyne expression we can employ to describe Spenser's approach to the problem. Spenser's language anticipates the imagery frequently employed in the depositions taken after the Ulster Rising of 1641.[67] Jonathan Dollimore and Alan Sinfield, citing the description of the Munster famine, say 'even those who, like the poet Edmund Spenser, defended torture and murder expressed compunction at the effects of English policy'.[68]

Mutability in Munster did not simply prepare the way for plantation. The transformation of the landscape was effected by activists intent upon securing livelihoods from the depopulation and plantation of the region. This is not to deny that Ireland's richest territory was already in the process of alteration and modernization under its Old English lords. The speed of change, though, was determined by the massive intervention of the New English in the period. Spenser's part in both stages of the metamorphosis of Munster ought not to be underestimated.

I want to conclude this analysis of the Munster plantation with a quotation from a seventeenth-century pamphlet on the proposed Cromwellian transplantation of the Irish to Connaught which ends on a positive note, with a happy prospect of the future set against the horror of recent events:

> And what a pleasing sight will it be to England, instead of meagre naked Anatomies, which she received driven from *Ireland* in the beginning of a War, to empty her self of her young Swarms thither in the beginning of a Peace? If Antiquity deceive us not, that Land was once called the Island of Saints; and if Novelty deceive us not again, it may find as strange a change to good, as it had a fall to ill; God has made (in the name of Instruments) the good or ill of thousands beneath, to hang upon the breath of a few that are above.[69]

Gookin has in mind the English refugees who fled from Ireland during the conflagration of the 1640s, having suffered a fate similar to that of the displaced Irish of Spenser's *View*, those grim and ghostly figures which haunt the passage on the Munster famine. Reminding his readers of the troubled past, and looking ahead with optimism, the writer

forgets that it was in just such an atmosphere of exhaustion following
a long and bitter conflict that Spenser's ill-fated Irish sojourn began.

IV DUBLINERS

To illustrate the context in which educated Englishmen thought fit
to discuss colonization, I want now to move from the reality of
Munster, a province decimated by 'Captain Travel, Captain Sickness,
Captain Cold, and Captain Hunger', a reality I tried to convey through
the representations of contemporary New English colonists in the last
section, to the fantasy of another country composed of those selfsame
gentlemen discoursing of that Trojan Horse of 'civility' they considered
themselves to be bringing to the Irish.[70]

'Spenser's Ireland has not altered', so begins Marianne Moore's
romantic remembrance of the poet's Irish experiences.[71] As with all
poetry there is history, truth and myth here. The myth of an Ireland
untouched by Spenser's intrusion is not merely the product of
successive generations of critical revision, nor is it simply the result
of the persistent obfuscation of history in Spenser studies. Rather, the
roots of this blindness to change reside in the persistent pastoral
idealizations of Ireland to be found in the poet's own writings. In *Colin
Clouts Come Home Againe* and the *Two Cantos of Mutabilitie*, Spenser
set up an image of a proverbially primitive province far removed from
the corruption and careerism of court politics.

This idea of rural Ireland as an attractive alternative to the incessant
jockeying for position so evident in the English metropolis is
communicated most poignantly in Lodowick Bryskett's *A Discourse
of Civill Life*, written in the first half of the 1580s, and published in 1606.
Dedicated to Lord Grey, late Lord Deputy of Ireland, this translation
of a continental courtesy handbook is introduced via the standard
literary device of an 'occasion'. The translation, we are told, was read
in Bryskett's house on the outskirts of Dublin. Thus the original nexus
of the English Pale provides the immediate context for a sophisticated
discussion of the process of civility. Together with Spenser's communal
colonial fictions, Bryskett's gathering of Dublin literati established a
tradition of a quaint, backward Ireland, an eternally uncomplicated
setting against which the more advanced concepts of English culture
could be advanced. Ancient, infantile, inane, untouched, even under
English influence – this is the received impression of Spenser's Ireland.
The overall effect created by such literary representations of English

culture in Ireland is to suggest that, far from being modified, or mediated by the colonial milieu, English civility could comport itself outside of England whilst appearing almost entirely impervious to that Irish 'subculture' towards which it only very occasionally gestured.

The Bryskett conference sees a small clique of urbane young men, for the most part aged around thirty, predominantly Oxbridge-educated, and occupying a series of key posts in the New English colonial system, assemble at the house of a provincial administrator on the outskirts of Dublin, sometime in the early 1580s. Bryskett's *A Discourse of Civill Life*, famous for its early reference to Spenser's *The Faerie Queene* as work-in-progress, has as its 'pretext' for the translation of Giovanni Battista's cult of civility, a gathering of friends and colleagues at Bryskett's 'home' within Ireland's English Pale. The colonial context provides the perfect foil for a discussion of the relative merits of manners and morality in the constitution of an ideal subject.[72] Frederic Ives Carpenter wrote in 1922: 'An attempt to reconstruct this society and to show the life of the times in Ireland in connection with Spenser would not be an impossible task and should be a highly interesting one.'[73] I shall attempt here to sketch the beginnings of such a reconstruction.

The young urban professionals present at Bryskett's house a mile and a half from Dublin in the spring of 1582 were captains Christopher Carleil (c.1551–1593) and Nicholas Dawtrey; Thomas Digges (d.1593); Sir Robert Dillon (d.1597); one Dormer, the 'Queenes Sollicitor'; John Long, 'Primate of Ardmagh' (1548–1589); Sir Thomas Norris (1556–1599); Thomas Smith, 'the Apothecary'; Warham St Leger; Edmund Spenser (c.1552–1599) and, of course, Bryskett himself. Apart from St Leger, these were men of Spenser's generation, whose place in Irish society was dependent upon the pace and progress of the policy of plantation. What kind of men were they? How do their careers compare with Spenser's? From the smallest fragments of information, it is possible to piece together a composite picture of the discursive pretext for Bryskett's translation.

Lodowick Bryskett (c.1545–1611) matriculated at Trinity College, Cambridge on 27 April 1559, but does not appear to have taken any degree. By 1571 he was occupying the post of Clerk of the Council in Ireland under Sir Henry Sidney. Between 1572 and 1575 he accompanied Sidney's famous son, Philip, on his continental travels. On returning to Ireland he secured an appointment as Clerk for the Chancery of the Faculties in Ireland. At the time of the alleged audience at his Dublin residence, Bryskett was Secretary of the Munster Council. The higher office which he was disappointed in his efforts to attain, that of Secretary of State, which fell vacant on the death of Sir John Challoner on 11 May 1581, went instead to Sir Geoffrey Fenton. Had it not been for Grey's loss of favour at court and his eventual recall Bryskett might have obtained the position he desired, a position for which, as the dedication to the *Discourse* makes clear, Grey had recommended him. Bryskett's opinion of Grey at the time of the Smerwick Massacre is expressed in a letter to Walsingham dated from Dublin, 21 April 1581:

> Her Majestie had never here a more willing, a more zealous, nor a more sufficient minister for suche an enterprise then this L. Deputie, nether was there ever any here more lykely to prosper in any action that he shall take in hand, as a man living in the feare of God, and so consequently assured of his blessing.[74]

Bryskett appears not to have found a patron as generous as either Sidney or Grey after the recall of the latter, but by 1606, the year of the publication of the *Discourse*, he was a major landowner, with estates in Dublin, Cavan and Cork.[75]

Christopher Carleil, the son of a London vintner, has a typical New English pedigree. He was educated at Cambridge in the 1560s. In the 1570s, he saw active service in the Low Countries. As the son-in-law of Sir Francis Walsingham, he participated in the early 1580s in English efforts to colonize America. He was the author, in 1583, of *A discourse upon the entended voyage to the nethermoste partes of America*, which is to be found in Hakluyt's *The principal navigations, voyages, traffiques & discoveries of the English nation*. In 1584 he was appointed supreme commander of the garrison at Coleraine. He lost this post the following year, seemingly due to a disagreement with Perrot. In July 1588, he was installed as constable of Carrickfergus in Antrim.[76]

Little is known of Nicholas Dawtrey's early life or education. He arrived in Ireland in the 1560s, but he first appears in crown documents in September 1581, where he is reported as commander of a company of one hundred horse in Clandeboye, in east Ulster. Four years later we hear of him being despatched to the Scottish court on official business. He shared Carleil's disaffection with Perrot, as indeed did Spenser, and he did not resume his Irish commission. In 1588 he acted as Sergeant Major General of the Queen's troops at Tilbury. Throughout the 'crisis' years of the 1590s, he contributed a series of position papers on Ireland to the government in the hope of once more attaining office there. He died in his 'adopted country' in 1601. Dawtrey was the subject of a curious piece of antiquarian excavation by one of his descendants in the 1920s, who claimed that his ancestor was a role model for Shakespeare's Falstaff. Dr Hiram Morgan has exhumed a lengthy prose dialogue on Ireland penned by Dawtrey in 1597, entitled 'A Booke of Questions and Answars concerning the Warrs or Rebellions of the Kingdome of Irelande', which deals in some detail with the problem of military strategy.[77]

Thomas Digges matriculated as a pensioner of Queen's College, Cambridge in May 1546. He duly proceeded BA five years later. Digges was a colleague of John Dee, whose mathematical genius he shared. We recall that Dee wrote the preface for Henry Billingsley's translation of Euclid's *Geometrie*, and that Billingsley was one of the original undertakers in the Munster plantation. On the 14 April 1582 he was made a member of an advisory committee set up to review the fortifications at Dover. He married Agnes, a daughter of Sir Warham St Leger. It was probably during his courtship of Agnes that he came into contact with the select circle of colonial officials immortalized by Bryskett's *Discourse*.[78]

Sir Robert Dillon was sworn in as Second Justice of the germinal presidency of Connaught on 15 June 1569. By virtue of the patronage of Lord Deputy Grey he was elevated to the office of Chief Justice on 28 June 1581, replacing his great-uncle Sir Robert Dillon (c.1500–1580).[79]

'M. Dormer the Queenes Sollicitor', has been identified as George Dormer, an Oxford educated lawyer, and a native of Ross in county Cork. It seems he wrote in ballad royal *The Decaye of Rosse*, a tale, incidentally, narrated by Stanyhurst in the *Chronicles*. He was made the Queen's Justice for Wexford on 17 July 1585.[80]

John Long was born in London and educated first at Eton then at King's College, Cambridge, where he was admitted as a scholar on 13 August 1564. He became Primate of all Ireland on 13 July 1584 having been nominated by Perrot one week earlier. He was admitted to the Privy Council in Ireland within a year of securing the Primacy. Long died at Drogheda in 1589.[81]

Sir Thomas Norris entered Magdalene College, Oxford in 1571, and graduated BA on 6 April 1576. By December 1579 he was considered sufficiently mature, at the tender age of twenty-three, to lead a troop of horse in Ireland at the outbreak of the Desmond Rebellion. In August 1582, Norris was made colonel of the forces in Munster. Two

years later, he was embroiled in Perrot's campaign against the
McDonalds of Antrim. From 1585–6 he was the MP for Limerick, and
in December 1586 he was appointed acting President of Munster in
lieu of his brother, John, whilst the latter was engaged with the Earl
of Leicester and Sir Philip Sidney in the Netherlands.[82]

What scant information there is concerning 'M. Smith the
Apothecary' describes him as the compiler, around 1561, of a dossier
on the Gaelic bards, familiar subjects of scorn for the literati of the
Dublin administration. The aim of Smith's catalogue of crimes
endorsed or encouraged by the bards was to justify legislation targeted
toward the praise poets.[83]

Warham St Leger arrived in Ireland in 1574, possibly as part of the
entourage of the first Earl of Essex, in the company of Barnaby Rich,
Thomas Churchyard and Barnaby Googe. He was most closely
connected with the recently planted counties of Leix and Offaly
abutting the Dublin Pale. By 1597 he had been knighted and raised
to governor of Leix.[84]

The actions and ambitions of the younger generation of New
English adventurers appear to have played a prominent part in the
unfolding tragedy of Elizabethan Ireland. The polite society assembled
at Bryskett's Dublin residence should serve as a reminder that the very
feasibility of such advanced literary projects was dependent upon the
Renaissance recolonization of Ireland. This *reconnaissance* provided
an alternative, or an indispensable supplement, to the unreliable
system of patronage, to the constrictions of court politics, to the
mutability and machinations of Oxbridge, and to the cut-throat
careerism of the metropolis. The fact that Bryskett chose Dublin as
the putative location for his *Discourse* is not at all fortuitous, but,
rather, reflects the historical reality of a self-consciously sophisticated
English civility cultivated on the margins of English society.

V INVENTING ENGLAND

Which brings me to the title of this chapter, a variation on Roy Foster's
'Varieties of Irishness', and a cautionary note drawn from Declan
Kiberd's *Inventing Ireland*.[85] 'Spenser and Ireland' is a dangerous
coupling. There is an ever-present risk that an exclusive or all-
encompassing focus on Ireland and Irishness will let England off the
hook. Ireland takes attention away from the contingent nature of

English identity. Bruce Avery has argued that Spenser's objective in the *View*:

> is to institute a new sort of Anglo-Irish, nationalistic identification between soil and subject. His first task is to break the Irish identification with their own land ... In the gap between the Irish and their land produced by this geographical chiasmus he will insert British landlords and British garrisons, the former to keep the Irish at one remove from the soil and the latter to maintain the borders drawn by the English colonial map.[86]

The tendency of critics has been to follow blindly the trajectory of the colonial gaze.

Andrew Hadfield maintains that 'a hybrid "national" group like the Anglo-Irish has a history which both absorbs *and* opposes English and Irish traditions'.[87] Yet hybridity, a key term in recent post-colonial theory, has not been a significant feature of debate surrounding Spenser's Irish experiences. Nor has a term such as 'ambivalence' been much in evidence. Indeed, critics working on 'Spenser and Ireland', whether defensive or polemical, have tended not to view the problem in the sophisticated manner demanded by Hadfield. Instead, we get Spenser the humanist being defended against Spenser the colonist, as though these domains did not overlap. Spenser's hybridity, his vacillation between margins and metropolis, has to be worked through.

The question of nomenclature is a vexed one. Some historians have sought refuge in objectivity. Ciarán Brady writes:

> I have used the term 'Anglo-Irish' here and throughout in preference to 'Old English' because the latter came into use only in the late 1590s and was employed then in a particularly strict sense to denote a significant reorientation that was taking place in the attitude of the descendants of the Anglo-Normans towards the English government in Dublin. 'Anglo-Irish' is, moreover, closer to the terms 'Anglo-Hiberni', 'English-Irish' and 'English of Irish birth' most commonly employed by contemporaries. As such, it seems less confusing to use this relatively neutral term for purely descriptive purposes.[88]

In response to Canny's criticisms that this is an artificial distinction that does not pay adequate attention to historical context, Brady replies:

> Canny charges me ... with disrespect for literary scholars in my use of the term Anglo-Irish. I have already noted the difficulties attached to the term 'Old English' ... suffice it to say here that in retaining 'Anglo-Irish' I am merely following the conventions laid down in the standard *A New History of Ireland*.[89]

But *A New History of Ireland* is a text, not scripture. Walter Ong points out that it is 'culture' that separates the English from the Irish:

> In *A View of the Present State of Ireland* the difference between the Irish and the English is again stated frankly in cultural terms. The English themselves, before they had acquired culture, labored under the same vices as the Irish, so much so that it is impossible to say whether the Anglo-Irish who were Spenser's contemporaries were the victims of retrogression or of mere stagnation.[90]

But here again the hyphenated expression 'Anglo-Irish', historically anomalous, disguises tensions between the Old and New English communities.

Brady notes that: 'The spread of rebellion in the north and west between 1593 and 1596 gave rise to a renewal of arguments for a thorough and permanent resolution to England's problem in Ireland.'[91] Brady goes on to refer to 'England's difficulty in Ireland'.[92] What of England's English problem? Who was truly English – the Old English, the New English, or those who stayed at 'home', in 'England proper'? For some of the New English, 'it was the religiously obdurate Old English rather than the primitive Gaelic Irish who were the principal obstacle to the achievement of a truly reformed society in Ireland'.[93] Yet one looks in vain in the *View* for signs of anti-Catholicism in Spenser's discussion of the Old English. Again, it's a question of culture, of language and customs, and not, by and large, a matter of religious difference.

Nicholas Canny wants to emphasize that it was fundamentally a question of religion:

> The task of the New English was also rendered more difficult by their conviction ... that the Old English society in Ireland, no less

than that of the Gaelic Irish, was in need of fundamental reform. This conclusion was inescapable for any committed Protestant who took account of the fact that the Old English population of the Pale and in the towns had become fully evangelized Catholics and were therefore less likely than the Gaelic Irish, who were recognized to be poorly instructed, in any faith, to be brought to an acceptance of Protestant doctrine.[94]

Canny insists that it is Spenser's antipathy towards the Old English that is the most important aspect of the *View*:

the novelty of Spenser's *View* is not, as Bradshaw has suggested, the invective which it directed against Gaelic institutions but rather the vicious attack which it launched against the leaders of the Old English community and the policies which they had previously advocated. Nor, it must be emphasised, did the New English Protestants escape unscathed, and Spenser, like his contemporary Sir William Herbert, devoted much effort to detailing how their compatriots had been lured from Christian civility by the ungodly license which was so pervasive in Ireland.[95]

Brady points up the paradox that before the split between the two English communities in Ireland the Old English had advanced reforms similar to those advocated by Spenser:

It is an irony, though hardly one which Spenser himself would have appreciated, that several proposals for which the *View of the Present State of Ireland* became notorious had long before been espoused by a group for whom he harboured an especial dislike: the Anglo-Irish feudal magnates.[96]

Note that they are not only 'Anglo-Irish', an incongruous term, as Canny has shown, in early modern Ireland, but they are 'feudal magnates'. This implies that the Old English were literally living in the past, as Spenser and the New English would have it. Call me old-fashioned if you will – call me a feudal magnate, even – but don't call me Anglo-Irish. Brady has no sooner acknowledged the complicity between Spenser's New English and the Old English than he undermines it:

Such similarities between Spenser and his Anglo-Irish enemies are, of course, largely superficial: for it is evident that the magnates who presumed that they should take a leading role in the new conquest were the very group whom Spenser wished to exclude from all participation in the reconstruction of English rule in Ireland.[97]

But the fact that two bodies can't occupy the same space does not preclude their being identical. It's the 'laws of physics'.

Canny's persistence in calling the Old English by their proper name, or at least by the name given by Spenser, is not itself unproblematic. Canny elaborates thus:

The term 'Old English' is used here as it was by Edmund Spenser to denote the descendants of the Anglo-Norman settlers of the twelfth century. Brady eschews this term and chooses instead the term 'Anglo-Irish'. The reasons given for this choice of designation are cited ... but he fails to allow for the fact that the term 'Anglo-Irish' has won almost universal acceptance among historians and literary scholars to describe the Protestant descendants of the Elizabethan and Cromwellian conquerors of Ireland. It is out of respect for the work of these scholars that I leave them the term 'Anglo-Irish' and use 'Old English' for descendants of the Anglo-Normans. That Spenser included the Old English of the Pale within his general prescription is clear from *View*, lines 3319–50 [*Variorum* edition]. Elsewhere, as in lines 1996, 2938–40, Spenser was more circumspect in what he said of the Old English of the Pale, but he never allowed that they were truly civil.[98]

Canny is not the only critic to appreciate the complexities of Spenser's colonial milieu. Patricia Coughlan reminds us that 'Irish divisions are not readily to be understood as simple ethnic polarities'. For example, in the mid-seventeenth century: 'Paradoxically a common religion uneasily united the "Old English" elite – Catholic of Norman origin – with the native aristocracy.'[99] This unity could be dated to 1579, and the final meltdown in relations between the Old and New English. What was forged from the crucible of the Desmond Rebellion, with its horrific famine, was a new sense of Englishness. As Stephen Greenblatt says: 'The colonial violence inflicted upon the Irish is at the same time the force that fashions the identity of the English.'[100]

Contemporaries, too, were sensitive to these cross-cultural anxieties. Edmund Campion, in his *Historie of Ireland* (1571), writes:

> It is further to be knowen that the symple Irish are utterly another people then our Englishe of Ireland, whom they call dispitefully *boddai Sassonis* and *boddai Ghalt*, that is Englishe and Saxon chorles, because of theire Englishe ancestours planted heare withe the conquest and sithens withe the descent hathe lasted nowe fowre hundred yeares.[101]

Thus in 1571 the Irish apparently did not distinguish between Old and New English but despised both. Within a generation the distinction would materialize and rigidify, as the Old English Catholics fell in with the 'native' Irish.

'Irish' and 'English' are not constants in Spenser's day – or today, for that matter – but are ever-changing terms. Eva Gold comments: 'When Spenser considers the blurring or outright dissolution of a boundary of another sort in *View* – the boundary between the English and the Irish – he reveals what is really threatened by Ireland and the Irish: identity as an Englishman.' Gold goes on to say that: 'Much of Spenser's harshest criticism is directed against the Anglo-Irish, the descendants of the English families long settled in Ireland.'[102] The problem here is that the so- called 'Anglo-Irish' in the period refer to themselves, and are alluded to by others, as 'Old English', and thus Spenser's identity crisis becomes an English one, even an Anglo-English one. Gold concludes that: 'The corollary to the retention of English identity is, for the English in Tudor Ireland, the obliteration of Irish identity.'[103] It is one of the many ironies of 'Spenser and Ireland' that what has been most successfully obliterated is English identity.

4

'Who knowes not Arlo-hill?':
Changing Places in
The Faerie Queene

What would the act of reading Ireland in *The Faerie Queene* entail? Which particular image of Ireland should we set alongside Faeryland? How do we inveigle Spenser's 'bizarre dislocation of chronology' into the framework of a history of early modern Ireland, given that this history itself is by no means self-evident?[1] 'Comparatively few know anything of the "Faerie Queene", but its name and the name of its author.'[2] The establishing shot of this, perhaps the most visual poem in the English language, conveys no clear idea of location:

A Gentle Knight was pricking on the plaine. (*FQ.*I.i.1)

The closing sequence, set on Spenser's Kilcolman estate, sends the reader back to that uncoordinated opening in search of clues to the location of the poem's action.

Geoffrey Elton's description of Ireland in the period bears an uncanny resemblance to the Faeryland of Book V:

The ordinary state of Ireland was war, cattle raids, the burning of the countryside, the murder of its people. Outside the Pale there was hardly anything like peace and order, and the tribes lived in conditions reminiscent of 'heroic' poetry.[3]

An earlier critic argued that the Renaissance innovation evident in the encounters between Spenser's knightly adventurers and the 'rascal many', rare in medieval romance, are 'almost a direct transcript from the life and warfare of the English army in Ireland'.[4]

Spenser, in his dedicatory sonnet to Grey, spoke of:

Rude rymes, the which a rustick Muse did weave
In savadge soyle, far from Parnasso mount.

In the dedicatory sonnet to Ormond, the Earl is urged to:

> Receive most noble Lord a simple taste
> of the wilde fruit, which salvage soyl hath bred,
> Which being through long wars left almost waste,
> With brutish barbarisme is overspredd:
> And in so faire a land, as may be redd,
> Not one *Parnassus*, nor one *Helicone*
> Left for sweete Muses to be harboured ...
> Such therefore, as that wasted soyl doth yield,
> Receive dear Lord in worth, the fruit of barren field.

There is nothing new in viewing *The Faerie Queene* as, literally, the product of Ireland. The astute reader may find a pun on Faeryland in Spenser's description of Ireland as so 'faire a land, as may be redd'.

Our knowledge of Spenser's familiarity with Ireland centres on the poignant allusion to the Fens of Allen in Book II, the river schemata of Book IV, *Colin Clouts Come Home Againe*, and the *Mutabilitie Cantos*.[5] Smith concludes: 'Even if Spenser's sources for his river stories are unwritten or no longer extant, there can be little doubt that he drew heavily on the topographical lore he picked up in Ireland.'[6] The 'bog of *Allon*' is named in the *View* as one of those parts of Munster abutting 'Mountaines, or *Irish* desarts' which were once planted with English but were, through laxity and lenience, 'displanted and lost'.[7] There may be a geographical resonance in the allusion in the *Mutabilitie Cantos* to Alain de Lille's medieval pastoral, the *Complaint of Nature*. Spenser's efforts to idealize Ireland's past through a narrative discourse of nostalgia and neglect, maps onto his lament for that lost Latin text.[8]

We will never know precisely what chart Eudoxus had before him when he produced that famous multiple pun, probably the most classic example of Spenser's propensity for wordplay, in the midst of a sombre exchange on where best to locate the provincial garrisons tabled by Irenius:

> I see now all your men bestowed, but what places would you set their Garrison that they might rise out moste conveniently to service? and though perhaps I am ignorant of the places, yet I will take the *Mappe* of *Ireland*, and lay it before me, and make mine eyes (in the meane time) my Schoole-masters, to guide my understanding to judge of your plot.[9]

I have always found this a deeply disturbing montage, a morbid anatomy in the course of a clinical dissection of the country. The astonishingly flexible train of thought that can run rapidly through '*Mappe*', 'eyes', 'Schoole-masters' (being both 'schoolmasters' and 'skull masters'), 'understanding' (possibly an extension of the grave imagery – '*under*standing', that is, standing under), followed by 'judge' and, finally, the profoundly ambiguous term 'plot', both plan or project, and, eerily, final resting place, leaves one wondering whether the *View*, without woodcuts or typographic design, is yet the most visual of Spenser's texts.

George McLean has argued that the whole basis of the *View*, and, by virtue of their accepted reciprocity, Book V of *The Faerie Queene*, is 'territorial history', a unique Elizabethan synthesis of local history, national nostalgia, and chorography.[10] The question of place in Spenser's work, in light of his tenuous status as a landowner in Munster, is an intensely unstable one.[11] William Gladstone, jotting down his first impressions of *The Faerie Queene*, noted its pronounced lack of a sense of place: 'N. B. No locality'.[12] Gladstone's puzzlement is shared by most visitors to Spenser's undiscovered country. Anne Fogarty draws on Michel Foucault in order to harness a model for reading Faeryland:

> Foucault's concept of the heterotopia may be used in order to set up an initial comparison between the different narrative worlds of *The Faerie Queene* and the *View*. In a posthumously published article, he propounds the theory that societies maintain themselves by incorporating within their structures 'other spaces', or oppositional sites, in which the many facets of their ideologies and belief systems may be simultaneously represented, contested and inverted. While these counter-sites may involve an idealizing moment, Foucault ultimately distinguishes them from the non-place of utopia and prefers instead to refer to them as heterotopias, that is places of Otherness or difference.[13]

We have no sustained scholarship on the geography of *The Faerie Queene*, only a few suggestive comments by some of its most sensitive readers. C. S. Lewis testifies to the Irishness of the poem in a passage which is as powerful as it is personal:

> There is a real affinity between his *Faerie Queene*, a poem of quests and wanderings and inextinguishable desires, and Ireland itself – the

soft, wet air, the loneliness, the muffled shapes of hills, the heartrending sunsets. It was of course a different Ireland from ours, an Ireland without potatoes, whitewashed cottages, or bottled stout: but it must already have been 'the land of longing'. *The Faerie Queene* should perhaps be regarded as the work of one who is turning into an Irishman.[14]

Here, the startling conflation of text and context is given an intensely private gloss. One is reminded of Greenblatt, whose concept of 'self-fashioning', particularly as practised in his essay on Spenser, is far from innovative as applied to Colin Clout. Indeed, some critics have argued that Spenser himself is the original architect of such a theory of self-fashioning.[15]

Of course, Greenblatt would claim that this is exactly the value of his approach, namely, that it reveals the degree to which Renaissance writers fashioned for themselves a public persona, that is, the extent to which individual identity is not an essential property, but, famously, a social construct. Greenblatt's reading of the Bower of Bliss episode is exemplary:

> I can point briefly to three reiterations by the culture of important elements of the destruction of the Bower of Bliss: the European response to the native cultures of the New World, the English colonial struggle in Ireland, and the reformation attack on images.[16]

My own feeling is that this 'New Historicism' draws its sustenance from the useful insights into Spenser's private achievements and personal attitudes which were a by-product of the old historicism of the inter-war years. Ironically, where that earlier historiography opened Spenser's Irish experiences to a general critique of the Anglo-Irish colonial experience, Greenblatt concludes his eloquent intervention into the debate with a gesture towards a pervasiveness which is as ultimately personal as that evoked by Lewis:

> Spenser's own career is marked by conflicting desires to turn his back on Ireland forever and to plant himself ever more firmly in Munster; if the latter course scarcely represented an abandonment of English civility, it may nonetheless have felt like the beginning of a threatened transformation. I do not propose that Spenser feared such a metamorphosis on his own behalf – he may, for all we know, have been obscurely attracted to some of the very things he

worked to destroy, though of this attraction our only record is his poetry's fascination with the excess against which it struggles – only that he was haunted by the fact that it had occurred over generations to so many of his countrymen. The enemy for Spenser then is as much a tenacious and surprisingly seductive way of life as it is a military force, and thus alongside a ruthless policy of mass starvation and massacre, he advocates the destruction of native Irish identity.[17]

Greenblatt backs up his point about Spenser's 'conflicting desires' with a reference to Guyon's hasty departure from the Bower of Bliss.[18] This is arguably inappropriate, since the allegorical suppression of the 'degenerate' medieval colonists represented in that episode is an instance of resolution rather than uncertainty. The 'Ireland' that Guyon turns his back on is the one forged by the Old English. There is no 'conflict of desires' here, only a consistency and rigour in Spenser which is not shared by his critics. Furthermore, I perceive no contradiction between turning one's back on one manifestation of 'Ireland', and planting oneself 'ever more firmly in Munster'. Munster was no more immutable than Ireland. As for the possibility of his being seduced by Gaelic culture, Spenser's envy of the exalted status of the bards, as well as his admiration for their work, is as undisguised as it is undeniable.[19]

The most recent version of the 'seduction and destruction' story is intermittently laced with the kind of rich detail one would expect from such experts on early modern Ireland. Yet the overall impression is of a collection of literary commonplaces inserted into a very general historical framework. Brady's 'humanist crisis', Bradshaw's 'puritan ethos', and Canny's concept of 'colonial ideology' are all, in my judgement, equally inappropriate models. Spenser, as John King has recently argued, was no puritan; humanism, as Terence Ranger, Lisa Jardine and Katherine Walsh have pointed out, is far from incompatible with colonialism, and it is, as Steve Ellis asserts, the peculiar provincialism of Spenser's views, their local and contingent character, rather than their implication in any transatlantic colonial milieu, which is most marked.[20]

It is appropriate that 'culture' and 'colonialism' share the same root, because Ireland cultivated not only varieties of Englishness, in terms of non-metropolitan identities, but also in terms of the production of new literatures. Spenser's epic found its conditions of possibility in Ireland. As one nineteenth-century critic remarked:

Whatever Spenser may have done to it before he left England with Lord Grey, the bulk of the *Faerie Queene* was composed on what to Spenser and his friends was almost a foreign land – on the conquered and desolated wastes of wild and barbarous Ireland.[21]

Nicholas Canny and Andrew Carpenter observe that:

Although Edmund Spenser thought of himself as an Englishman in Ireland ... he chose to set important episodes of his major poetic work, *The Faerie Queene*, in Ireland. In doing so, he became the first English poet to make use of the Irish landscape and of Irish mythology.[22]

Ireland was both a place of exile and a source of inspiration, a cultural backwater and a well of English undefiled.

There are numerous examples of the kind of source material that Spenser might have drawn on. Some years ago, Professor Roland Smith unearthed a document entitled 'A proclamation that every horsmane should were redd Crosses. Dated at limiricke the vi November 1579'.[23] This is the month and year when Paul McLane conjectures that Spenser was in Ireland.[24] Leicester would shortly be appointed to a special commission to examine Irish affairs.[25] The text cited by Smith suggests an immediate pretext for *The Faerie Queene*:

By the lo: Justice
   William Pelham
fforasmuch as the said lo: Justice expresse pleasure is, that all horsemen that are to intende her Ma[tis]: service in this assemblid Armie, shalbe knowne from others: Not beinge of the same retinewe his lo: ordereth, publisheth, and Comandeth in her Ma[tis]: Name, that all the said horsemen both Englishe and Irishe, shall presentlie provide in redines two rede crosses, either of Silke or Cloth, the one to be fastened on the breste, and the other on the backe of Eache such horseman as is usuall, and to conteyne in lenght viij inches, and in bredthe one Inche, and a halfe, to be Worne upon every horsemans uppermoste garment w[ch] he purposeth to serve in, be it habergine, Jacke or other upper garment, for defence, What so ever upon paine for not havinge such a crosse, as is before mentioned by Wensdaie morninge next, eache horseman to forfaicte xx[s], & that the provoste Marshall of her Ma[tis]: Armie shall leavie,

and take upp eache such forfaiture to be disposed at the pleasure of the said lo: Justice Yeven at Limiricke the vj Novembr 1579.[26]

Surely this proclamation provided Spenser with an urgent spur to resuscitate the myth of Saint George? Smith refers to an illustration by Barnaby Googe of the interview between Walter Devereux, the first Earl of Essex, and Turlough Lynagh at the Blackwater in 1574, which shows the English soldiers wearing the guidon of St George.[27] Smith further observes that the English practice of wearing a red cross was known to the Scots:

> If the Irish records are silent, the Scottish chronicles reveal that as early as 1544 it was not only 'usuall' but 'the note of the English' to 'bere a crosse of seynt George' for purposes of recognition. In that year, according to the *Diurnall of Remarkable Occurents*, 'the Inglishmen ... causit all thame that thai fand betuix [Kirktown and Sowtray] weir ane reid croce'. According to Lindesay of Pitscottie, many Scots took the oath of assurance. Later the assured Scots were required to wear red crosses 'fast sewed' on their jacks or coats, under penalty of being taken for enemies.[28]

The Scottish Chronicle in Holinshed draws upon Leslie's *Historie of Scotland* where there is reference to the Scottish 'bordirmen, qhua in a gret number bure the rid croce, quhilke was noted to the Inglis men of weir, and was as a takne to ken thame by'.[29]

There is another plausible Irish source for Spenser's militant nationalist mythology. Kenneth Ferguson has uncovered a statute of 1474 authorizing a chivalrous order of thirteen prominent Palesmen to form a Brotherhood:

> Which brothers by the said authority shall have full power to them and to their successors for ever annually to assemble them and every of them or the greater part of them on Saint George's Day in the city of Dublin to choose by their wisdom and discretion the most able person of said thirteen to be captain for the year then next ensuing, to have the rule of the said brothers for that year.[30]

In Poynings' parliament of 1494, the Brotherhood was abolished, having altered from its original design as a means of policing the Pale through its own chief citizenry, and become a personal bodyguard employed by the acting viceroy in pursuit of his own ends.

The Brotherhood may have been one of the sources for *The Faerie Queene*. In the 'Letter to Raleigh' Spenser proclaims that:

> The beginning therefore of my history, if it were to be told by an Historiographer, should be the twelfth booke, which is the last, where I devise that the Faery Queene kept her Annuall feaste xii. dayes, uppon which xii. severall dayes, the occasions of the twelve severall adventures hapned, which being undertaken by xii. severall knights, are in these xii books severally handled and discoursed.

Spenser's self-conscious return to the chivalric ideals of the past matched contemporary colonial strategies.

Steve Ellis asserts that the *View*:

> was above all a persuasive rationalization of the particular circumstances in which the New English now found themselves, hence its continuing popularity in planter circles.[31]

He might have added that *The Legend of Justice* fails to resolve in any satisfactory form the problems described in the *View*, hence its continuing unpopularity with just about everyone.[32] *The Faerie Queene* has been described as 'the most unreadable poem in the English language'. Its continued dissociation, not simply from Spenser's Irish experiences, but from the mainstream of English politics and history, renders it the most unread poem in the English language.[33]

Alongside the 'domain of lyric' proposed by Paul Alpers for *The Shepheardes Calender*, I would want to locate a 'dominion of epic' in *The Faerie Queene*:

> By the modest boldness everywhere evident in *The Shepheardes Calender*, Spenser achieved a qualified but nonetheless genuine independence, of which the legal concept of *demesne* (= 'domain') is a suggestive representation.[34]

Critics frequently play down the relationship between Spenser's pastoral eclogues and his panoramic epic. One might discern an awkward shift from nation to empire.[35] Yet *The Faerie Queene* commences with a claim for continuity:

> Lo I the man, whose Muse whilome did maske,
> As time her taught, in lowly Shepheards weeds,

Am now enforst a far unfitter taske,
For trumpets sterne to chaunge mine Oaten reeds,
And sing of Knights and Ladies gentle deeds;
Whose prayses having slept in silence long,
Me, all too meane, the sacred Muse areeds
To blazon broad emongst her learned throng:
Fierce warres and faithfull loves shall moralize my song.
(*FQ.I.Proem*.i)

The disappointed courtier and suitor for Irish service and estates in *The Shepheardes Calender* has emerged as a fully-fledged colonist, leaving 'homely spoken' lyric behind in order to 'blazon broad' an epic tale of 'fierce warres and faithfull loves'. The change in demeanour and the acquisition of an Irish *demesne* are not unrelated. As John Breen contends:

> Spenser's 'Faery land' is the imaginative world of *The Faerie Queene*, dedicated to the 'Queene of England France And Ireland'. In his writings, Spenser stakes a claim for Elizabeth's sovereignty and dominion over Ireland, for in the Ireland of the *View*, as in 'Faery land', the Queene rules the land.[36]

Spenser, according to Donald Bruce, perceived both an Irish 'Otherworld' and an 'Underworld'.[37]

Otherness and subordination were constructed in terms of gender. Spenser's Ireland, whether as Irena or otherwise, is feminine. As Clare Carroll notes: '*A View* represents the Irish as a feminized, culturally barbaric, and economically intractable society that must be subjected to complete cultural and economic destruction and reorganization by the English colonists.'[38] In Book V, Tom Healy argues, 'Ireland is presented as a place whose feminine nature makes the country require a more powerful masculine presence to keep it from the savagery of the giant who is unmistakably a Roman Catholic monster.'[39] Artegall is freed by Britomart, 'whose chastity gives her great military powers'.[40]

There is always the risk that the question of gender, central to every discourse of colonialism, will be relegated to that of a figure or trope. Clare Carroll rehearses this risk thus:

> Even more provocative questions about the ideology of gender, particularly as it intersects with social status, are raised by those

recent critics who set out to analyze the poem in relation to *A View*, but still metaphorize the historical context.[41]

Carroll gives an example of the tendency to move from gender to colonialism rather than recognizing their complicity:

> Greenblatt explained the text in relation to the social context, by linking the burning of houses and the felling of groves in the destruction of the Bower of Bliss with the colonial policy of Lord Grey, which Spenser defended in *A View*. However, his explanation did not connect this violence with sexual exploitation. Marguerite Waller has criticized Greenblatt's text because, as she writes: 'it exercises the very cognitive imperialism it deplores'.[42]

Yet Greenblatt does acknowledge the complex dialectic that links metaphor with history: 'As the fashioning of a gentleman is threatened in book 2 of *The Faerie Queene* by Acrasia, so it is threatened in Ireland by the native women.'[43]

The gendering of Ireland is also a gendering of action. Artegall's 'domestication' is a case in point, for what enslaves him is inaction, and in this we see a critique of Elizabeth or Gloriana, as much as a criticism of Ireland or 'effeminacy' – something not necessarily feminine – *as such* – if it ever appears *as such*. The confining of Artegall, however, is stated in terms that are palpably misogynist:

> Amongst them all she placed him most low,
> And in his hand a distaffe to him gave,
> That he thereon should spin both flax and tow;
> A sordid office for a mind so brave.
> So hard it is to be a womans slave.
> Yet he it tooke in his owne selfes despight,
> And thereto did himselfe right well behave,
> Her to obay, sith he his faith had plight,
> Her vassall to become, if she him wonne in fight.
>
> Who had him seene, imagine mote thereby,
> That whylome hath of Hercules bene told,
> How for Iolas sake he did apply
> His mightie hands, the distaffe vile to hold,
> For his huge club, which had subdew'd of old
> So many monsters, which the world annoyed;

His Lyons skin chaungd to a pall of gold,
In which forgetting warres, he onely joyed
In combats of sweet love, and with his mistresse toyed.

Such is the crueltie of womenkynd,
When they have shaken off the shamefast band,
With which wise Nature did them strongly bynd,
T'obay the heasts of mans well ruling hand,
That then all rule and reason they withstand,
To purchase a licentious libertie.
But vertuous women wisely understand,
That they were borne to base humilitie,
Unlesse the heavens them lift to lawfull soveraintie. (*FQ*.5.23–5)

The representation of Ireland as a female figure is always bound up
with monstrosity and perversion, or with servility and victimhood.
Richard Bellings, responding in 1635 to the published version of the
View, wrote:

> This is, gentle reader, the same vexing griefe which severely pinched
> Ireland's inward bowels, cut her veins, dismembered her joints, and
> so confounded by degrees her vital spirits, that by disquieting
> thereby the whole state of her commonwealth these past ages, she
> is now brought so low, that to speak truly of her ancient lustre, her
> spacious face is now turned by those her oppressing courses to the
> form of a filthy and deformed cadaver.[44]

Earlier critics were quick to note the way in which gender functioned
in a colonial context as a clear marker of identity and a means of
reinforcing patriarchal models of authority. Edwin Greenlaw wrote:

> It will be remembered that Artegall, disarmed by the beauty of
> Radigund, is made to assume the dress of a woman and to perform
> the menial tasks of a woman (v, 23–25; vii, 37–41). With this should
> be compared the sad state of Turpine, found by Artegall in the
> power of women, his hands tied behind his back (iv. 22). Here we
> have an arraignment of womanish methods applied to the solution
> of the Irish problem; Artegall clad in woman's garments and with
> a distaff in his hand is a fit representative, says Spenser, of the course
> advised by some.[45]

Irena is one those literary representations of early modern Ireland which humanize the land whilst dehumanizing its inhabitants. Sheila Cavanagh argues that the metaphoric separation of Ireland from the Irish 'illustrates the poet's consciousness of Ireland's divided nature'.[46] Irenius complements Irena. Both appeal to their respective sovereigns to rescue Ireland and reclaim it as a British dominion:

> Wherefore the Lady, which *Irena* hight,
> Did to the Faery Queene her way addresse,
> To whom complayning her afflicted plight,
> She her besought of gratious redresse,
> That soveraine Queene, *that mightie Emperesse*,
> Whose glorie is to aide all suppliants pore,
> And of weake Princes to be Patronesse,
> Chose *Artegall* to right her to restore;
> For that to her he seem'd best skild in righteous lore. (*FQ*.5.1.4; my emphasis)

Note Spenser's subtle reminder of the Queen's other role as Empress. Elizabeth's notorious parsimony was a perennial burr in the sides of her colonial courtiers. Irenius warns in the *View* that the want of supplies for the English army might 'happ to hazarde a kingedome', a phrase which proved tragically prophetic for Spenser's own Kilcolman estate, itself known as 'Haphazard'.[47]

Some critics, echoing John Donne's epistle to Henry Wotton, envisage Ireland exerting a powerful psychological pressure on Spenser, compelling him to submit to the 'Irish negligence'. C. S. Lewis is an early exponent of this theory, and Ciarán Brady a more recent convert.[48] Kenneth Gross is representative:

> Perhaps we must say that Ireland was to Spenser both *heimlich* and *unheimlich*; in it he confronted something like his own unconscious, or at least a 'salvage soyl' where nature, mind, and culture fought unresolvable battles.[49]

The idea of Ireland having an intensely personal effect on Spenser, rather than a pervasively political influence, is not confined to moral, or mythological criticism.

We know that Spenser exploited the Italian myth of place in order to institute a complex dialectic between the local and the legendary, the mundane and the mythical.[50] This literary interpenetration of the fabulous and the factual is what makes historical interpretation of *The Faery Queene* so difficult. Faeryland is at once intangible and intimate, foreign and familiar. Jacqueline Miller posits Faeryland as an 'ideal moral world', emphasizing the gulf between the uncompromising British history read by Arthur, and the mythopoetic chronicle of Faeryland perused by Guyon:

> His invented world is obviously not fact, clearly unverifiable by the standard criteria of authenticity; and this is made clear by the discrepancies between it and the account that precedes it.[51]

Miller's insistence upon the relationship between Spenser's mythology and history is crucial, since it governs the standard view that by separating the two narratives 'the poet guarantees himself and his Faeryland a space to inhabit where there are no pretensions (and hence no demands for) correspondence to the structure of actual experience'. But she stresses that the 'explicit contrast' is one of 'dynamic alternation, not static opposition'.[52]

Faeryland is not merely an ideal Elizabethan England, but a site of struggle for Tudor imperial aspirations. Recent work on the 'British problem' suggests that it was on the fringes of English society in Ireland, in the North, and in Wales that the question of cultural identity was most pressing.[53] The most polished articulations of colonial identity display a sense of urgency and exasperation conspicuously absent from the political discourse of the metropolis. These texts point to a critique of Faeryland which places the poet's fictive domain within the context of the drive towards a politically united kingdom.[54]

Judith Anderson suggests a correspondence between *The Faerie Queene* and the *View* by way of a mythopoetic understanding of 'antiquity'. She argues that Spenser's pronouncements on Irish antiquities in the *View* are not mere digressions, lacking in historical fact, but complex literary fictions, supplementing the chronicle of British history previewed in *The Faerie Queene*:

> To a modern historical temper, Spenser's indulgence is frivolous or merely decorative; to a poetic temper, by no means so sharply, readily, or consistently distinguished from a historical one in the sixteenth century, it is both pleasing and imbued with latent significance.[55]

Anderson compliments Spenser on his literary strengths, rather than faulting him for his historical weaknesses.

In the *View*, Irenius justifies his reliance upon Irish material in searching out the antiquities of Ireland:

> Those *Bardes* indeed, *Caesar* writeth, delivered no certaine truth of any thing, neither is there any certaine hold to be taken of any antiquity which is received by tradition, since all men be lyars, & many lye when they wil, yet for the antiquities of the written Cronicles of *Ireland*, give me leave to say something, not to justifie them, but to shew that some of them might say truth. For where you say the *Irish* have alwayes bin without letters, you are therein much deceived; for it is certaine, that *Ireland* hath had the use of letters very anciently, and long before *England*.[56]

This does not square with the received view of the poet as an unrelenting enemy of Irish culture. Roland Smith traced the influence of the Gaelic history, the *Leabhar Gabhala*, through Holinshed, by way of Stanyhurst, to Spenser, showing how the Renaissance industry of *translatio studii* modernized and mythologized versions of the past in order to enhance the present.[57]

Clare O'Halloran has commented upon the way in which Irish writers reacted to Spenser's 'primitivist paradigm':

> Native Irish writers projected their desire for change on to a mythic past which was sophisticated politically and culturally, rather than primitive; and destroyed by outside aggression and not by its own inadequacies. Their view of ancient Ireland in effect mimicked the model of modern England instead of rejecting it.[58]

Geoffrey Keating was one of the first to oppose the myth of Irish barbarism prior to English colonization, presenting that nation instead with 'a glorious precolonial past which contrasted with their present situation as colonial subjects'.[59]

Jeffrey Knapp uses the concept of self-fashioning to map out the process of national self-determination in Renaissance England. The appropriation of antiquity in the interests of a nationalist nostalgia for a lost empire and cultured disdain for the inhabitants of projected colonies produces a double vision:

This process of self-definition by negatives helps account not only for Spenser's archaisms or the 'imaginative refeudalization' generally of Elizabethan culture, but for Irenius's extreme opinion in *A View of the Present State of Ireland* that 'it is but the other day since England grew civil'.[60]

Thus patriotic sentiment and imperialist aspirations merge in a myth of progress and a legend of forgotten dominions.

The universalism of imperialism and the localism of colonialism merge in the cultural identity of a 'dominant minority'.[61] Critics have long been aware of the means by which a colonial retreat, as a refuge from repression, can become a base for the incitement to imperialist discourse. A. B. Giamatti argues that the birth of empire occurs through myths of an expatriate culture repatriated.[62] Jane Tylus records the Virgilian echoes in Colin Clout's two withdrawals, first in the December Eclogue of *The Shepheardes Calender*, and then in Book VI of *The Faerie Queene*.[63] Julia Lupton explores the way in which Spenser's roles as outcast and homemaker recall Virgil's Eclogue I.[64]

Of course, Spenser was not merely recovering a history, but discovering a poem:

> Right well I wote most mighty Soveraine,
> That all this famous antique history,
> Of some th'aboundance of an idle braine
> Will judged be, and painted forgery,
> Rather then matter of just memory,
> Sith none, that breatheth living aire, does know,
> Where is that happy land of Faery,
> Which I so much do vaunt, yet no where show,
> But vouch antiquities, which no body can know.

> But let that man with better sence advize,
> That of the world least part to us is red:
> And dayly how through hardy enterprize,
> Many great regions are discovered,
> Which to late age were never mentioned.
> Who ever heard of th'Indian *Peru*?
> Or who in venturous vessell measured
> The *Amazons* huge river now found trew?
> Or fruitfullest *Virginia* who did ever vew? (*FQ*.II.i.1–2)

Virginia, named after the virgin queen, is contrarily described as 'fruitfullest'. Spenser anticipates realist attacks on his 'feigned common wealth', and counters by recalling recent contact with hitherto undiscovered countries. The reading of the world referred to here presages a textual colonization in the socio-political realm which has its concomitant in Spenser's epic poetry, where a 'wel-eyed' reader might just make out the contours of an Irish Faeryland or a Faery Ireland, 'By certaine signes here set in sundry place' (*FQ*.2.1.4.2).

Declan Kiberd has suggested provocatively that:

> The notion 'Ireland' is largely a fiction created by the rulers of England in response to specific needs at a precise moment in British history.[65]

Mary Hamer has described the process whereby Ireland was constructed as a recognizable physical entity by English map-makers from the Jacobean plantation of Ulster to the Ordnance Survey of the nineteenth century.[66] Lest we think this notion of 'Ireland' as a cultural construct symptomatic of a modish preoccupation with literary theory, consider the complex view of Rome, the seat of classical learning and the scourge of English Protestantism, conveyed in Spenser's *Ruines of Rome*:

> Thou stranger, which for *Rome* in *Rome* here seekest,
> And nought of *Rome* in *Rome* perceiv'st at all,
> These same olde walls, olde arches, which thou seest,
> Olde Palaces, is that which *Rome* men call.
> Behold what wreake, what ruine, and what wast,
> And how that she, which with her mightie powre
> Tam'd all the world, hath tam'd herselfe at last,
> The pray of time, which all things doth devowre.
> *Rome* now of *Rome* is th'onely funerall,
> And onely *Rome* of *Rome* hath victorie;
> Ne ought save *Tyber* hastning to his fall
> Remaines of all: O worlds inconstancie.
> That which is firme doth flit and fall away,
> And that is flitting, doth abide and stay.[67]

The closing couplet might be applied to Spenser's flitting to Ireland, where he and his fellows hoped to preserve a cultural identity under threat both at home and abroad, best sustained in the halfway house of English Ireland. David Norbrook situates the poem succinctly:

> Spenser's 'feigned commonwealth', Faerie Land, is not ... a precisely imagined political entity like Sidney's Arcadia; it is a cloudier realm, more romanticised and idealised.[68]

Alastair Fowler notes the critical emphasis on 'the poem's undramatic quality', the way in which 'it seldom offers a direct naturalistic representation of objective reality as it would appear to an observer'.[69]

For the reader, *The Faerie Queene* is not merely an unforgettable spectacle of writing, but a memorable experience of reading, and often a confused, disorientating, and heterogeneous one. *The Faerie Queene* is not a prose history, nor does it pretend to that status. The most successful readings of the text that remain sensitive to its status as a poem, but are nonetheless conscious of Spenser's standing as a 'poet historicall', are those which focus on particular passages, usually textual cruces or lacunae. These include Stephen Greenblatt's influential interpretation of the Bower of Bliss, Roland Smith's observations on the origins of the symbol borne by the Red Cross Knight, and Clarence Steinberg's comments on the use of Irish emblems in Book II.[70] Steinberg says of Atin, Pyrochles and Cymochles that a strong clue to an Irish identity for the trio is in their resemblance to characters in the Cuchulain tale in the Irish epic *Táin bó Cúlaigne*'.[71] Steinberg makes the point that Spenser's allegory was darkened by his use of Celtic mythology, but that this was quite in keeping with his cultural project:

> One might ask why Spenser would employ such Gaelicism if he did not, or could not, expect his readers to decode it. An obvious reply is that he liked 'darke conceites' and that these just happened to be among the darkest. Spenser probably wished to promote an interest in Irish antiquities, however, not only because they were products of a northern tongue, but also because, as he tells us on several occasions, this material can be put to good use.[72]

In a similar vein, Roland Smith asked of Spenser's 'continued Allegory, or darke conceit':

> When Spenser wrote these words in the Letter to Raleigh ... did he realize, ironically, that much of *The Faerie Queene* would be obscure

to his English readers because of its hidden Irish allusions? Surely, like his master Chaucer, the disciple was capable of having his tongue in his cheek![73]

Such close readings of specific episodes or images forestall the charge of reductionism one would expect to greet a reading which claimed that the poem was 'all about Ireland'. Yet something like this is argued by Greenblatt:

> Ireland is not only in book 5 of *The Faerie Queene*; it pervades the poem. Civility is won through the exercise of violence over what is deemed barbarous and evil, and the passages of love and leisure are not moments set apart from this process but its rewards.[74]

In what sense can we speak of 'Ireland' as being 'in book 5'? Is there not the risk that the usual restriction of 'Ireland' to Book V might be supplanted by a diffuseness, a tendency to see Ireland everywhere?

The move away from Book V as sole source of Irish material is an advance, however, on earlier criticism, which devalued that book on the grounds of its Irish content and context. According to A. C. Hamilton:

> In the Belgae, Burbon and Irena episodes it is hardly possible to allow that there is anything beyond the painfully obvious topical allusion.[75]

In this reading, the complexity of Book V is disallowed on the grounds that certain contemporary references transgress the rules of allegorical representation. Conversely, Sean Kane has suggested that:

> The difficulty of the Legend of Justice is compounded if we think of its author as an essentially apolitical animal, awkward outside of an inward and personal fairyland ... Yet Book Five is the culmination of the endeavour of reconciling classical and Christian value which is the whole project of Spenser's epic.[76]

By insisting that Spenser is politically naive, critics continue to promote the fiction of Book V as 'bad poetry':

> Book V is the least liked of all ... and not without cause. Invention and narrative power are weaker, the verse is often flat, the peaks

of allegorical or pictorial concentration are lacking. The thematic material is less deeply felt than in I or III.[77]

Hough shares the popular view that Spenser is at his best when moving from particular exempla to universal truths.

The literary integrity of Book V has been preserved from the negative charge of allegorical transparency through a separation of Spenser's 'continued Allegory' into an historical allegory and a moral allegory. The condemnation of Spenser's historical allegory in Book V takes the form of a lesson on morality. This criticism ignores the fact that the poet's own eloquent justifications for Irish colonization are themselves above all dictated by *moral* considerations, based upon the Renaissance conception of moral philosophy as 'the philosophy of administration'.[78]

The ideology of civility and the moral philosophy of Book V are coincidental. As Robert Entzminger suggests, 'the moral upon which Spenser insists is that force is necessary to establish and maintain a workable society':

> Artegall's quest is logically prior to Calidore's, and Calidore assumes for the most part the successes of Justice that Artegall has won.[79]

Entzminger adds the caveat that 'Calidore's quest at the same time supplements Artegall's victories'. As indeed it must, when we recall that Book V closed with the Blatant Beast at large. Protestant propagandists were convinced of the power of print.[80] While the sword is not ruled out, the word is paramount.[81]

A. B. Giamatti invokes a notion of 'recreation', attuned to Spenser's political conception of love, in which the process of civility has at its centre, according to imperialist mythology, 'the artist who, by his morally informed power of mediation, recreates'.[82] This reading stresses the mediating power of recreation as an articulation of colonialism, rather than assuming that it mutely follows on from that process. Hugh MacLachlan has argued that the restraint shown by Guyon in the first eight cantos of Book II prepares the reader for his overthrow of the Bower of Bliss.[83] Greenblatt's reading of this episode ignores the explicit theme of Book II. Temperance was essential to Spenser's generation exactly because they perceived the lapse of the Old English as being due to a lack of social restraint. Greenblatt recognizes the colonial dimension of the Bower episode, but fails to alter his reading of Spenser's poem in the light of Guyon's rejection of a sensual solution to his quest, holding out for a higher reward than that offered by Acrasia. But it is precisely this determined resistance to the Irish 'lethargy' which governs the structure of feeling in *The Faerie Queene*.

For Spenser, 'love and leisure' are neither 'moments set apart' from the civilizing process nor its rewards, but pleasurable pitfalls placed between himself and access to the power of authority, promising in turn the authority of power. Spenser's idea of 'love' as political virtue, civil order, and loyal subjection clashes with the lewdness and lust of Acrasia.[84] Spenserian love is an active force, not a passive state, hence Guyon's refusal to languish in the Bower and his anguish at its paralysing influence (*FQ*.2.12.72–3). Ireland and Faeryland change places in *The Faerie Queene* because each zone is in the process of cultivation. Irish names 'caconymous to English ears' were Anglicized under Elizabeth:

> this pouring of new administrative wine into old territorial bottles might have been expected to serve a useful political purpose by neutralising the regional loyalties of the Irish people.[85]

The Queen complained about the renovation of Ireland, its 'strategic geography', in a letter to Lord Deputy Sidney, observing that 'one day places are described to be of importance to be fortified, and another day they are held merely inutile'.[86]

Bagwell's words are worth recalling whenever one feels inclined to wax lyrical about Spenser's poetic ideals:

> If the readers of Spenser's verses, and still more his treatises, find fault with his truculence, they should forget that he was a poet, and remember that he was trying to improve forfeited lands.[87]

While I harbour doubts about the distinction assumed here between two concepts of culture which share a common root – culture as literary text and culture as tilling land – I admire Bagwell's brusque and businesslike realism. Yet improving forfeited lands is not a process confined to history. The coining of new counties and the litigation over land titles suggests that legal theory and textual practice converged in the absorption of 'borderlands' by the Renaissance state.

If Ireland is reduced to one tragic vision in the *View*, it detonates into a thousand fragments in *The Faerie Queene*. The place of Ireland in Spenser's epic is, like the place of words themselves, constantly subject to displacement and metamorphosis. Ireland dominates the poem in the way that the poet would have wished his sovereign to dominate Ireland. Spenser's project is nothing less than the making of Irish colonial society. 'Ireland' is not only where *The Faerie Queene* was written, it is where the forms for its visions of Faeryland were discovered. This dramatically alters the sense of a reading of the poem, making it more politically critical of English imperialist efforts than has hitherto been appreciated. In the 'feigning of a common wealth' one may discern the outline of a colonial poetics, supporting and sustaining, but also supplementing, a colonial politics. If this sounds all too close to the charges of perversion and pervasion that I have levelled against the Old and New Historicist accounts of Ireland's influence on the poem – either Ireland is only in Book V and that book is bad poetry, or Ireland is everywhere, an amorphous Other – then it may be because the truth lies somewhere in between, in the shimmering vision that is Faeryland.

5

'And nought but presed gras where she had lyen': Royal Absenteeism and Viceregal Verses

In this chapter I shall argue that the nature of the viceregal system in Ireland – unique in European politics in the early modern period – complicates the relationship of court and colony, and undermines the idea that Spenser had to choose between the two. My argument will subvert the critical history that would see Spenser's career as a planter in Ireland as a consolation prize for a disappointed courtier. My contention is that Spenser's acquisition of an Irish estate represents the fusion of two political vocations. The core/periphery model of Anglo-Irish history ignores the fact that the English viceroy in Ireland effectively ruled as an absolute monarch. This post displaced the crown from centre to margin, resolving, or at least suspending, the tensions arising from royal absenteeism in Ireland, and in the process creating a surrogate monarchical authority that retained and maintained loyal followers like Spenser. Ireland was an *alternative* to the court in terms of being a site from which the metropolis could be criticized, but it was also, crucially, an alternative *court*, viewed as a locus of power and patronage in its own right.

Early in the *View*, Spenser emphasized the importance of a strong monarchical presence in imposing a conquest. Contrasting the state of England at the time of the *'Norman Conquerour'* with the present state of Ireland, Irenius argues that William:

> found a better advantage of the time, then was in the planting of them in Ireland, and followed th'execution of them with more severity, and was also present in person to overlooke the Magistrates, and to overawe these subjects with the terrour of his Sword, and the countenance of his Majesty. But not so in Ireland,

for they were otherwise affected, and yet doe so remaine, so as the same Lawes (me seemes) can ill fit with their disposition, or worke that reformation that is wished. (p. 8)

Here is the solution to that vexed textual crux, 'even by the sword', by which Irenius means the sword of state backed up by real sovereign power, viceregal force administered with royal approval:

for by the sword which I named, I did not meane the cutting off all that nation with the sword, which farre bee it from mee, that I should ever thinke so desperately, or wish so uncharitably, but by the Sword I mean the royall power of the Prince, which ought to stretch it selfe forth in the chiefest strength to the redressing and cutting off those evils, which I before blamed, and not of the people which are evill. (p. 66)

This is a troubling passage, and I do not propose to decipher it here, merely to suggest that the problem of viceregal authority is central to the issue of the 'Sword'. If the monarch must be absent, then another must act with the full weight of monarchical authority.

There is no shortage of monographs on Elizabeth I. She is probably the most publicized figure in English Renaissance culture, vying for prominence with Shakespeare. No such extensive bibliography exists on her princely delegate in Ireland. The office of Lord Deputy in early modern Ireland was one of the most powerful positions in European politics, yet it remains a neglected area of study among English and Irish historians alike.[1] The Irish viceroy could dispense justice and patronage to a greater degree than any other comparable official on the continent.

One of the most striking illustrations of viceregal power in Elizabethan Ireland is to be found in John Derricke's *The Image of Irelande*. A woodcut depicting a scene from Sir Henry Sidney's deputyship, the submission of Rory Oge O'More, portrays Sidney in full royal regalia, crowned and enthroned. A more poignant portrait of viceregal aspirations one could not hope to discover. Derricke's woodcut tells of two submissions by Turlough Luineach O'Neill, and consequently shows Sidney in two positions, embracing O'Neill in the background and receiving him again in the foreground. The text accompanying the illustration closes with these lines:

Loe where he sittes in honors seate, most comely to be seene,
As worthyer to represent, the person of a queen.[2]

One can only surmise as to the Queen's response to such impersonations. Derricke's verse and woodcut are not the sole surviving evidence of the viceroy's regal pretensions. As early as Sidney's second deputyship (1568–71), Sir Edmund Butler had 'feared that Leicester would marry Elizabeth and make Sidney king of Ireland'.[3] The image of Sidney decked out in such splendour must have jarred on a queen constantly reproached by English planters struggling to survive in Ireland for her parsimonious attitude to the funding of settlement there. It must also have influenced her reaction to Leicester's efforts to create an 'alternative court at the Hague' during his governor-generalship in the Netherlands (1586–7).[4] She may have recalled her father's servant, Thomas Cromwell, styling himself *Pro-Rex*. Finally, in light of the Essex Rebellion, coming as it did in the wake of the Earl's brief spell as viceroy, we can see with hindsight that Elizabeth was right to be wary of giving too much authority and resources to her Irish deputies.

Few critics have viewed Spenser's epic environment as influencing in any decisive way the role of Elizabeth, represented, among others, in the figure of Gloriana. Maureen Quilligan grants a significance to the poet's choice of location for the *Two Cantos of Mutabilitie*:

> The very setting in Ireland ... queries Elizabeth's policy at the point where Spenser was disposed to be most personally critical.[5]

If by placing the final fragments of *The Faerie Queene* in an Irish context Spenser intends to question, perhaps even to provoke, his Queen, then he is also paying homage to the *memory* of his adopted home, a memory tainted by royal displeasure and neglect. Norbrook noted that 'for Spenser ... the monarch is a remote figure'.[6] The postscript to *The Faerie Queene* brings her closer to 'home'.

Andrew Hadfield has read the Faunus episode as 'an allegory of the English presence in Ireland, a counterpart to the *View*'s analysis of the helplessness of attempts to assert control unless vice-regal authority is re-established'.[7] Harry Berger Jr has argued for a triadic pattern for the *Mutabilitie Cantos*, 'from pagan through medieval modes of imagination to the lyric (and renaissance) present'.[8] I see in this triple play a cultural progression from ancient Gaelic civilization, through the feudal establishment of an Old English settlement, to the Renaissance reconquest. But this is more than a mere chronology, more than a poeticized narrative discourse. Irish antiquity, Old English degeneration, and New English civility are parts of the same political whole. The present exists side by side with the past, 'eterne in mutabilitie', constancy within currency. Aidan Clarke has further compounded matters by arguing for a quadrilateral pattern, pointing out that the English court must be added to the Irish/Old English/New English political triangle.[9]

Jeffrey Fruen, situating Elizabeth in the poem devoted to, and constitutive of, 'the eternitie of her fame', notes that:

> through all its thirty thousand lines, the titular heroine of the poem remains conspicuous almost solely by her absence ... How can the faery queen be said to be integral to, much less unifying in, a narrative not itself conspicuously integrated, and in which she was scarcely mentioned until the final book?[10]

Fruen answers this crucial question by adverting to the established tradition of biblical typology in which Christ figured as a purpose rather than a presence in the text.

Marie Axton has explored the question of kingship in the reign of Elizabeth, showing how 'a legal metaphor defining the relationship between sovereign and perpetual state' became an urgent political necessity in the context of a kingdom ruled by a virgin queen.[11] She suggests that Spenser was aware of this contemporary quandary and fashioned the most problematic princely personage in *The Faerie Queene* accordingly: 'History, "faerie" and legal precept were united in the figure of King Arthur.'[12] Consider the conclusion to the summary of the British role in Ireland given by Irenius in the *View*:

> Finally it appeareth by good record yet extant, that king *Arthur*, and after him *Gurgunt*, had all that Iland under their alleageance and subjection.[13]

As always with Spenser, historical truth matters less than strategy, movement, or what one might call 'the poetry of history'. According to James Vink:

> For Gurgunt to have intervened in the affairs of Denmark, Scotland, *and* North Ireland ('Easterland') would make sense from the viewpoint of Elizabethan policy, as well as from that of earlier periods.[14]

Spenser always has his eye on the prize, on the big picture, and on probability and relevance rather than strict fact. Indeed, the reference to Arthur, which I broke off in mid-sentence, concludes:

> hereunto I could add many probabilities of the names of places, persons, and speeches, as I did in the former [that is, the former parts of this criss-cross of origin-myths], but they should be too long for this, and I reserve them for another.[15]

The history proper is postponed. What matters for the moment is the sense of a British investment.

Proof of the significance accorded to the myth of Arthur's subjection of Ireland can be found in the lengthy refutation devoted to it by Peter Walsh in *A Prospect of the State of Ireland* (1682). Walsh ridicules the 'vain relations' of Campion and Hanmer in repeating those:

> Fables of their great *British* Heroe King *Arthur's* forcing the *Irish* Kings to pay him Tribute: and their appearing at his great Court and City of *Caer Leon* upon *Usk*: and the Irish Monarch that (as they idly fain) was contemporary and tributary to him, to have been called *Gillimer*. In any of the *Irish* Annals, Chronicles, Histories, there is not a syllable of any part of these matters; no not so much of *Arthur's* attempting once at any time on *Ireland* or picking or having any quarrell with any of the Kings or Lords there.[16]

Walsh traces this myth to Geoffrey of Monmouth, and notes that it came from him, via Giraldus Cambrensis, to the Elizabethans. Buchanan had perpetuated the myth in the Irish section of his *History of Scotland*. Walsh cites Keating's preface to his History of Ireland for an earlier attack on the Arthurian legend.[17] Spenser's choice of principal protagonist in *The Faerie Queene*, far from being 'furthest from the daunger of envy, and suspition of present time' as the 'Letter to Raleigh' attests, was guaranteed to provoke those for whom the story of Arthur's conquest of Ireland was an affront. 'Arthur' was at once a Welsh Prince who had subdued Ireland, and the name of a male monarch, and the name of Lord Grey. Ware's note to Spenser's claim in the *View* reads:

> Concerning King Arthur's conquest of Ireland, see Geffry of Monmouth, and Matthew of Westminster, at the yeare 525. where he is said to have landed in Ireland with a great army, and in battel

to have taken Gilla-mury prisoner, and forced the other Princes to subjection. In our Annals it appeares that Moriertach (the sonne of Erca) was at that time King of Ireland, of which name some reliques seeme to be in Gilla-Mury, Gilla being but an addition used with many names, as Gilla-Patrick, &c. But in the Country writers (which I have seene) I find not the least touch of this conquest.[18]

Clare Carroll notes that Spenser uses the myth of Arthur's subjection of Ireland in order to circumvent 'the fact that it was ironically Pope Adrian IV who granted Ireland to the English during the twelfth century':

Instead Spenser asserts the prior claim of Arthur. By tracing the genealogy of power to Arthur, Spenser appeals to the Tudor myth of their Welsh descent from Arthur, a myth also employed in *The Faerie Queene* 3.3, where it is prophesied to Britomart that she will marry Artegall, the hero of Book 5. The mention of the priority of the English [sic] claim to Ireland through Arthur in *A View* indicates that Spenser's genealogy in *The Faerie Queene* is invested with a historical and political validity as well as a mythopoetic force. It is Artegall who takes the place of Arthur in the genealogy of the Tudors in *The Faerie Queene* 3, and also Artegall who, in Book 5, undertakes the quest to free Irene [sic], or Ireland. At least since the eighteenth century, Artegall has been recognized as referring to Arthur Lord Grey of Wilton, the Lord Deputy of Ireland under whom Spenser served.[19]

Arthur, 'before that he was king', is a viceroy of sorts, whether or not he is modelled on Lord Grey.

David Miller has applied Marie Axton's analysis of the Queen's two bodies to *The Faerie Queene*, and 'the poem's two bodies'.[20] Where Axton confined her study to the drama, Miller extends the theory of a major constitutional problem, the succession crisis, inducing 'a precarious balance of power between the king and the state', to a reading of Spenser's poem.[21] Miller argues that:

This incarnation of empire is the central 'figure' of Spenser's *Faerie Queene* its founding trope as well as its title character. Conceived and designed to abet the glorification of the body politic in Elizabeth, Spenser's epic reflects a distinctly imperial and theocentric poetics.[22]

Jeffrey Fruen qualifies Miller's assertion that 'Elizabeth *is* Gloriana' by invoking her other allegorical personae in the poem.[23] Judith Anderson suggests that Spenser's representation of Elizabeth bears 'witness to a sophisticated subjectivity'.[24] Robin Wells argues for the epideictic function of the poem, its promotion of 'the cult of Elizabeth'.[25] Louis Montrose has argued along similar lines for a less literal, more textual idea of 'the Queen's subject', in this case Edmund Spenser, and 'the Queen-as-subject', in this case Gloriana.[26] Leonard Tennenhouse has examined the implications of the theory of the Queen's two bodies for Jacobean tragedy, particularly as it determines a politics of gender.[27]

There is a danger that the critical preoccupation with representations of Elizabeth in Tudor culture, especially prevalent amongst American critics, might erase the historical Queen, or raise her to the level of an icon. There is no banal sense in which Elizabeth *is* Gloriana. Miller is being deliberately provocative. Such a formulation does justice to neither figure, literal or literary. The 'Letter to Raleigh' warns the reader against any such one-to-one correspondences:

> In that Faery Queene I meane glory in my generall intention, but in my particular I conceive the most excellent and glorious person of our soveraine the Queene, *and her kingdome in Faery land*. And yet in some places els, I doe otherwise shadow her. For considering she beareth two persons, the one of a most royall Queene *or Empresse*, the other of a most vertuous and beautifull Lady, this latter part in some places I doe expresse in Belphoebe, fashioning her name according to your owne excellent conceipt of Cynthia, (Phoebe and Cynthia being both names of Diana). (my emphasis)

No critic to my knowledge has registered the significance of the words I have highlighted. If, in a formulation I would hesitate to endorse, Faeryland *is* Ireland, might not a central tension of Spenser's 'darke conceit' be that the poet is reconstituting the body of the Queen in England, and the body of her colonial kingdom in Ireland? Could it be that the planter poet's eccentricity in relation to the court concentrates his 'theocentric poetics'?

To the legal fiction of the Queen's two bodies, and the literary theory of the poem's two bodies, I want to add the political fact of the viceroyalty. England had declared itself an 'empire' in the Act of Restraint of Appeals in 1533, a word which in this context 'designated a sovereign territorial state which was completely independent of the pope and all foreign princes'. My contention is that the Act of Restraint of Appeals and the declaration of kingly title in Ireland inspired Spenser's 'epic tribute to early absolute monarchy under Elizabeth'.[28] Spenser's celebration of absolute monarchy and lamentation of limited viceroyalty interpenetrate. Elizabeth and Ireland – royal biography and imperial geography – change places in *The Faerie Queene*, first one, then the other, commanding the affection of its author, and the attention of its reader. The typically Spenserian solution to this political dilemma comes in the poem's open-ended conclusion, an elegant indictment of the official resistance to colonial investment, expressed through a witty satire on 'antipastoral sentiment'.[29]

While I concur broadly with Fruen's idea of Christian encomium, I should like to take Gloriana's absence in a more literal, and perhaps more ironic sense. The actual absence of the monarch from Ireland, except in name, I would argue, influenced Spenser's representation of Elizabeth in a work which was composed in her absence. There is perhaps a touch of earthy humour, a thing not unknown to our author, especially in his capacity as the colloquial Colin Clout in the apparition of one of the Queen's 'doubles' in the *Mutabilitie Cantos*, at the very point at which the poet anchors his text in the geography of his Kilcolman estate. Helena Shire perceives an appropriate inevitability in the pastoral setting of the debate between eternity and inconstancy:

> The great scene of Book VII canto vii shows Nature confronted by the Titaness Mutabilitie, child of chaos, force of rebellion and violent change: she argues her place in the cosmic scheme. She is arraigned before a council of gods, not on Olympus but on Arlo Hill. It is not by chance but by grand design that the argument of the whole heroic poem has drawn ever nearer home ... In Aherlow/Arlo, 'a nest of robbers and outlaws', the issue of mutability was fought out in bloody actuality.[30]

Another critic holds that the choice of location 'queries Elizabeth's policy at the point where Spenser was disposed to be most personally critical'.[31] Diane Parkin-Speer suggests that: 'We might recall Spenser's knowledge of and concern about land conveyance cases in Ireland when examining Mutabilitie's actions and her legal case.'[32]

There is an impudence in Spenser's choice of place for this confrontation. It is as though the poet were saying: 'If Elizabeth will not summon Spenser then Spenser will summon Elizabeth.' One can draw an analogy between Spenser's invocation of Elizabeth in the

April Eclogue of *The Shepheardes Calender*, 'Eliza, Queene of Shepheardes', and her incarnation as Diana in the *Mutabilitie Cantos*.[33] Lisa Jardine has remarked upon the significance of Spenser's instituting the imperial myth of Gloriana at precisely the point at which he leaves the source of imperial power and moves to the site of colonial struggle.[34]

Stevie Davies and Douglas Brooks-Davies echo Fruen, seeing *The Faerie Queene* as 'an elaborate encomium on Elizabeth and her realm, and a repository of late Tudor commonplaces concerning monarchy'.[35] What realm? Ireland or England? Or both? The same critics go on to argue that the poem is haunted by 'that familiar Renaissance ghost, the ideal prince (king, governor, magistrate)', as conceived by writers such as Erasmus, Thomas Elyot, Philip Sidney and James VI.[36] No mention is made here of Machiavelli, perhaps because his presence would have undermined the idea of an encomium. Is Elizabeth being offered a model, or offered *as* a model?

I want to develop the notion of a double identity at the heart of the English monarchy, of a divided royal persona, and suggest that the nature of viceregal government in Ireland, together with Ireland's dubious status as both 'kingdom and colony', adds a further layer of tension to *The Faerie Queene*. From the time of Henry II, the king of England had styled himself *Dominus Hibernia*, or lord of Ireland. In 1541, Henry VIII's Irish parliament turned a lordship into a kingship:

> an act that the king of England, his heirs and his successors be kings of Ireland.
>
> Forasmuch as the king our most gracious dread sovereign lord, and his grace's most noble progenitors, kings of England, have been lords of this land of Ireland, having all manner kingly jurisdiction, power, preeminence, and authority royal, belonging or appertaining to the royal estate and majesty of a king, by the name of lords of Ireland, where the king's majesty, and his most noble progenitors, justfully and rightfully were, and of right ought to be kings of Ireland, and so to be reputed, taken, named, and called, and for lack of naming the king's majesty and his noble progenitors kings of Ireland, according to their said true and just title, style and name therein, hath been great occasion that the Irish men and inhabitants within this realm of Ireland have not been so obedient to the king's highness and his most noble progenitors, and to their laws, as they of right, and according to their allegiance and bounden duties ought to have been.[37]

The act goes on to declare that the king of England *and* Ireland will carry the 'majesty of a king imperial', and that the Irish kingdom would be held 'as united and knit to the imperial crown of the realm of England'. It is Elizabeth's role as 'king imperial', and inheritor of an 'imperial crown', which most crucially concerns Spenser.

Ireland's ambiguous position in the Tudor political system has been charted by Karl Bottigheimer:

> Nominally, Ireland was a kingdom of the English monarchy for nearly four hundred years, but unlike England and Scotland where the triumph of monarchy followed hard-won military and political consolidation, the promotion of Ireland to a kingdom in 1541 was little more than an overzealous declaration of intent.[38]

Brendan Bradshaw raised what had been an issue of secondary importance for English historians to the level of a 'constitutional revolution'.[39] Ciarán Brady points out the gap that opened up between ideal and real in this revolution in name only, stating that:

> the king of Ireland never existed, except in legal theory, as a real and distinct individual. He was from the beginning absorbed within the person of the English monarch and his role within the mixed entity was a decidedly secondary one ... Thus even theoretically Ireland's new constitutional status was seriously qualified: neither a colony nor yet an independent sovereign entity, Ireland was a curious hybrid, a kingdom whose own sovereign denied its autonomy.[40]

The act of kingly title did little in the way of creating a stable centre of power and patronage. Again, Brady indicates the limits of the new legislation:

> Since there was no resident Irish monarch, there was no Irish court. After 1534 the king's representative, the English viceroy, might dispense a little favour of his own, but at most he offered only an indirect avenue to the English court.[41]

There is a vast and varied panorama of contemporary views on royalty and viceroyalty in early modern Ireland. A surrogate sovereign, he was the titular king of Ireland in the eyes of its loyal subjects. If we accept that a recognizably English society existed in

Ireland, and acknowledge that the office of Lord Deputy carried with it powers exceeded only by Elizabeth herself, then we might well proclaim that England, far from verging on being an absolute monarchy in the period, was in fact a *diarchy*.

Brady brings a touch of realism to the question of the 1541 act and its implications for the viceroyalty:

> It was the ironic fate of the viceroys of Tudor Ireland that, in their failure to establish a model state of their own in the land, they should have contributed so much to the emergence of a polity of far more enduring historical significance: they had aimed to fashion a kingdom in Ireland, and had laid instead the foundations of a colony.[42]

The author of a late seventeenth-century treatise proclaimed that 'no Vice-Roy in all *Europe* hath greater Power, or comes neerer the Majesty of a King in his Train and State'.[43] This explains Languet's conviction that the young Philip Sidney was well-nigh royalty because of his father's post in Ireland.

The 'kingdom and/or colony' debate currently raging within Irish historiography has important consequences for theories of kingship in early modern England, and its representation in Renaissance literature. Since the alteration in the royal style by parliament on 18 June 1541 there was, theoretically, no English Pale. All Ireland was officially under English control. The Papal Bull of 7 June 1555, issued by Pope Paul IV, making Ireland a Catholic kingdom, complicated further the question of kingdom or colony.

Writing in the wake of the 1541 legislation, Andrew Boorde described Ireland as a 'kingdomship longing to the kyng of England'.[44] Bale put it bluntly: 'If Englande and Irelande be undre one Kinge they are both bounde to ye obedience of one lawe undre him.'[45] Spenser was unimpressed:

> for by this Act of Parliament whereof wee speake, nothing was given to K. *Henry* which he had not before from his Auncestors, but onely the bare name of a Kinge, for all other absolute power of principality he had in himselfe before derived from many former Kings, his famous Progenitours and worthy Conquerors of that Land.[46]

Shakespeare's Richard II asked rhetorically: 'Is not the King's name twenty thousand names?' (III. 2. 85). Spenser did not find anything intrinsically regal in an unrecognised title. A kingdom in phrase but not in fact was no kingdom at all:

> The which sithence they first conquered and by force subdued unto them, what needed afterwards to enter into any such idle termes with them to be called their King, when it is in the power of the Conqueror to take upon himself what title he will, over his Dominions conquered. For all is the Conquerours, as *Tully* to *Brutus* saieth.[47]

Spenser's pessimistic impression of the change in nomenclature is not shared by a later commentator:

> because in the vulgar conceit the name of King is higher than the name of Lord; assuredly the assuming of this Title, hath not a little raised the Sovereignty of the Kings of England in the minds of this people.[48]

For Richard Cox, the office of viceroy is to be judged for its political execution, not its literary expression, 'since their Power is measured by their Commission, and not by their Denomination'.[49]

Elizabeth Bellamy argues that *The Faerie Queene* '"lets itself be read" because its ultimate quest is the poet's unsuccessful effort to nominate Elizabeth'.[50] She cites Raleigh's second commendatory verse 'Behold her Princely mind aright, and write thy Queene anew' noting the play on 'right' and 'write', but ignoring the implication that a change of mind and policy is in order.[51] Arguably, the ultimate quest of Spenser's epic is not to nominate Elizabeth, but to denominate her viceroy. Bellamy reveals the way in which Spenser, in a stunning paranomasic reversal, conceals the name of his sovereign in the 'Sabaoths sight' of his final stanza, 'ELIZABETH', also enshrined in the typography of the poem's original dedication.[52] I would supplement this meaning, as indeed one must always do with Spenser, adding to that Sabbath sight the apocalyptic vision of the 'Lord of hostes', a vision in which Milton, for one, may have perceived the image of Oliver Cromwell, future curse of the Irish nation.[53] Approving Cromwell as governor of Ireland on 22 June 1649, parliament declared that 'civil and military power shall be for the present conjoined in one person'. A decade later, on 7 June 1659, realizing that there was little to choose between a royal tyrant and a viceregal one, parliament resolved that Irish rule 'shall be by commissioners nominated and authorised by parliament, and not by any one person'.[54]

For Spenser, the dialectic of court and colony was crystallized in the symbol of the crown, and the sceptre stretching ultimately to the '*Armericke* shore', but before that to the banks of the Bregoge, where the viceroy wields 'The club of Justice dread, with kingly power endewed' (*FQ*.V.i.2.9). In an awkward moment in the *View*, Irenius translates a call to suppress Ireland 'even by the sword':

> for by the sword which I named, I did not meane the cutting off all that nation with the sword, which farre bee it from mee, that I should ever thinke so desperately, or wish so uncharitably, but by the Sword I meane the royall power of the Prince, which ought to stretch itselfe forth in the chiefest strength to the redressing and cutting off those evills, which I before blamed, and not of the people which are evill. For evill people, by good ordinances and government, may be made good; but the evill that is of itselfe evill, will never become good.[55]

Spenser claims that the royal power behind the viceregal sword is as important as its actual physical force.[56]

Recalling Greenblatt's intuitive remark about the language of colonialism, one might suggest that Spenser's theory of language and his view of Ireland converge in a myth of delegation and displacement. If Ireland 'pervades the poem', it does so in the same way that Elizabeth dominates it – by proxy. We recall Arthur's dream:

> When I awoke, and found her place devoyed,
> And nought but presed gras where she had lyen. (*FQ*.I.ix.15.12)

Royal absenteeism was a perennial problem practically and psychologically in colonial Ireland.[57] The Anglicization of the viceroyalty from 1534 was one way to confirm English sovereignty. The act of kingly title of 1541 was another. The reorganization of Leix and Offaly in the early 1550s as Queen's and King's Counties underlined Ireland's status as a crown colony.[58] Legal and regal imperialism were intertwined in a process of domination through denomination. The cultural imperialism of Spenser's epic poem reinforced this colonial project. Gloriana may have given her name to *The Faerie Queene*, but Arthur, viceregal pretender to the British throne, presents himself as the rightful ruler of Faeryland, and as 'that familiar Renaissance

ghost, the ideal prince'.[59] A ghost is someone who isn't there, and in
Ireland the status of the prince was necessarily ghostly. What haunts
the pages of *The Faerie Queene* is the spectre of sovereignty without
the presence of a sovereign. Donald Bruce points out that Arthur's
phantom love in his dream is 'not, as he surmised, his paramour but
his descendant'.[60]

In Spenser's time, viceregal government experienced, during the
tenure of Sir William Fitzwilliam (1588–94), an acute crisis of
sovereignty:

> under the eyes of a viceroy who renounced all responsibility for
> the problems he had inherited, the spirit of Tudor reform expired.
> And as conditions in Ulster rapidly deteriorated and everywhere
> else Irish lords and English captains confronted each other in an
> atmosphere of increasing hostility, the idea of establishing a model
> English kingdom in Ireland fell from sight – a victim neither of
> ideological change nor political convulsion, but of exhaustion,
> disillusion and neglect.[61]

It is in keeping with the ambivalence of the Irish colonial situation
that Spenser may have been both promoting the office of viceroy as
a model of monarchical authority, and advocating that metropolitan
sovereignty be exercised in Ireland. In 'The Funerall', John Donne
draws on the image of viceregal power:

> Who ever comes to shroud me, do not harme
> Nor question much
> That subtile wreath of haire, which crowns my arme;
> The mystery, the signe you must not touch,
> For'tis my outward Soule,
> Viceroy to that, which unto heaven being gone,
> Will leave this to controule,
> And keep these limbes, her Provinces, from dissolution.[62]

Viceregal authority was a means of keeping provinces from
dissolution. Eva Gold rehearses the familiar argument that 'the queen
is not – as is sometimes assumed – simply absent from book 6. Rather,
we see the poem enact the displacement of the queen from a central
position in the text.'[63] Gold maintains that when Spenser puts the
queen in parentheses in 6.10.4 – (Save onely Glorianaes heavenly

hew/To which what can compare?) – he is marking a boundary of royal authority: 'Like the walls and fences Spenser advocates for Ireland in the *View*, parenthesis is a figure that both reflects and attempts to control disorder.'[64] Thus, Gold argues: 'The place of queen Elizabeth in book 6 remains unsettled, subject to a continuing effort to displace her or to contain her presence.'[65] The question of sovereignty vacillates between place and person:

> as Spenser's place in Ireland is dependent on the containment or the displacement of the Irish, so his claims to the territory that is the poem become dependent on the displacement of the queen. The placing and displacing of the queen in canto 10 of book 6 suggests that Spenser is beginning to define the poem as a place apart from the queen – that, in fact, the queen has become a kind of trespasser in the poem. With this, Spenser also suggests that he is beginning to define his identity as a poet apart from his relation to the queen.[66]

If viceregal power may be in conflict with royal authority, so too might 'verseregal' power, that is the vice of the poet historical who assumes the role of royal representative, but advocates an abstract and absolute sovereignty that does not quite square with the approach of a particular incumbent:

> The *View* rehearses the need to displace the Irish so the English can consolidate their possession of territory; the poet of book 6, by contrast, seeks to displace the queen in order to lay claim to the space of the poem. So, too, with the issue of identity: Spenser's identity as poet in book 6 is in competition with the queen.[67]

If the 'present state' cannot offer hope of change, then the future must contain the promised transformation: 'The reformation in Ireland remains unrealized in the *View*, and all moments of resolution in book 6 are undone.'[68] The colonial context is a viceregal one, and the place of the colonial poet is highly ambiguous with respect to metropolitan sovereignty. Gold concludes that:

> The treatment of the queen in book 6, along with the disturbing presence of the 'mighty Pere' on its border, suggests that Spenser in the last complete book of *The Faerie Queene* is fashioning a sense of poetry and of identity apart from the queen and court.[69]

As Brady has argued, the persistent strategy of the Palesmen in the 1570s was to appeal directly to Elizabeth over the heads of her deputies:

> In practical terms alone this direct appeal to the queen and the London government seriously weakened the credibility of the Irish viceroy at court and rendered him vulnerable to all manner of intrigues. More seriously it overtly denied the viceroy's claims to be fully representative of sovereignty in Ireland to whom alone all requests for favour and redress should be addressed and from whom alone communication would be made to the crown. But most serious of all, in their requests for royal intervention in Ireland the common-wealth men explicitly charged the Dublin governor with wilfully disregarding their status as free-born subjects which was the very basis on which their authority within the Irish kingdom rested.[70]

While the Old English looked to the court and Elizabeth, the New English turned to her viceroy for support. The figure of the lord deputy filled the vacuum created by an absentee monarch. This was the point at which, as Richard McCabe has argued, the 'perilous muse' of Machiavelli came into play:

> Machiavelli is deemed valuable in that his observations provide an apparently objective historical perspective upon Spenser's own. His call for a more 'ample and absolute' power could not, therefore, be dismissed as the product of eccentricity or faction. The logic of conquest endorsed it. In Spenser's view, Tudor England owed its advanced level of civilization to the regulating presence of the monarch whereas Ireland, denied such a central authority, had declined into a state of 'salvage' regression. Since it was impossible for the English sovereign to reside in the conquered territory, as Machiavelli had recommended in *The Prince*, the Lord Deputy was to receive the powers of Vice-Regent.[71]

Yet while he wishes the viceroy to have absolute authority, in keeping with Machiavelli's prescription, Spenser insists that he be subject to severe strictures should he abuse that power. This is the point that Milton picks up on in his reading of the *View*. With absolute power goes absolute responsibility, though McCabe is right to emphasize that: 'In times of moral necessity compassion can be a vice.'[72] Such times may call for a viceroy, and a vice-like grip on the sword of state. Of Grey, McCabe remarks: 'His was a Cromwellian dream a century before Cromwell.'[73] According to McCabe, Spenser is adamant 'that there is no Irish sovereignty independent of the English crown'.[74] In the absence of an English court, however, it was for the viceroy to impose that sovereignty.

Critics are still divided as to Spenser's purpose in writing the *View*. To whom was it addressed? Which 'learned throng' did he have in mind? David Baker insists that:

> Spenser surely meant the *View* as a royalist polemic. He was a royal servant, not just by employment, but as a self-appointed apologist and theorist.[75]

My own feeling is that Spenser is something of an incipient republican. Influenced by Bodin, Buchanan and Machiavelli – as Fenton was by Guiccardini – Spenser was not rewarded 'land and position' by Elizabeth, as Baker would have it, but received these prizes at the hands of Grey, who was rebuked for dispensing favours too freely. Spenser mentions Machiavelli in the *View*, and also praises Buchanan, whom Elizabeth loathed. Spenser was a frustrated courtier who lived most of his creative life away from court. It was both easy and hard for a colonist to be a courtier – easy because they were suitably distant from court to tolerate its corruptions, and hard, because they could speak so freely, fearlessly and dispassionately, of those corruptions. Baker's contention that 'Spenser means to vindicate Elizabeth's colonial policy – despite her better impulses if need be – to expose and then negate the contradictions in the royal view of Ireland', assumes that a 'colonial policy' and a 'royal view of Ireland' were compatible.[76] On the contrary, sovereignty, royal and viceroyal, was a contested domain.

Baker maintains that Spenser is a royalist to the end:

> The solution Spenser expects is the immediate and definitive establishment of English law on royal authority. This would require an incontrovertible demonstration from the throne of the absolute centrality of the prince's will and the utter dependence of every legal doctrine on its conformity to that will for its validity.[77]

Must the prince be enthroned? Might not the prince be a royal *representative* who goes forth and acts with true regal authority,

absolute and unequivocal? The contradictions that Baker finds in the
View are structural problems within any colonial context. Where does
power reside? As Baker would have it:

> The *View*, in sum, is a contradictory invocation of authority; it
> summons the 'presence' of the Queen to invest her system of law
> with her own inherent sovereignty. But in order to convince
> Elizabeth of the necessity for her authorizing 'presence', Spenser
> must repeatedly point up the malignant effects of her 'absence' from
> the legal system, while, at the same time, never explicitly
> acknowledging that her legal authority is lacking at all.[78]

This 'absence' is a necessity, for the monarch cannot be in two places
at the same time. She can, however, stretch forth her sword by
delegating power to an absolute authority outside herself, a viceroy.

The viceroy will of necessity be a phantom of sorts, a prosthetic
extension. Sir John Davies wrote on the entry of the Lord Deputy
into Ulster:

> They passed into the country of Cahane through the glannes and
> woods of Glanconkayne where the wild inhabitants wondered as
> much to see the King's Deputy as the ghosts in Virgil wondered to
> see Aeneas alive in hell.[79]

The apparition of royal authority haunts the pages of *The Faerie
Queene*, as a Celtic Arthur supplants a Saxon St George, only in turn
to be himself displaced. This raises questions of delegation, relegation
and representation. C. S. Lewis lamented the vacuum at the heart of
The Faerie Queene, its absent centre:

> It will be noticed that I have made no mention of Prince Arthur.
> The regrettable truth is that in the unfinished state of the poem we
> cannot interpret its hero at all ... Spenser's whole method is such
> that we have a very dim perspective of his characters until we
> meet them or their archetypes at the great allegorical centres of each
> book ... Spenser must have intended a final book on Arthur and
> Gloriana which would have stood to the whole poem as such
> central or focal cantos stand to their several books ... As things are,
> however, Arthur is inexplicable ... The poem is not finished. It is a
> poem of a kind that loses more than most by being unfinished. Its
> centre, the seat of its highest life, is missing.[80]

One may feel behind Arthur's elusiveness a greater absence, that of Gloriana, an absence felt both by Arthur and by the reader, as well as by Spenser in Ireland – if not the absence of the Queen herself, then the absence of that royal power that Irenius wished to see impose itself upon her Irish dominion.

I would maintain that Arthur's dream vision is an implicit critique of Gloriana, as a demand for support and patronage from a neglected viceroy to his monarch. Redcrosse and Una's readings of the episode confirm that the dream is a petition or position paper of sorts:

> Thus as he spake, his visage wexed pale,
> And chaunge of hew great passion did bewray;
> Yet still he strove to cloke his inward bale,
> And hide the smoke, that did his fire display,
> Till gentle Una thus to him gan say;
> O happy Queene of Faeries, that hast found
> Mongst many, one that with his prowesse may
> Defend thine honour, and thy foes confound:
> True Loves are often sown, but seldom grow on ground.
>
> Thine, O then, said the gentle Redcrosse knight,
> Next to that Ladies love, shalbe the place,
> O fairest virgin, full of heavenly light,
> Whose wondrous faith, exceeding earthly race,
> Was firmest fixt in mine extremest case.
> And you, my Lord, the Patrone of my life,
> Of that great Queene may well gaine worthy grace:
> For onely worthy you through prowes priefe
> Yf living man mote worthy be, to be her liefe. (*FQ.*I.xi.16–17)

The reverie is an appeal, from subject to sovereign, an effort to elicit a response from one who has yet to recognize the true value of colonial activity.

6

How Milton and Some Contemporaries Read Spenser's *View**

How influential was Spenser's *View* as a *representation* of Ireland following on from its publication in 1633? What part did it play in the atrocity literature of the 1640s and beyond? Little has been written on this topic, and I am very much aware of treading on unsurveyed territory. Indeed, not only is there a drastic shortage of secondary criticism on the subject of the later seventeenth-century interpretation of the *View*, but many critics, in discussing the document, appear to be unaware that its most decisive impact must surely have been in this period, and not in the thirty-seven years during which it circulated in manuscript form, however plentiful those manuscripts were. Judging by the twenty-odd surviving copies, the *View* must have been one of the most popular and widely known of such contemporary treatises. An exception to the general rule that sees Spenser's *View* as an Elizabethan document is Pat Coughlan, who has argued:

> Spenser's *View of the Present State of Ireland* (written in 1596, though not published until 1633) is indeed the founding text of modern English discourse about Ireland, and was a specific influence in the civil war decades on Englishmen's approach to Ireland. It affords a particularly appropriate source for a summary account of those received representations which are the basis of seventeenth-century English thought and action in respect of Ireland.[1]

The central argument of this chapter will be that whatever the influence of Spenser's prose dialogue in official circles prior to its publication, its commitment to print in Dublin in 1633 amplified its audience and caused it to play a much more central part in Anglo-

Irish politics of the 1640s and beyond than has hitherto been acknowledged.

The *View* made its typographical debut in a weighty volume of Irish historical tracts edited by the distinguished Dublin archivist Sir James Ware (1594–1660) which was dedicated to Sir Thomas Wentworth (1593–1641), Earl of Strafford and Lord Deputy of Ireland (1633–40). Strafford suffered a profound culture shock on his arrival in Ireland, which struck him as a breeding-ground for bourgeois individualism rather than loyal subjection to the English crown: 'I find myself in the society of a strange people, their own privates altogether their study without any regard at all to the public.'[2] Ware's collection included, in addition to Campion's Stanyhurst-inspired *History of Ireland*, *The Chronicle of Ireland* by Meredith Hanmer (1543–1604), whom Spenser must have known as Archdeacon of Ross in the 1590s. It was thus published as part of a compilation which comprised both Old and New English positions.[3] Our concern for the moment is the editorial policy adopted by Ware, who shows some discretion in gently chiding Spenser for the more inflammatory sections of the *View*:

As for his worke now published, although it sufficiently testifieth his learning and deepe judgement, yet we may wish that in some passages it had bin tempered with more moderation. The troubles and miseries of the time when he wrote it, doe partly excuse him, And surely wee may conceive, that if hee had lived to see these times, and the good effects which the last 30. yeares peace have produced in this land, both for obedience to the lawes, as also in traffique, husbandry, civility, & learning, he would have omitted those passages which may seeme to lay either any particular aspersion upon some families, or generall upon the Nation. For now we may truly say, *jam cuncti gens una sumus*, and that upon just cause those ancient statutes wherein the natives of *Irish* descent were held to be, and named Irish enemies, and wherein those of *English* bloud were forbidden to marry and commerce with them, were repealed by act of Parlament, in the raigne of our late Soveraigne King *James* of ever blessed memory. His proofes (although most of them conjecturall) concerning the originall of the language, customes of the Nation, and the first peopling of the severall parts of the Iland, are full of good reading, and doe shew a sound judgment.[4]

The preface, although it registers the scholarly antiquarian's reservations about the impropriety of certain of Spenser's opinions, presumes that these are now redundant, and should be passed over in favour of its supposed historical worth. How wrong Ware was we shall shortly discover. His edition of the *View* could not have been undertaken at a more volatile moment in Anglo-Irish affairs, and its dissemination coincided with an upsurge in English Protestant propaganda which, as the most elegant manifestation of that perspective, it provided with some cogent intellectual spine.

The earliest recorded review of Spenser's treatise which I have been able to locate is a manuscript report by Richard Bellings written around 1635.[5] The original document, MS.24.G.i6, is in the Library of the Royal Irish Academy, Dublin, but the relevant passage is reproduced *in extenso* in the first volume of John Gilbert's *History of the Irish Confederation* (1882). Bellings is, famously, the author of *A sixth book of the Countess of Pembroke's Arcadia*, a continuation, from an Irish perspective, of Sir Philip Sidney's pastoral prose. His reading of *the View* is the most immediate evidence we have of the stir it caused on its appearance in print. Here is the key extract:

> In a book intituled 'A View of the state of Ireland' written dialogue-wise between Eudoxus and Ireneus by an ill-wisher of Ireland, Edmund Spenser, Esquire, in anno salutis 1596, and ever sithence kept dormant, as a destructive platform laid for utter subversion of this kingdom, and their aims thereby almost finished, it was printed at Dublin, anno 1633. Gentle reader, you may observe what ungodly projects there are set down for the absolute destruction of the Irish and this their country by Plantations, Displantations, Transplantations, dispersions and scattering of Ireland's poor natives, they being terms to all Christian countries most odious, yet to the Irish (by a long sufferance) made very familiar.
>
> It is there directed that in no place under any landlord of the English, no number of the Irish shall remain together, but they to be dispersed wide from their acquaintances and scattered far abroad through all the country, which rule hardly admitted man and wife to go together; and for others in their native country, they are made meere strangers and pilgrims.
>
> It is also there directed, that fostering with the Irish, marrying with them, their language and attire, are to be forbidden, forborne and extinguished; and, for the habit and language, Acts of Parliament are to that effect formerly passed ...
>
> It is moreover there directed, that great men in this land are to be grievously punished, and favourable grants, made to them in

time past, to be revoked; and why? Assuredly for any way favouring the Irish.[6]

Bellings' account of the contents of the *View* offers a useful insight into the earliest reactions of native intellectuals to a text which recalled the worst aspects of Elizabethan policy towards Ireland.

Arguably the most significant reading of the *View* in early modern, from a literary standpoint at least, was that of John Milton. What was Milton's impression of this most political of works from the pen of the poet he called 'our sage and serious Spenser'? Was his reading of the treatise dissimilar, as indeed one would expect, from that of contemporaries of different political persuasions? We have no way of knowing whether or not Milton had access while at Cambridge to one of the numerous manuscripts in circulation prior to publication, but evidence, hitherto unworked, exists for Milton's reading of the Ware edition of 1633. What we do know is that Milton read the *View*, not as an antiquarian exercise, but as a practical guide – clearly against the grain of Ware's prefatorial prompting. Two entries in Milton's common-place book suggest an intimate reading which offers a unique insight into the impact the work must have had on its appearance in 1633, the year of Strafford's appointment as Lord Deputy, in a volume whose publication coincided with that of Thomas Stafford's *Pacata Hibernica*, and with the composition of Geoffrey Keating's *History of Ireland*.[7]

The first of Milton's notes appears under the heading *Astutia politica*, and reads: 'The wicked policies of divers deputies and governours in Ireland. See *Spenser* dialogue of Ireland.'[8] Here, one can only assume that Milton is referring to the following passage in the printed version of the *View*; Irenius has just been expounding upon the corruption of certain minor officials, and concludes with a critique of English captains which makes Falstaff seem like a model officer. Eudoxus wishes, understandably, to know why such misdemeanours are countenanced by the viceroy:

IREN. But how can the Governour know readily what persons those were, & what the purpose of their killing was, yea & what will you say if the Captaines do justifie this their course by ensample of some of their Governours, which (under *Benedicite*, I doe tell it to you) doe practise the like sleight in their governments?
EUDOX. Is it possible? take heed what you say Ireneus.

IREN. To you onely *Eudoxus,* I doe tell it, and that even with great hearts griefe, and inward trouble of mind to see her Majestie so much abused by some who are put in speciall trust of those great affaires: Of which, some being martiall men, will not doe alwayes what they may for quieting of things, but will rather winke at some faults, and suffer them unpunished, lest they (having put all things in that assurance of peace that they might) they shoulde seeme afterwards not to be needed, nor continued in their governments with so great a charge to her Majestic. And therefore they doe cunningly carry their course of government, and from one hand to another doe bandie the service like a Tennis-Ball, which they will never strike quite away, for feare lest afterwards they should want.
EUDOX. Doe your speak of under Magistrates Ireneus, or principall Governours?
IREN. I doe speake of no particulars, but the truth may be found out by tryall and reasonable insight into some of their doings. And if I should say, there is some blame thereof in the principall Governours, I thinke I might also shew some reasonable proofs of my speech. As for example, some of them feeling the end of their government to draw nigh, and some mischiefes and troublous practice growing up, which afterwardes may worke trouble to the next succeeding Governour, will not attempt the redresse or cutting off thereof, either for feare they should leave the Realme unquiet at the end of their government, or that the next that commeth, should receive the same too quiet, and so happily winne more prayse thereof, then they before. And therefore they will not (as I said) seeke at all to represse that evill, but will either by graunting protection for a time, or holding some emparlance with the Rebell, or by treatie of Commissioners, or by other like devices, onely smother and keepe downe the flame of the mischiefs, so as it may not breake out in their time of government, what comes afterwards they care not, or rather wish the worst. This course hath beene noted in some Governors.[9]

Faction, as Ciarán Brady has consistently and coherently argued, plays a leading part in viceregal politics, and Spenser was not alone in making such criticisms.[10] The author of another treatise, probably a New English neighbour of Spenser's – written after the destruction of the Munster plantation in 1598, shared the poet's scepticism when it came to confidence in the viceregal system:

Doe not, O Queene, as yore Chiefe governours in that contry hathe done alwayes: Lett not yore care be to make fayre weather with them for the dayes of yore raigne only.[11]

The strategies of successive chief governors had been to prolong the agony of Ireland in their own interests.[12]

Spenser goes on to recall the past problems arising from a divided viceroyalty:

when the government of that Realme, was committed sometimes to the *Geraldines*, as when the house of *Yorke* had the Crowne of *England*, sometimes to the *Butlers*, as when the house of *Lancaster* got the same. And other whiles, when an *English* Governour was appointed, hee perhaps found enemies of both.[13]

This exchange is especially crucial, and must surely have given Milton much food for thought in the context of Strafford's almost universal unpopularity in Ireland. It is passages like this which may have come back to Milton when he was commissioned by Cromwell's parliament to write the *Observations upon the articles of peace with the Irish Rebels* (1649).[14]

The second entry in Milton's common-place book is much more specific, and a page reference for the Ware text is provided. It appears under the banner of *De disciplina militari*, and reads: 'Provision for souldiers after the warrs to be consider'd. *Spenser's* dialogue of Ireland from p. 84. &c.'[15] Here, Milton is drawing on a neglected aspect of Spenser's *View*, its exceptionally pragmatic approach to the question of what was to be done with the English standing army then becoming a standard feature of the Irish landscape.

The passage in the published edition of the *View* to which Milton refers in this note is that which begins with a question from Eudoxus concerning the proper course of action to be taken in the demobilization of English forces following the projected victory against Tyrone, a question which closes with an evocation of the social disorder which might ensue from a too hasty disbandment of such a substantial force. We recall that Essex arrived in Ireland in 1599 at the head of the largest army to leave England during the reign of Elizabeth.[16] This entry plausibly touches on one of the principal fears of the crown in its consideration of Irish policy, namely, the danger of having so many armed men at such a remove from the kingdom and under the supreme command of a sub-monarch. On the one hand, no viceroy doubted the degree to which he was placing himself in a vulnerable position by assuming such a treacherous office so far from the court and its intrigues. On the other hand, no monarch, least of all Elizabeth, relished the thought of having a disconsolate viceroy using Ireland as an alternative power base.[17]

Clearly, one who controlled an army as experienced and formidable as that deployed in Ireland was potentially the most worrisome of 'overmighty subjects'. In Milton's day, Strafford would have been the deputy who was most immediately brought to mind by this section of the *View*. This is ironic in light of the fact that Sir James Ware chose to dedicate it to the new viceroy, a figure who proved unpopular with every grouping in Irish colonial society.[18] Strafford's execution on 12 May 1641 was one of the most lucid markers of the political power concentrated in the hands of one of those communities, the New English, then coming under the rubric of 'Old Protestants'.[19]

Surprisingly, Nicholas Canny appears not to have been aware of the *View's* dedication to Strafford in 1633, or of the fact that its editor presented it as being of purely, or primarily, antiquarian interest:

> The continued popularity and relevance of Spenser to planters in Ireland explains why Spenser's *View*, which had previously circulated in manuscript, was finally published in Dublin in 1633, and we can assume that it provided wonderful consolation to the New English planters when they struggled with Thomas Wentworth ... to retain political and social control over the country of their adoption.[20]

I am not so sure that we can attribute the *View's* publication to its popularity, but there is a rather delicious irony in the fact that it indubitably did furnish the New English with ammunition against the most authoritarian of viceroys, whom Milton, having copied out the gist of the passage on corrupt governors, castigated in the *Observations* as an instrument of royal tyranny.[21]

If there is some irony in the fact that a text dedicated to Strafford provided the New English with powerful arguments against him, then there is further irony in the fact that Strafford's absolutism was anticipated favourably in the *View*. Indeed, one of the reasons Irenius gives for the inconsistency and corruption of successive viceroys is that they are not endowed with sufficient power, and are thus susceptible to bribery, slander and a sense of self-preservation which compels them to pursue policies aimed at the maintenance of the status quo. To remedy this reduction of the chief governor to the role of a pacifistic prevaricator, Spenser recommends a considerable extension of his powers: 'And therefore this should be one principall in the appointing of the Lord Deputies authority, that it should bee more ample and absolute then it is, and that he should have uncontrouled power, to doe any thing, that he with the advisement of the Councell should thinke meete to be done.'[22] Significantly, this is the only point in his discourse at which Spenser finds it prudent to make a specific allusion to Machiavelli: 'And this (I remember) is worthily observed by *Machiavel* in his discourses upon *Livie*, where he commendeth the manner of the *Romans* government, in giving absolute power to all their Councellors and Governours, which if they abused, they should afterwards dearely answere.'[23] Strafford was given just such wide-ranging authority, and he suffered for abusing it with the loss of his head.[24] The double bind of absolute power and absolute responsibility spoken of by Irenius was his downfall. Milton, the advocate of regicide, must have recognized the radicalism implicit in Spenser's incipient 'vice regicidal' discourse.

To return to Milton's citation, and to Spenser's solution to the problem of military subvention and reorientation. Eudoxus, we remember, was sketching a scenario of discharged soldiers returning to England and spreading domestic discontent, a scenario supported by the evidence of social historians:[25]

> that you should take some order for the Souldiour, which is now first to bee discharged and disposed of, some way: the which if you doe not well foresee, may growe to as great inconvenience as all this that I suppose you have quit us from, by the loose leaving of so many thousand Souldiours, which fro thenceforth will be unfit for any labour or other trade, but must either seek service and imployment abroad, which may be dangerous, or else perhaps imploy themselves heere at home, as may bee discommodious.[26]

Irenius responds by setting out a proposal for, not simply a garrison milieu, but a civil settlement peopled by soldiers, who were expected to turn their swords to ploughshares in the aftermath of the complete conquest he envisaged:

> You say very true, and it is a thing much mislyked in this our Common wealth, that no better course is taken for such as have beene imployed i service, but that returning whether maymed and

so unable to labour, o otherwise whole and sound, yet afterwards unwilling to worke, or rather willing to set the hang-man on worke ... For it is one speciall good of this plot, which I would devise, that 6000. Souldiers of these whom I have now improved in this service, and made thoroughly acquainted both with the state of the Countrey, and manners of the people, should henceforth bee still continued, and for ever maintayned of the Countrey, without any charge to her Majestic, and the rest that either are olde, and unable to serve any longer, or willing to fall to thrift, as I have seene many Souldiers after the service, to prove very good husbands, should bee placed in part of the landes by them wonne, at such rate, or rather better then others, to whom the same shall be set out.[27]

Irenius proceeds to map out, in some considerable detail, the territory which he would have allocated to the English army, with South Leinster and Ulster highlighted, justifying Spenser's description in the crown document which nominated him for the office of Sheriff of Cork on 30 September 1598 as 'a man endowed with good knowledge in learning, and not unskillful or without experience in the service of the warrs'.[28] Spenser's knowledge of Irish geography has been discussed elsewhere in great depth by the editor of the Variorum edition of the *View*.[29] Moving on from maps to models, Irenius assures Eudoxus of the advisability of his prescribed course of action by citing the classical precedent of imperial Rome, arguing that:

this was the course which the *Romanes* observed in the Conquest of *England*, for then, planted some of their Legions in all places convenient, the which they caused the Countrey to maintaine, cutting upon every portion of land a reasonable rent, which they called *Romescot*, the which might not surcharge the Tennant or Free-holder, and might defray the pay of the Garrison ... and the want of this ordinance in the first conquest of *Ireland* by *Henry the Second*, was the cause of the so short decay of that government, and the quicke recovery of the *Irish*.[30]

This passage must have lodged in Milton's mind with a forcefulness more immediate than others. One would imagine the principal proponent of Cromwell's armed republic finding the problem of military discipline a pressing political reality.

In 'Of Education' (1646), an essay in the form of an open letter to Samuel Hartlib, Milton echoes closely Spenser's concern for order in the English army, when he comes to address the question of training an officer class to assume command of what he appears to accept as a permanent fixture in the English political system. Milton, in this essay, seems to me to envisage a military academy more than anything else. Having run through the various exercises which will prepare the cadets for active service, citing the Roman custom of 'scrambling' troops without warning in order to ready them for rapid deployment, he announces that, on graduating, they will 'come forth renowned and perfect commanders in the service of their country':

> They would not then, if they were trusted with fair and hopeful armies, suffer them for want of just and wise discipline to shed away from about them like sick feathers, though they be never so oft supplied; they would not suffer their empty and unrecruitable colonels of twenty men in a company to quaff out or convey into secret hoards the wages of a delusive list and miserable remnant; yet in the meanwhile to be overmastered with a score or two of drunkards, the only soldiery left about them, or else to comply with all rapines and violences. No, good men or good governors, they would not suffer these things.[31]

The dream of a professional army, led by educated officers, who were also 'gentlemen', which had been a New English vision throughout a century of colonial struggle, was made a reality, not by regal imperialism, not by the myth of Gloriana made manifest, but by radicals and republicans. This is one of the supreme paradoxes of English history, just as it is one of the unacknowledged components of English Renaissance literature.

George Story (d.1721), who served as chaplain with the Williamite army at the Battle of the Boyne, in *An Impartial History of the Wars of Ireland* (1693), drawing on the *Discovery* of Sir John Davies, recites the four fundamental defects found in royal armies previously despatched to Ireland, these being weakness, inadequate pay, premature dissolution – twice under Richard II, the last English monarch to head such a force in person – and poor governance. Having quoted the proverb 'He that wou'd England win, Must with Ireland first begin', Story goes on to present a concise analysis of the *View* which suggests that it was still regarded as a primary text of some import:

> There was a view of *Ireland*, writ by *Spencer*, I take it, towards the latter end of Queen *Elizabeth's* Reign, and amongst other things, he

has this Remarque. 'Several Irish Families (says he) are already become English, and more would, if the English would do their parts, in supplying the Country with Learned, Pious, and painful Preachers, who could Out-Preach, and Outlive the Irish Priests: For Religion must not be forcibly imposed upon them with Terrors and sharp Penalties (as now is the manner) but rather delivered and intimated with Mildness and Gentleness, so as it may not be hated before it be understood ...' thus far *Spencer* seems to be in the right of it; that True Religion is not to be planted by Penal Laws, or the Terrour of Punishment, which may fill a Church with Temporizing Hypocrites, but never with Sincere Professors; for tho' Humane Laws are a good Hedge about Religion, and an Encouragement to Vertue, yet that which is solely founded upon such, binds the Conscience no longer than those Laws are in force.[32]

Far from being the puritan extremist some critics would have us regard him as, this near contemporary Protestant cleric thought Spenser the most moderate of religious reformers. It is in his secular proposals, particularly those pertaining to military and administrative matters, that Spenser assumes a radicalism in advance of his age.[33]

Milton's post-publication perusal of the *View* suggests a purposeful, pragmatic, political approach. What, then, of Milton's own contribution to the growing volume of English literature on Ireland? Published in an atmosphere as charged as that which prevailed in the year the *View* was suppressed, the government-sponsored *Observations* is a text on which few Milton scholars would want to dwell unduly. Yet it is a document which critics cannot continue to ignore while Spenser is still pilloried for his part in the subjection of Ireland. Milton holds that the 'Irish Papists', as he terms them, are incorrigibly regressive:

who rejecting the ingenuity of all other Nations to improve and waxe more civill by a civilising Conquest, though all these many yeares better shown and taught, preferre their own most absurd and savage Customes before the most convincing evidence of reason and demonstration: a testimony of their true Barbarisme and obdurate wilfulnesse to be expected no lesse in other matters of greatest moment.[34]

He goes on to speak of the late king's crime in failing to avenge 'the bloud of more than 200000. of his Subjects, that never hurt him, never disobeyed him, assassinated and cut in pieces by those *Irish Barbarians'*.[35] Milton's estimate of the Protestant fatalities exceeds that of the most imaginative contemporary English commentators, although Sir John Temple did cite the figure Of 300,000 either 'expelled out of their habitations' or 'destroyed some otherway'.[36] Hughes records that Milton's death-toll, though greatly exceeding Clarendon's 'forty or fifty thousand', is 'far below Sir John Temple's 300,000'. Here, Hughes is mistaking Temple's combined figure of deceased and displaced for an enumeration of the total slain. The fact remains that Milton's exorbitant claim is greater than, or equal to, that of any contemporary reporter.[37]

Where Spenser's discourse apparently fell foul of the censorship imposed upon it by an absolute monarchy, Milton's tract was specially commissioned by the Cromwellian Republic, proof of the dangers of a too simplistic and one-sided view of censorship in the period.[38] Is it not ironic that the utter extirpation of the Irish desired by Spenser under his beloved Gloriana could only be attained when the English throne was vacant, and unqualified executive power was placed in the hands of the viceroy?[39]

My own feeling is that Spenser is a rather reluctant royalist, one might even say, an opportunist monarchist. The persistent myth of the unerringly loyal courtier is a fiction which ought to be exploded once and for all. It does no justice to the advanced nature of Spenser's political thought. While I am far from suggesting that the arch-royalist and pronounced puritan we have inherited is really a radical republican, and an atheist to boot, I am not so distant from a reconstruction of Spenser as more than a mere mouthpiece for the presumed policies of the presiding regime. That charge would be levelled with more justice at Milton. What I will say is that Spenser's intellectual preference for Buchanan and literary patronage under Raleigh certainly exposed him to democracy and disbelief as viable alternatives to royal absolutism and religious extremism. No proto-socialist sceptic, none the less, he was much more than the old-fashioned imperialist lackey Marx described in the now notorious barb against 'Elizabeth's arse-kissing poet'.[40]

Interestingly, the launching of Milton's career as a pamphleteer coincides with the Ulster Rising of 1641. One wonders how much his reading of Spenser influenced Milton's decision to establish himself as a political theorist. The *Observations*, perhaps predictably, are excluded from most selections of Milton's prose. As far as I am aware, the only existing monograph on the *Observations* is that presented by

Professor Merritt Hughes on the tercentenary of its publication. This essay, entitled 'The Historical Setting of Milton's *Observations on the Articles of Peace*, 1649', cannot be faulted for its thorough exposition of the urgent political context in which the document was drafted. It is palpably deficient, though, on the question of the wider implications of Milton's position on Ireland, a position which, as we have seen, was evidently influenced by a close reading of Spenser's *View*. Hughes' apology for Milton is quite in keeping with a dominant trend in Spenser criticism which tries, unsuccessfully, to separate the enlightened English Renaissance gentleman from the ardent colonial proponent, so that, in Milton's case, we are left with an image of 'the courageous author of *Areopagitica* struggling to break the bonds of the political propagandist'.[41] I am suggesting that the Milton of the *Areopagitica* and the Milton of the *Observations*, like the Spenser of *The Faerie Queene* and the Spenser of the *View*, are one and the same. There are no more two Miltons than there are two Spensers. There are, though, two views of representation, and two views of responsibility.

If Professor Hughes is occasionally prone to engaging in apologetics, in his otherwise meticulous analysis of Milton's *Observations*, then Christopher Hill, in a recent article entitled 'Seventeenth-Century English Radicals and Ireland', is similarly defensive in his remarks upon the attitudes of Milton and his fellow 'radicals' to Ireland. Professor Hill, in my judgement, errs immediately he exclaims that 'even relatively liberal thinkers *assumed* the total inferiority of the Irish and their culture' (my emphasis).[42] That 'even', like Spenser's notorious phrase, 'even by the sword', conceals a multitude of sins. Not 'even', but 'especially', is the appropriate adverb. It was not, after all, Elizabeth, or Charles I, for that matter, who wished to see a complete conquest of Ireland. The relationship between court and colony in the period was such that the Crown, whatever imperial themes and colonial dreams it entertained, displayed little of the commitment to the politics of plantation evinced by its estranged 'radicals', from Bale, Raleigh, Spenser and Davies, through to Milton, Cromwell, Petty, and beyond to Berkeley. Those figures making breakthroughs in religion, science, literature, law, politics, economics and philosophy, were also those most emphatically in favour of making breakthroughs in the New World, or, to be more precise, the New English world.

Hill compounds the problem by cordoning off Milton, as an innocent bystander, from the carnage of 'propagandists': 'The grotesque exaggerations of propagandists were accepted by perfectly rational and balanced Englishmen, including John Milton.'[43] 'Accepted' by them? Accelerated, more like. One cannot simply exonerate a writer of Milton's standing from the charge of inciting violence against the Irish – and let there be no doubt that every English writer who published 'evidence' of Irish atrocities was doing precisely that – on the spurious grounds that he, the most erudite of political thinkers, was duped by some faceless, nameless 'propagandists'. That way, no one is to blame; no question of moral responsibility is raised. We simply register our surprise that one so 'gentle', so 'rational and balanced', as Milton was, could 'accept', unwittingly, the 'grotesque exaggerations of propagandists'. This 'rational and balanced' Milton is the same one who read the *View* with such care, and who systematically argued against religious toleration for Catholics in the *Observations*.

Only if we see Milton as somehow taken unawares, like so many modern English historians, by events in Ireland can we possibly sustain the incongruous vision of such a mature mind momentarily impaired by the intrusion of, on the one hand, the cataclysmic events of 23 October 1641, and, on the other hand, the baying for blood of those who are inevitably located beyond the Pale of English literature, namely, the 'propagandists'. When does Milton cease to be the gull and become the hawk? That is to say, at what point does the relayer of propaganda become a propagandist? It is not simply, as Hill would have it, that Milton suffers from some sort of lapse of reason, or loss of balance, succumbing, reluctantly, to 'the Irish negligence'. Rather, from the moment 'Lycidas' appeared, in November 1637, mourning the death on the Irish seas of Edward King, son of Sir Henry King, the infamous arsonist of Boyle Abbey, Milton was steeped in the politics of English colonialism. His reading of the *View*, a work written by an author he acknowledged as a greater teacher than Aquinas, reinforced cultural prejudices probably first imbibed in his undergraduate days at Cambridge.[44]

If any doubt remains regarding Milton's colonial disposition, consider the following passage from 'Of Education' (1644):

Besides these constant exercises at home, there is another opportunity of gaining experience to be won from pleasure itself abroad: in those vernal seasons of the year, when the air is calm and pleasant, it were an injury and sullenness against nature not to go out and see her riches and partake in her rejoicing with heaven and earth. I should not, therefore, be a persuader to them of studying much then, after two or three years that they have well laid their grounds, but to ride out in companies with prudent and staid guides to all the quarters of the land, learning and observing all places of strength, all commodities of building and of soil for towns and tillage, harbours, and ports for trade. Sometimes taking sea as far as to our navy, to learn there also what they can in the practical knowledge of sailing and sea-fight.[45]

In envisaging the cream of England's youth pricking forth to pastures new as part of an ongoing learning process, Milton is picking up on a familiar Renaissance theme. Colonialism, the proper pursuit of the educated, is, reciprocally, an education in itself.

The *View*, written under Elizabeth, became a standard Cromwellian text on Ireland. It was seized upon by the Irish and the Old English as a piece of vicious propaganda, and defended by radical Protestants like Milton as a timely reminder of the vicissitudes of Irish politics. Its controversial nature is evidenced in a letter from Oliver Cromwell dated Whitehall 27 March 1657, which argues in favour of William Spenser, second son of Sylvanus:

To Our Right Trusty and Right Well-beloved Our Council in Ireland.

A petition hath been exhibited unto us by William Spenser, setting forth that, being but seven years old at the beginning of the rebellion in Ireland (1641), he repaired with his mother (his father being then dead) to the city of Cork, and during the rebellion continued in the English quarters. That he never bore arms or acted against the Commonwealth of England. That his grandfather, Edmund Spenser, and his father were both Protestants, from whom an estate of land in the barony of Fermoy, in the county of Cork, descended on him which, during the rebellion, yielded him little or nothing towards his relief. That the said estate hath been lately given out to the soldiers in satisfaction of their arrears, only upon account of his professing the Popish religion, which, since his coming to years of discretion, he hath, as he professes, utterly renounced. That his grandfather was that Spenser who, by his writings touching the reduction of the Irish to civility, brought on him the odium of that nation, and for these works, and his other good services, Queen Elizabeth conferred on him the estate which the said William Spenser now claims. We have also been informed that the gentleman is of civil conversation, and that the extremity of his wants have brought him – have not prevailed over him to put him upon indirect or evil practices for a livelihood. And if, upon inquiry, you shall find his case to be such, we judge it just and reasonable, and do therefore desire and authorise you that he be forthwith restored to his estate, and that reprisal lands be given to the soldiers elsewhere: in the doing whereof our satisfaction will be greater by the continuation of that estate to the issue of his grandfather, for those eminent deserts and services to the Commonwealth that estate was first given him. We rest your loving friend. Oliver P.[46]

The recent debate around the censorship of the *View* suggests that history really does repeat itself, the first time as tragedy and the second as farce.

I want to conclude with extracts from two later responses to Spenser's *View*, both from different perspectives than that of Milton. The first comes from Peter Walsh (c.1618–1688), an Irish Franciscan and native of Kildare. Walsh refers more than once to Spenser in *A prospect of the state of Ireland* (1682). On one particular occasion, after a lengthy disquisition on the falsity of the Arthurian legend and of the English fiction of Egfrid and Edgar having Ireland in utter subjection, and a comparably detailed refutation of Spenser's genealogy of the O'Byrnes, O'Tooles and MacSwines, Walsh has this to say:

> In both particulars how mightily Spencer is out, and without any support either from History or Criticism, *Keting* in his Preface, has very sufficiently, if not abundantly shewn. And therefore I will say no more of *Spencer*, than that although in writing his *Faerie Queene* he had the right of a Poet to fancy anything; nevertheless, in the Historical part of his Dialogue (written by him, anno 1599) he should have follow'd other Rules. I say *Historical part*, &c. For I am willing to acknowledg, that where he pursued the *Political* main design of this Dialogue, which, was to describe the ways and means to reduce *Ireland* (a design well becoming him as Secretary to *Arthur Lord Grey of Wilton* and Deputy of *Ireland* under Q. *Elizabeth*) none could surpass him: no man could except against him, save only those that would not be reduc'd.[47]

I should point out that Walsh appears to have been unpopular amongst those of his own religious persuasion, and that his most abiding objection to Spenser and his associates appears to have been, not their anti-Irish sentiments, but their negative attitudes towards the Old English. Although by marking Charles II's achievement in subduing a civilized nation rather than a race of barbarians he does, to be fair, praise the native Irish by way of extending a careful compliment to the king.[48]

Sir Richard Cox prefaced his *Hibernia Anglicana* with a brief review of the historiography of Ireland which included a passing reference to the *View*, which he seems not to have rated as history proper:

> But those tracts that have been written of later times, have most of them another Fault; they generally write true, but not observing Chronology; they jumble Times, Persons and Things together, and so confound the Story. Sir James Ware was the first that mended this Error, and is undoubtedly the best Author that has undertaken the Irish History; but he has only the four Reigns of Henry VII, Henry VIII, Edward VI, and Queen Mary. Campion and the rest have but a Scrap here and there, and that it Self very imperfectly. And Camden's Annals, Fever Clun's, and others, that were mostly collected by Monks, are very faulty, and have no coherence; Spencer's View of Ireland is very well, and Sir John Davys his Discourse is better; but both are Commentaries rather than Histories.[49]

Spenser's 'commentary', whatever its faults, cannot be considered apart from the broad conflict which turned English colonial rule in Ireland upside down between 1534 and 1660. The *View* has to be approached both through its previews, those discourses and experiences which influenced, informed, and inspired it, and its reviews, those reactions and representations prompted by its circulation in manuscript, and, more importantly, its appearance in print. One of the implications of this reading of the *View* is that while the long-term causes of the 'English' Civil War may have been all but abolished, the long-term causes of the British crisis of the 1640s can only be understood within a context which takes into account the cumulative pressures on the English polity from its Irish colony. Milton's reading of Spenser suggests a continuity in English colonial theory in a period of conflict and change.[50]

The complexities of British history are seldom brought out in mainstream English historiography. Lawrence Stone, in *The Causes of the English Revolution, 1529–1642*, offers a classic instance of the modern Anglocentric position, devoting a brief passage to 'two chance events' that sparked off civil war in England. One was the death of the moderate leader-in-waiting, the Earl of Bedford, the other was the 'Irish Rebellion'. Both 'chance events' are dealt with summarily under the heading of 'The Triggers, 1640–42'. This is English historiography before the 'British Problem' was acknowledged:

> With hindsight one can see that the Irish situation had been becoming more and more explosive for a decade, but to contemporaries the rebellion, with its accompanying massacres and the loss of all English control outside the port towns, came like a bolt from the blue. Its timing could not have been more unfortunate, since the plain need to crush it made necessary the resurrection of central power in its most extreme and dangerous form, an army. Ever since the collapse of the government in 1640, there had been a vacuum of power, a situation which, had it not been for the Irish Rebellion, might have been allowed to continue for some time until the political crisis had been settled. But now there arose the necessity of raising an army, and therefore the question of who was to control it.[51]

The Ulster Rising was neither a 'chance event', nor 'a bolt from the blue'. Milton's reading of Spenser suggests that the slow-burning fuse of culture has to be measured against the sudden impact of historical events.

7

The *View* from Scotland: Combing the Celtic Fringe*

I IRELAND'S SCOTLAND: THE INVISIBLE OTHER

In a book ostensibly concerned with Spenser and Ireland it may seem strange to encounter a chapter on Scotland. 'Spenser and Scotland' is an incongruous pairing, but, I hope to show, an appropriate one. Those critics who, like Artegall in Book V of *The Faerie Queene*, have 'Irenaes quest pursewed', have been engaged to some extent in a con-quest, and one that does not begin to do justice to the con-texts of 'Spenser and Ireland'. It was while looking at texts by Bacon and Milton that I became aware of the extent to which what I had hitherto placed within an English-Irish, or 'Anglo-Irish' framework, was in fact very much bound up with questions of Britishness and British identity as it was composed of, and in turn decomposed, the attendant national identities of England, Scotland, Ireland and Wales.[1]

Now, this was clearly the case with Bacon's *Certain Considerations Touching the Plantations in Ireland* (1609) and with Milton's *Observations upon the articles of peace* (1649). Both these texts had, it was true, been read in a purely 'Irish' context, but could obviously be viewed as part of something which has come to be known as the 'British Problem', a recent approach to the historiography of the seventeenth century that tries to broaden the perspective previously adopted of seeing England as the centre of activity, the benchmark against which the histories of the other nations that constituted the nascent British state were to be measured.[2]

There has been a tendency, both in literary or cultural studies, and in the historiography of the early modern period, to overlook this 'British' context – with all of its tensions and complexities – in favour of a pronounced Anglocentrism.[3] The seventeenth century has been described by one Scottish historian as the 'Century of the Three Kingdoms', and one can indeed see why this century should be singled out for special attention.[4] This is the period in which the great revisionist process of the last few years has concentrated. The so-called, for so long, '*English* Civil War' is now recognized as a British – or perhaps more accurately, an Anglo-Celtic – conflict, a series of cross-border disputes within a multiple kingdom. The chief focus of this new historiography has, perhaps predictably, been on the period between the Scottish invasion of England in 1638, through the Ulster Rising of 1641, to the 'English Revolution', as it was once known, and, beyond, to the Restoration of 1660.

How does Spenser's work impinge upon Scotland? First, his prose dialogue *A View of the Present State of Ireland*, was written in 1596, ten years before the invention of the Union Jack, and as a pre-Union text it offers a fascinating sidelight on the 'British Problem'. Secondly, the *View* was not published until 1633, and despite being treated primarily as an Elizabethan discourse on Ireland – which to some extent it remains – it is also, and importantly, a document whose moment of impact was not Elizabethan but Caroline, and ultimately Cromwellian.[5]

So in this chapter, as an act of atonement, I want to elaborate another context, a Scottish one, and show the way in which Scotland features in a major canonical English text on Ireland that has not, as far as I'm aware, been picked up on. Indeed, 'Spenser and Ireland' is a phrase that harbours a double complicity and simplification, with denunciation vying with defence as the dominant critical genre.[6] I come here neither to bury Spenser nor to praise him, but to point out the precariousness of some of the familiar binaries.

As we have seen, the early modern period witnessed a struggle for supremacy between *varieties of Englishness*, as the Old English, Catholic descendants of the twelfth-century settlement gave way to post-Reformation Protestant planters like Spenser.[7] The modern period has seen a preoccupation with *varieties of Irishness*, challenging the idea of a monolithic Irish nation.[8] Between times, in the space of a hyphen, it might be appropriate to speak of *varieties of Scottishness*. Posting something through that letterbox between 'Anglo' and 'Irish' is not easy.

'Spenser and Scotland' is not, I shall maintain, as perverse a conjunction as it might first appear. An Englishman who settled in Cork and never, as far as we know, ventured north of the border, Spenser was nonetheless astute enough to recognize, and address at some length, the existence of a Scottish dimension in Anglo-Irish politics. In fact, his national epic *The Faerie Queene*, written in Ireland, was banned in Scotland when James VI took exception to the representation of his mother, Mary Queen of Scots, in Canto 9, Book V, published in 1596, the likely year of the *View*'s composition.[9] The objections of James VI to Spenser's poem, and his request to Elizabeth that it be seized and destroyed and the poet punished, may have had some bearing on the failure of the *View* to find its way from manuscript to print for forty years.[10] Spenserians have long been aware of this means by which Scotland, or Scottish interests, impinged upon Spenser. They have been less aware, or less eager to note, that in the *View* Spenser cites the Scottish humanist George Buchanan as his principal intellectual influence.

Having described his own historical method, Irenius pays his dues to his sources, ending with the most important: '*Buchanan*, for that hee himselfe being an *Irish* Scot or Pict by nation, and being very excellently learned and industrious to seeke out the truth of all things concerning the originall of his own people, hath both set downe the testimony of the auncients truely, and his owne opinion together withall very reasonably, though in some things he doth somewhat flatter' (p. 29). Ware has a note to this in his appended 'Annotations': '—*an Irish Scot or Pict by nation*. Bede tells us that the *Picts* were a colony of *Scythians*, who first comming into *Ireland*, and being denyed residence there by the *Scots*, were perswaded by them to inhabit the North parts of *Britaine*. But Mr *Camden*, out of *Dio, Herodian, Tacitus*, &c. and upon consideration of the customes, name and language of the *Picts*, conceives not improbably, that they were naturall *Britons*, although distinguished by name' (p. 122). James Vink also points out that: 'The terms "Picts" and "Scots" were used indiscriminately, even in Roman times, for the peoples in the northern fringe of the British Isles.'[11]

The former tutor of King James, as a proto-republican, was of course no friend to either James or Elizabeth. Spenser's praise and use of Buchanan in the *View* may be another reason for its apparent suppression. No treatment of Spenser and Scotland can ignore the influence of the Scottish humanist George Buchanan (1506–1582), Scottish historian, scholar and translator, born at Killearn in Stirlingshire, studied in Paris and at St Andrew's, where he took his BA in 1526 returning to Paris in 1528 to teach there for ten years. Returned to Scotland in 1537. Professor at Bordeaux from 1539 to 1542, where he had Montaigne as a pupil, then travelled to Portugal. Back in Paris by 1553, and in Scotland in 1561. Became Principal of St

Leonard's College, St Andrew's in 1566, and Moderator of the General Assembly in 1567. Subsequently made Keeper of the Privy Seal and tutor to the young King James. Author of *De Jure Regni Apud Scotos*, written in 1567 to justify the deposition of Mary, but not published until 1579. His translation of Psalms into Latin brought him wide renown as a Latinist. His *History of Scotland*, in Latin, was published at Edinburgh, 1582. An associate of the Leicester–Sidney circle, Buchanan was singled out by Spenser in the *View* as his chief intellectual influence.

Here, I want to focus upon two passages in the *View*, one on origins and one on policy, both of which are informed by a consideration of a crucial Scottish component. That this Scottish aspect arises in the administrative and strategic section of the text as well as the antiquarian disquisition on identity formation is revealing. The initial exchange between Spenser's two interlocutors, Irenius and Eudoxus, occurs during a discussion of the early history of Ireland. Eudoxus asks Irenius what he thinks of the current Irish claims to Spanish descent. Irenius first relates these claims to the present position of Spain as a European and world power, then dismisses them as myth-making, together with all other origin-myths, including the English tale of Brutus.[12] He then proceeds to map out, in a kind of cultural cartography, the ethnic make-up of Ireland. This is where Scotland, or the Scots, make their second appearance (I shall speak in due course of their first sighting). Irenius says that the 'Scythians', hearing of Ireland, 'arrived in the North part thereof, which is now called *Ulster*, which first inhabiting, and afterwards stretching themselves forth into the Land, as their numbers increased, named it all of themselves *Scuttenland*, which more briefly is called *Scutland*, or *Scotland*'.

This sudden shift from Spain to Scotland in the search for Irish origins takes Eudoxus by surprise: 'I wonder (*Irenaus*) whether you runne so farre astray, for whilest wee talke of *Ireland*, mee thinkes you rippe up the originall of *Scotland*, but what is that to this?' Irenius's response is hardly designed to clear the confusion: 'Surely very much', he tells Eudoxus, 'for *Scotland* and *Ireland* are all one and the same'. Eudoxus is aghast: 'That seemeth more strange; for we all know right well that they are distinguished with a great Sea running between them, or else there are two *Scotlands*.' Irenius reassures Eudoxus, with a mocking and elaborate show of patience, that he is not seeing double:

Never the more are there two *Scotlands*, but two kindes of Scots were
indeed (as you may gather out of *Buchanan*) the one *Irin*, or *Irish
Scots*, the other *Albin-Scots*; for those *Scots* are *Scythians*, arrived (as
I said) in the North parts of *Ireland*, where some of them after
passed into the next coast of *Albine*, now called *Scotland*, which (after
much trouble) they possessed, & of themselves named *Scotland*; but
in processe of time (as it is commonly seene) the dominion of the
part prevaileth in the whole, for the *Irish Scots* putting away the
name of *Scots*, were called onely *Irish*, & the *Albine Scots*, leaving
the name of *Albine*, were called only *Scots*. Therefore it commeth
thence that of some writers, *Ireland* is called *Scotia major*, and that
which now is called *Scotland*, *Scotia minor*. (p. 28)

In Holinshed's *Chronicles* Stanihurst wrote: 'as Scotland is named
Scotia minor, so Ireland is tearmed Scotia major'.[13] Another writer
that Spenser may have in mind is Johannes Major, or John Major (or
Mair) of Scotland. A key feature of Major's history is his rejection of
the British origin myths being marketed by English historians. He is
particularly keen to scotch the brute that the Scots, like the Welsh, are
descended from Brutus. Indeed, although he styles himself a 'Scottish
Briton', Major insists that 'the Irish are descended from the Spaniards
and the Scottish Britons from the Irish'. Where Spenser will claim that
the Irish are really Scots, Major contends that the Scots are really Irish.[14]
Where the proto-unionist Major seeks the unification of Britannia
Major, the English nationalist Spenser desires the subordination of
Scotia Major and Scotia Minor.[15]

Eudoxus is now satisfied, and indeed proceeds to recap and clarify:
'I doe now well understand your distinguishing of the two sorts of
Scots, & two *Scotlands*, how that this which is now called *Ireland*, was
anciently called *Erin*, and afterwards of some written *Scotland*, & that
which is now called *Scotland* was formerly called *Albin*, before the
comming of the *Scythes* thither; but what other nation inhabited the
other parts of *Ireland*?' (p. 28). Irenius then outlines the other groups
in Ireland. Eudoxus summarizes, before going on to praise 'This
ripping of Auncestors':

Now thus farre then, I understand your opinion, that the *Scythians*
planted in the north part of *Ireland*: the *Spaniards* (for so we call them,
what ever they were that came from *Spaine*) in the west, the *Gaules*
in the south: so that there now remaineth the east parts towards

England, which I would be glad to understand from whence you doe think them peopled.

Iren. Mary I thinke of the *Brittaines* themselves, of which though there be little footing now remaining, by reason that the *Saxons* afterwards, and lastly the *English*, driving out the Inhabitants thereof, did possesse and people it themselves. (p. 33)

So, the English drive out the British, and the Irish can with more justification claim an affinity with the Scots than the Spanish. Moreover, the Old English come in for more severe criticism than the Gaelic Irish. Irenius shocks Eudoxus again by declaring that the chief abuses of the Irish are grown from the English, and indeed that the Old English are more reprehensible than the native Irish, 'which being very wilde at the first, are now become more civill, when as these from civility are growne to be wilde and meere *Irish*' (p. 105). Here, 'Irish' is not simply another word for 'wild', but a term of opposition, in this case opposition to another wave of colonizers.

The Old English put out the British and are themselves now 'degenerate'. The Scots, or Scythians, are the other culprits. The Irish customs that Irenius abhors, and which critics often read as evidence of anti-Irish sentiment, are Scythian. Eudoxus speaks of 'the *Scythians*, which you say were the *Scottes*' (p. 34), and Irenius, commencing his account of Irish customs, proposes to begin 'first with the *Scythian* or *Scottish* manners', and with '*Boolying*' , the 'pasturing [of cattle] upon the mountaine, and waste wilde places' (p. 35). Also from the Scythians – or Scots – come the '*Mantles*' and '*Glibbes*', and the war-cry '*Ferragh*' (pp. 37–9). Of the last, Irenius says:

And here also lyeth open an other manifest proofe, that the *Irish* bee *Scythes* or *Scots*, for in all their incounters they use one very common word, crying *Ferragh, Ferragh*, which is a *Scottish* word, to wit, the name of one of the first Kings of *Scotland*, called *Feragus*, or *Fergus*, which fought against the *Pictes*, as you may reade in *Buchanan, de rebus Scoticus*. (p. 39)

The next Scythian or Scottish custom is the use of a short bow. In a helpful marginal note, Sir James Ware tells us: 'The originall of the very name of *Scythians* seemeth to come from *shooting*.' Next comes the long shield, the absence of armour and helmet, 'trusting to the thicknes of their glibbs the which (they say) will sometimes beare off a good stroke, is meere *Scythian*, as you may see in the said Images of the old *Scythes* or *Scots*, set foorth by *Heriodanus* and others' (pp. 40–1). Irenius seals his argument thus: 'By which it may almost infallibly be gathered together, with other circumstances, that the Irish are very Scots or Scythes originally, though sithence intermingled with many other Nations repairing and joyning unto them' (p. 41). Irenius goes on to claim that both the 'wild *Scots*' and the Irish drink blood and swear by their swords (p. 41). They worship the sun (p. 41). A wronged Scythian will sit on an ox hide until others join with him in his quarrel: 'And the same you may likewise reade to have beene the ancient manner of the wilde *Scotts*, which are indeed the very naturall *Irish*' (p. 42). Throughout these passages, Irenius time and again makes it clear that he is speaking of the Irish of the 'North', not the Irish *per se*. Moreover, the whole discussion rests on the assumption that there is no such thing as the Irish as such. They are a mixture of many nations, and, in the North in particular, are originally Scots. Again, Irenius, having moved on to Gaulish and British customs, says that the use of the long shield, Gaulish as well as Scythian, is something he has observed only in the North: 'But I have not seene such fashioned Targets used in the Southerne parts, but onely amongst the Northerne people, and Irish-*Scottes*, I doe thinke that they were brought in rather by the *Scythians*, then by the *Gaules*' (p. 44).

Now, at this stage, it would be tempting to conclude that Spenser is a proto-unionist who is surreptitiously limiting Ireland's Spanish provenance and strengthening the claim of Scotland, thus anticipating the Ulster plantation of the early seventeenth century that will tie Scotland to England through the colonization of the North of Ireland. Spenser's endorsement of a Scottish investment in Ireland could be read as a prelude to a proposed union. It could be argued that Spenser had burned his bridges with Scotland, when one recalls that *The Faerie Queene* was, as I pointed out, by this time proscribed there. However, opposition to Mary Queen of Scots and opposition to Scotland were not the same thing. Moreover, fear of an independent Scotland getting a further foothold in Ireland need not conflict with a desire in the long term to see an enlarged political configuration that would include all three nations.

If Munster was Spenser's base, then Ulster was the province that most vexed him, as it had Sidney senior. In the *View* Ulster, as the haunt of O'Neill, the least Anglicized region of Ireland, and the inlet to Scotland, is a trouble spot that merits great attention. The Scottish Question is posed once more when Irenius outlines the problem of Ulster, the most ungovernable province of Ireland from an English perspective, made manifest in the 1590s with the rebellion of Hugh O'Neill, Earl of Tyrone.[16] Various methods of reform are aired, and Eudoxus blithely enquires of Irenius: 'what say you then of that advice ... which (I heard) was given by some, to draw in Scotts to serve against him? how like you that advice?' This elicits a yelp of protest from Irenius, who harks back to his earlier conflation of the Scots with the Irish of the North:

> for who that is experienced in those parts knoweth not that the *ONeales* are neerely allyed unto the *MacNeales* of *Scotland*, and to the Earle of *Argyle*, from whence they use to have all their succours of those *Scottes* and *Redshanckes*. Besides all these *Scottes* are through long continuance intermingled and allyed to all the inhabitants of the north: So as there is no hope that they will ever be wrought to serve faithfully against their old friends and kinsmen: And though they would, how when they have overthrowne him, and the warres are finished, shall they themselves be put out? doe we not all know, that the *Scottes* were the first inhabitants of all the north, and that those which are now called the north *Irish*, are indeed very *Scottes*, which challenge the ancient inheritance and dominion of the Countrey, to be their owne aunciently: This then were but to leap out of the pan into the fire: For the chiefest caveat and provision in reformation of the north, must be to keep out those *Scottes*. (pp. 79–80)

Ware's rather optimistic marginal note at this point reads: 'The causes of these feares have been amputated, since the happy union of *England* and *Scotland*, established by his late Majesty.' This text, one has to remember, was written seven years before the Anglo-Scottish Union of the Crowns and ten years before the Ulster Plantation, and was published five years before the Scottish invasion of England. Spenser's insistence upon Scythian origins for the Irish was underpinned by a fear of Scottish intervention in Ulster.

Despite Ware's optimism, the North, and Ulster, continued to be a site of Anglo-*Scottish* conflict, as well as the scene of a complication of interests, from Milton to Maastricht. But it was not the Union alone that allayed Spenser's fears and warded off the awesome spectre of a pan-Celtic alliance against Little England, for the Scots who settled in Ulster after the Anglo-Scottish Union of Crowns in 1603 were not those whom Spenser feared – the Irish Scots, Highlanders and Islanders whom John Major had earlier categorized as 'Wild Scots', and contrasted with the 'domestic' or 'household' variety found in the civilized lowlands. This is one reason why the term 'Ulster Scots' does not begin to do justice to the subtle nuances of the Scoto-Irish context. Not only does Scotland get lost in the hyphen of 'Anglo-Irish' history, but so too does the fact that, as Jenny Wormald has pointed out, the traditional Irish connection with the Western Isles was superseded, deliberately, as an extension of James VI's policy of planting lowland Scots in the Western Islands as part of a putative civilizing process.[17]

It is worth noting in passing that Steve Bruce, in a recent essay on 'The Ulster Connection' with Scotland, glosses over the way in which the Anglo-Scottish Union of Crowns changed utterly the tenor of Scoto-Irish interaction.[18] This was not the logical extension, as Bruce would have it, of a cross-cultural exchange stemming from the fifth century, but a transformation of a relationship between two nations by a third, England, in the interests of a British identity that would disempower Scotland and Ireland at a stroke while maintaining English sovereignty. In the wake of the Union – the first of three, one recalls – Erin was crucified between two thieves, Albion and Albany. As Alasdair Gray, the Scottish novelist, puts it in his wonderful little book *Why Scots Should Rule Scotland*: 'Jamie arrived at a tactic which could only be deployed by a Scottish king ruling Ireland with an English army: the colonization of Ulster.'[19] I have argued elsewhere at length on the manipulative nature of the plantation of Ulster, laid bare by Francis Bacon.[20] The Union inflected everything.[21] For me, the Union is similarly responsible for prejudice and discrimination. Bob Purdie has argued, in 'The Lessons of Ireland for the SNP', that 'the roots of the Irish problem lay in the Act of Union of 1800'. My own feeling is that this perspective overlooks the significance for Ireland of the seventeenth- and eighteenth-century Anglo-Scottish Acts of Union. Purdie further contends this it is significant that while in Ireland the emphasis is on 'the border', in Scotland one speaks of 'the Borders'.[22] What Purdie fails to address is the extent to which the Borderers, those Scots who posed the greatest danger to England, were planted in Ireland by a newly-formed British polity to serve a double placatory purpose.

Current attempts to address the Scottish part in the Anglo-Irish problem are fraught with difficulty. On the one hand, there are those who prefer to speak in terms of 'Ulster and Scotland'. Whether the emphasis is on the Scotticization of Ulster or the Ulsterization of Scotland, there is an attempt to set Scotland up as a means by which

Northern Ireland can maintain its links with the 'mainland', to use another anomalous term. On the other hand, there are those, like Mary Robinson, who have spoken of strengthening connections between 'Ireland and Scotland'. Here, one senses a move to isolate England by turning the Anglo-Celtic axis in favour of the latter term.[23] The political codes remain heavily marked, but the overall connections being made can only be an advance on the sterile oppositions of yesterday.

Spenser's injunction not to allow Scots access to the North of Ireland became, within a decade of his prohibitive discourse, an imperative in the interests of solving competing Anglo-Scottish claims to that territory. Henceforth, Scotland would shrink to a hyphen, and the English Pale around Dublin would become, in the course of history, and through an act of upward displacement, a British (*née* Scottish) Pale around Belfast. Beyond the Pale lay another. The haemorrhage of identity that followed on from the Union – remember that both Scottish and English opponents feared loss of sovereignty – was bandaged up in 'Scotia Major', now 'Britannia Minor'.

But why, the reader may ask, reassert the Scottishness of Ireland/Ulster? Michel Foucault remarked: 'The purpose of history, guided by genealogy, is not to discover the roots of our identity but to commit ourselves to its dissipation.' It is not in order to promote a singular politics of identity, but to advocate an understanding of the multiplicity and confusion of origins that I have tried to unravel this Scottish thread in Spenser. Few in Ireland, North or South, have been keen to assert a Scottish dimension. For Republicans and Nationalists this would be to acknowledge a 'British' stake or investment. James Joyce neatly summed up one Irish perspective on Scotland when he wrote in 'Gas from a Burner' (1907): 'Poor Sister Scotland, her doom is fell! She has no more Stuarts to sell.' Scotland has shot her bolt. (Scythians, according to Spenser's editor, Sir James Ware, derived their name from 'shooting'.) For Unionists and Loyalists, the priority was 'Britishness', with crown, government and army firmly identified as 'British'. Scotland was thus regarded by both sides – in a struggle where none appeared able to count beyond two – as an accomplice in Empire, England's sidekick, a subordinate National Region, to use BBC-speak. Despite this, an interest in Scottish language and culture persisted, and rich seams were mined beneath the troubled surface of 'Anglo-Irish' or 'British–Irish' conflict. The peace process has put Scotland back on the agenda, coupled with the drive towards devolution and/or independence in Scotland, and the larger European context that militates against English insularity may augur well for Scottish–Irish relations, as well as instituting a new area in Anglo-Irish, and of course, Anglo-Scottish relations. These hyphens have to be negotiated, not in order to return to some unique origin or essence, but, rather, to arrive at a politics of plurality and difference rather than polarity and deference.

What are the limits of Anglo-Irish identity? One limit or horizon is that this term implies a unitary Englishness and a monolithic Irishness. Other identities, traditions, histories and ethnicities get left out of the grand oppositional narrative. The example of Scotland is salutary, but there are others. The term Anglo-Irish is freighted with conflictual histories. It is used nowadays to refer to relations between England (or, to be precise, Britain) and Ireland (or, to be precise, the Irish Republic). Its other meaning is to refer to Irish literature in English. And the third meaning, the one that is used in relation to Spenser, is to denote the Protestant Ascendancy.

Now, identity is a minefield, and old workings can yield underfoot, but they can also give rise to an open cast identity in place of ethnic closure. We all know the story of how the Anglo-Normans became the Old English after the advent of the post-Reformation Protestant planters known as the New English. The Old English became, in the seventeenth century, the New Irish, and the New English became the Old Protestants. In the eighteenth century the New Irish were simply Catholics, and the Old Protestants were the Ascendancy. After partition, the Irish of the Irish Republic contained the Anglo-Normans, Old English, New English, and so on, all Irish now, while in Northern Ireland, six counties of Ulster, there were the Nationalists or Republicans – Irish Catholic – and the Ulster Unionists, Loyalists, or British, with the term 'Ulster Scots' sometimes invoked. The Catholics were Irish and the Protestants of the south were Anglo-Irish while the settlers in the north went from Ulster Scots to British, and so on. Finally, after partition, Ulster (or six counties thereof) was British and the other twenty-six were, unproblematically, Irish. Simple, isn't it?

All too simple. Don't forget Foucault. One remembers in order to forget. It was Joyce who wrote, in 'Ireland, Island of Saints and Sages' (1907): 'What race, or what language ... can boast of being pure today? And no race has less right to utter such a boast than the race now living in Ireland. Nationality (if it really is not a convenient fiction like so many others to which the scalpels of present-day scientists have given the coup de grâce) must find its reason for being rooted in something that surpasses or transcends and informs changing things like blood and the human word.' All nations are mixed, and this should be a cause for celebration, not mourning.

II SCOTLAND'S IRELAND: DARKNESS VISIBLE

Playing 'spot the Scot' in modern historiography on early modern Ireland is a futile game. Yet the original sources, sources so much favoured by historians, are ample testimony to the claim of Scotland to attention. Irish historians are generally reluctant to acknowledge the place of Scotland in a history they prefer to see in 'Anglo-Irish' terms. Ciarán Brady, to take one example among many, manages to avoid any reference to the Scots, preferring to see Spenser as resistant exclusively to the 'Anglo-Irish'. Alternatively, Brady is more at home speaking of 'Normans' in Spenser's text – few and far between – than discussing 'Scots' – who abound.[24]

Spenser's purpose in the *View*, according to David Baker, is 'to tell the intolerable truth of Ireland'.[25] I prefer to say truths rather than truth, and myths rather than truths. One of those myths/truths was that Ireland was, in Spenser's view, originally Scotland. This is a 'truth' of the *View* that few commentators – Irish historians and English literary critics – have been particularly keen to document. 'His dialogue', Baker concludes, 'is a resolute declaration of official truth, but in it can be heard the voices of more than a few unhappy ghosts'.[26] Certainly the ghost of Scotland haunts its pages, crying out to be heard, but without much success.

According to Brendan Bradshaw, for example, Richard Beacon 'shows as little interest as Herbert in the possible implications of ethnography for the Irish problem, omitting, like the latter, to speak of the racial origins or characteristics of the native race'.[27] But Spenser's purpose in producing an Irish genealogy is directed to the present. He wishes to prise Ireland away from Spanish and Scottish incursions by at once interrogating, recognizing, demeaning, and challenging the claims of those nations.

This challenge has gone largely unnoticed, since critics have preferred to allow Ireland to occupy ground which in Spenser's treatise and poem is open to many nations and identities. Consider the following remark by Ciarán Brady:

'The Legend of Justice' is a veritable paradise for the seeker after contemporary allusions, and throughout its cantos thinly veiled references to the dominant fears of late Elizabethan England have been gleaned: dynastic instability, social discontent, the war with Spain and of course the running sore of Ireland.[28]

Brady might have added the uncertain state of Scotland as it related to England's future and as it impinged on the running sore of Ireland, but once again the Scottish dimension is underplayed. To be fair to Brady, he does go on to allude to Spenser's 'pitiless condemnation of Mary, Queen of Scots (Duessa)', but by now, having ignored the representation of the Scythians as Scots and the insistence that the Scots be kept out of Ulster, Brady is unable to link the condemnation of Mary Stuart to Spenser's general attitude to Scotland.

Of course, it is not enough to say that as well as being anti-Irish, Spenser was anti-Scottish. Indeed, I have been struggling throughout this book to convince the reader that mere rebuke is no adequate response to Spenser's Irish experience or its textual residues. Fear of a pan-Gaelic alliance fuelled the ideologies of both English planter communities. Nicholas Canny has observed that 'Old and New English were united by their mutual contempt for the Gaelic inhabitants of the island.'[29] This anti-Gaelic sentiment extended to Gaelic Scots. Clare Carroll says that the *View* is divided into three parts, and that 'the first section ... criticizes the previous English reform strategy'.[30] The text begins in fact with an ethnography and a rehearsal of a history of conquests. Moreover, it signals a Scottish dimension that few scholars wish to acknowledge. I have already pointed to the link between Spenser's Scottish genealogy for Ireland, and his later insistence that the Scots be kept out of Ulster. Here I want to return to the opening of the *View*, and look at a passage I purposefully omitted from that earlier discussion.

The first reference to the Scots comes in fact within its first few pages, and intervenes between the antiquarian excursus that inscribes the Scots at the origins of Ireland, and that history of the present that sees the Scots as a menace in the North. Again, it is a question of con-quest and con-text, for between the 'original' influx of Scots into Ireland and the contemporary threat of Scottish activity in Ulster in the 1590s, Spenser inserts the invasion in 1315 led by Edward Bruce, brother of Robert Bruce, King of Scotland. Spenser was probably drawing on *Holinshed* for his reading of this episode, where there are two accounts of it. Frank Covington argues that since the account in the Scottish section is short and from a Scottish perspective, the longer version of events in the Irish section – written from an English perspective – was most likely to be Spenser's source.[31] Here is the passage as it appears in Ware's edition. Note that Edward the Bruce is first mentioned in an aside, which Eudoxus picks up on, a form of exchange that anticipates the subsequent allusion to Scotland and Ireland being all one. Here, Irenius is concluding an account of the overrunning of the Pale under Edward IV, and the encroachment of the 'O'Neill':

> In the which he soone after created himselfe King, and was called King of all *Ireland*, which before him I doe not reade that any did so generally, but onely *Edward le Bruce*. (p. 12)

Eudoxus interrupts:

> What? was there ever any generall King of *Ireland*? I never heard it before, but that it was alwayes (whilst it was under the *Irish*) divided into foure, and sometimes into five kingdomes or dominions. But this *Edward le Bruce* what was hee, that could make himselfe King of all *Ireland*?

What indeed, other than the brother of the King of Scotland who had just thrashed the English soundly at Bannockburn. Irenius responds as he will throughout the dialogue, firmly but with patience:

> I would tell you in case you would not challenge me anon for forgetting the matter which I had in hand, that is, the inconvenience and unfitnesse which I supposed to be in the Lawes of the Land.

Scotland is out of the way, and Irenius has come out of the way, or been led astray, by the intervention of Eudoxus. Eudoxus insists that this digression upon Edward the Bruce is timely and relevant, and promises to recall Irenius to his original plan in due course. Irenius relents, and pursues the Scottish angle thus:

> This *Edw. le Bruce* was brother of *Robert le Bruce*, who was King of *Scotland*, at such time as K. *Edward* the second raigned here in *England*, and bare a most malicious and spightfull minde against K. *Edward*, doing him all the scathe that hee could, and annoying his Territoryes of *England*, whilest hee was troubled with civill warres of his Barons at home. Hee also to worke him the more mischiefe, sent over his said brother *Edward* with a power of *Scottes*

and *Red-shankes* into *Ireland*, where by the meanes of the *Lacies*, and of the *Irish*, with whom they combined, they gave footing, and gathering unto him all the scatterlings and out-lawes out of all the woods and mountaines, in which they long had lurked, marched foorth into the *English* pale, which then was chiefly in the North from the point of *Donluce* and beyond unto *Dublin*: Having in the middest of her *Knockfergus*, *Belfast*, *Armagh*, and *Carlingford*, which are now the most out-bounds and abandoned places in the *English* Pale, and indeede not counted of the *English* Pale at all: for it stretcheth now no further then *Dundalke* towardes the North. (pp. 12–13)

That phrase 'doing him all the scathe' has to be a pun. The Scots, or Scythes, *scathe* the English. They do not emerge unscathed. Spenser speaks of those 'scatterlings' whom Edward Bruce drew against the English Pale. The term crops up in *The Faerie Queene*:

Who having oft in battell vanquished
Those spoilefull Picts, and swarming *Easterlings*,
Long time in peace his Realme established,
Yet oft annoyd with sundry bordragings
Of neighbour Scots, and forrein Scatterlings,
With which the world did in those dayes abound:
Which to outbarre, with painefull pyonings
From sea to sea he heapt a mightie mound,
Which from *Alcluid* to *Panwelt* did that border bound. (*FQ*.II.x.63)

Of this stanza, James Vink says:

Commentators assume that the 'Easterlings' are the 'Scatterlings', but no one knows where the Scatterlings were before they 'scattered' ... If 'Picts and Easterlings' is a doublet, showing the same tribe, then, similarly, 'Scatterlings' may be a subset of Scots.[32]

Vink goes on to explain the term 'Scatterlings':

The Picts were often taken to be those Scots who were seafaring, or resident on the islands, including Iona, Columba's seat. But why 'foreign' Scatterlings? ... Scots making incursions on England were 'foreign'.[33]

Of course the Scots were foreign, and have remained foreign within the domain of 'Spenser and Ireland'. From Brutus to Bruce, Salvaging Scotland – Scatterland or Scytheland – is no easy task. To return to Spenser's discussion of the incursion of the brother of the Scottish king upon the English Pale:

> There the said *Edward le Bruce* spoyled and burnt all the olde *English* Pale Inhabitants, and sacked and rased all Citties and Corporate Townes, no lesse then *Murrough en Ranagh*, of whom I earst tolde you: For hee wasted *Belfast, Greene-Castle, Kelles, Bellturbut, Castletowne, Newton,* and many other very good Townes and strong holdes, hee rooted out the noble Families of the *Audlies, Talbotts, Tuchets, Chamberlaines, Maundevills,* and the *Savages* out of *Ardes,* though of the Lo: *Savage* there remaineth yet an heire, that is now a poore Gentleman of very meane condition, yet dwelling in the *Ardes*.

Lord Savage was thus an Old English aristocrat literally savaged by the Scots and so reduced from nobility to gentility. The Scots salvaged Ireland for themselves. The Savages were, as Gottfried puts it, 'rooted out by the Scots'.[34]

Irenius now comes to the crux of his digression on Bruce and the Scottish invasion:

> And comming lastly to *Dundalke,* hee there made himselfe King, and raigned the space of one whole yeare, untill that *Edward* King of *England* having set some quiet in his affaires at home, sent over the Lord *John Birmingham* to bee Generall of the Warres against him, who incountring him neere to *Dundalke,* over-threw his Army, and slew him. Also hee presently followed the victory so hotly upon the *Scottes,* that hee suffered them not to breathe, or gather themselves together againe, untill they came to the Sea-coast.

In their flight, the Scots lay waste to the outer fringes of the English Pale, but Irenius ends on a positive note by singing the praises of the Pale in terms of its resources and prospects. Eudoxus is moved to say:

> Truly *Iren.* what with your praises of the countrey, and what with your discourse of the lamentable desolation thereof, made by those *Scottes,* you have filled mee with a great compassion of their calamities, that I doe much pitty that sweet Land, to be subject to

so many evills as I see more and more to bee layde upon her, and doe halfe beginne to thinke, that it is (as you said at the beginning) her fatal misfortune above all other Countreyes that I know, to bee thus miserably tossed and turmoyled with these variable stormes of affliction. (pp. 13–14)

The digression on Bruce becomes exemplary of an approach to history that Eudoxus regards as 'very profitable for matters of policy' (p. 15).

This early appearance of Scotland in the *View* has not gone entirely unnoticed. Gottfried noted Spenser's intimate knowledge of Ulster 'in the references to Irish encroachments during the Wars of the Roses and to the Scotch invasion at the beginning of the fourteenth century'.[35] Indeed it becomes evident from Spenser's argument that it was the Scots who empaled the English, or impaled them in a fixed identity. As Gottfried observes:

The clear division of English from Irish Ireland was only made shortly before the Scotch invasion, and the name *English Pale* did not appear before the fifteenth century; but Spenser is correct in placing the towns of eastern Ulster within the original boundaries of the Pale.[36]

It has been noted that the term 'Pale' was only used when the so-called English conquest had been limited to the 'Four Obedient Counties'.[37] By curtailing its progress, Scotland contributed to that process of 'impaling' English identity in Ireland.

If, as I have shown, Spenser is so keen to establish the Scottish origins of Ireland, why do critics persist in reading the debate in Anglo-Irish terms? Clare Carroll writes:

Spenser's comments on language in *A View* also express his concern with creating prior English origins in Ireland. For example, he reverts to a false etymology to explain the cry of the Irish as they retreat from battle; 'cummericke', for which no Irish equivalent has been found, comes from 'Briton, help'. The pun is on the Welsh word 'cummeraig', meaning 'Welsh', which in Spenser's mythology signifies Tudor. This quasi-paranomastic trope is translated into narrative action as the Briton knight Artegall saves Irene, or Ireland, to the enthusiastic shouts of the native people, glad to be free of the tyrant Grantorto, whose description is modelled on that of an Irish kern, or warrior. The Irish origins of Ireland are called illegitimate in *A View* and appropriated into a false British origin in both *A View* and *The Faerie Queene*.[38]

So in order to reinforce Englishness Spenser claims Welshness? One suspects that Spenser's early modern attention to national differences is here being subsumed within a modern conception of British identity. Carroll discusses Spenser's disquisition on Irish origins in the *View* and objects to his false derivations:

> While Spenser's construction of disparate economic groups within Ireland as one social category does not correspond to real conditions, he attempts to overcome this with a definition of the Irish as an antagonistic racial other, with the power to corrupt and subsume the Old English through social contact and intermarriage. Spenser describes the Irish as not only primitive and barbaric, but also as African and Asian, and pagan.[39]

The question is, is Spenser wrong? Is there a true origin that he is suppressing? My own feeling is that Spenser, as a poet historical, recognizes the contingency of history and the centrality of myth.

Thus we are kept in the dark as to the place of Scotland in Anglo-Irish history, and in the *View*. Covington insists that Spenser is making a joke when he derives 'Scot' from 'scotos', meaning 'darkness'.[40] Gottfried points out that the pun that makes this denigration of the Scots possible is borrowed from Stanyhurst and indeed turned against its original exponent.[41] J. W. Draper has illuminated the multiple origins of 'Scot':

> The Irish form, Scot, plural, Scuit, seems to have come from this source [that is, classical Latin]. The origin of the Latin has been variously traced: some have suggested a rare ON plural, skotar; and Rhys thought it from some form cognate to the Welsh ysgwthr, to cut or carve, and so to tattoo. The Greek word for darkness, to which Spenser refers, was written with an –o–, not –w–; and one has no reason to suppose either that there is any connection between that classic Greek word and the medieval Greek with an –w–, or that Spenser knew anything about the latter. In short, his derivation is probably guessed from a chance similarity.[42]

Spenser derives 'Kin-cogish' from English 'kin' and Irish 'cogish'. Draper argues that 'kin' is more likely to come from 'cin' for 'crime', and 'cogish' is an Anglicizing of the word 'comfocus', meaning 'relative', thus 'kin-cogish' is 'crime of relative'.[43] Perhaps the crime of the relative here is for England to keep Ireland away from Scotland, and for Spenser critics to be accessories after the fact. There is a skeleton in the cupboard, lurking in the darkness, a skeleton that goes by the name of 'Scotland'. As always with Spenser, textual strategy matters more than historical truth. The Irish are originally Scots, but the Scots who settled in Ireland did so before there was a Scotland, so in a sense the Scots are really Irish. Ireland is Scotia Major and Scotland Scotia Minor. There are two kinds of Scots. The Irish and the Scottish. Either way, it makes sense from an English perspective to keep both nations apart as far as possible, all the more so given their natural affinity.

An earlier strand of Spenser scholarship was happy to acknowledge the link that Spenser makes in the *View* between Scythians and Scots. Covington, for example, speaks of the poet's claim for 'the Scottish or Scythian origin of the Irish race'.[44] Covington also points out that Spenser had read Richard Stanyhurst's Latin text *De Rebus in Hibernia Gestis* (Antwerp, 1584).[45] In *De Rebus in Hibernia Gestis* Stanyhurst had rejected the myth that Scotia, an old name for Scotland, in the view of some antiquarians, came from 'Scota', the daughter of Pharaoh.[46] In the *View* Spenser wrongly attributes the myth to Stanyhurst. Covington refers to Irenius's explanation 'that both Scotland and Ireland were colonized in early times by the race of Scots'.[47] Spenser says all are not Spanish who came out of Spain. In the same way all are not Scots who dwell in Scotland.[48] In Holinshed, we learn of the Scots: 'They were also called Scoti by the Romans, bicause their Iland and original inhabitation thereof were unknowne, and they themselves an obscure nation in the sight of all the world.'[49] Roland Smith has pointed out that the Scythian origin is 'an "etymological invention", like Scota, to explain an old name for the Irish, *Scoti*'.[50]

'Spenser' and 'Ireland' are multiple and fragmented, invented and represented. Given Spenser's use of the past to inform the present, exemplified in his approach to the Scottish investment in Ireland, it is surprising that Gottfried, in his article on Spenser's historiography, should sum up thus:

> We can only conclude, therefore, that the antiquities are a completely separable element, a kind of historical decoration on the facade of the *View*; if they are also flimsy in character, they cause no weakening of its broad and solid structure.[51]

I have suggested in my uncovering of the Scottish strand of Spenser's antiquarian discourse that it is not merely decorative, but strikes at the heart of Anglocentric and Hibernocentric readings of the text.

III DISMANTLING SCOTLAND

In a footnote to *Castle Rackrent*, Maria Edgeworth discusses the antiquity of the mantle, arguing that Spenser 'proves that it is not, as some have imagined, peculiarly derived from the Scythians', but was in fact used by most nations, and quoting the relevant passages from the *View*.[52] If, as Edgeworth would have it, the mantle was not peculiar or proper to the Scythians – who are the Scots, remember, in Irenius's genealogy – but was of classical origins 'as you may read in Virgil', then it becomes harder to say what was characteristic of, or unique to the Irish.

I now want to take this reading of the place of Scotland in the *View* and use it as a lever with which to open up *The Faerie Queene* to a Scottish context. Written in Ireland, banned in Scotland, *The Faerie Queene* tells the story of the English nation from the perspective of an expatriate. The work of the English Renaissance poet and colonist who spent most of his literary career living as a planter in Munster, is often read in relation to early modern Irish politics and history. Written in Cork, his epic poem *The Faerie Queene* was banned in Caledonia on the instructions of James VI on the grounds that his mother, Mary Queen of Scots was defamed in Canto 9 of Book V, published in 1596. This section will argue that the place of Scotland in Spenser's corpus is more central than has hitherto been acknowledged. If the *View* itself is as much about Scotland as Ireland, if it deals with the complex interaction of Scotland, Ireland and England, then might his epic poem also bear traces of a three-way struggle? Critics of Spenser have set up a false opposition between English civility and Irish barbarity which ignores the tensions within the emerging British state. Far from being marginal or tangential, Scotland is the key third term in the formation of Anglo-Irish identity in the early modern period, and evidence of its role is to be found in Spenser's texts.

Some years ago, Paul McLane, picking up on a suggestive remark by Mary Parmenter, argued that the fable of the Fox and the Kid in the May Eclogue of *The Shepheardes Calender* was an allegory of the young King James VI (the Kid), duped by his French cousin Esmé

Stuart , Duc d'Aubigny (the Papist Fox), despite being warned by his tutor George Buchanan (the Goat).[53] McLane contends, rightly I think, that Spenser was as steeped in Scottish affairs as he was in French matters, and that the Duc d'Aubigny concerned him as much as the Duc d'Alencon.

Better known than this earlier link is the encounter with Scotland that came in the wake of the publication of all six books of *The Faerie Queene*. Dedicated to one monarch, it attracted the anger of another. The second part of Spenser's continued allegory was the subject of an exemplary political reading, a royal intervention, a crown communication and a judicial inquiry, all of which threatened to create an international incident in an already charged atmosphere of political suspicion and subterfuge. Ciarán Brady maintains that, although they raise related moral issues, Book V:

> remains a poem; the *View* is a prose dialogue. Their underlying intent, their mode of exposition and their effect upon the reader are correspondingly different.[54]

This is a modern literary fiction, not an early modern political fact. James Stuart was for none of these artificial demarcations. His reading of what was, after all, 'a mere poem', produced an international panic which was perhaps unprecedented in its day. What was it about Book V that could precipitate such top level activity at two courts, in two capitals?

On 20 January 1596 Books I–VI of Spenser's *magnum opus* were registered in London. Ten months later, on 1 November, Robert Bowes, the English agent in Scotland, wrote to Burghley from Edinburgh enclosing a missive he had lately received from Roger Aston, one of the king's representatives in Linlithgow, dated 31 October. Aston intimates therein the distress visited upon James VI by the contents of one specific section of *The Faerie Queene* (V. ix. 36–50), namely, the trial of Mary Queen of Scots:

> His Majesty has commanded me to certify you that so many as are there of the second part of the 'Ferry Quene' he will not have sold here and further he will complain to Her Majesty of the author as you will understand at more length by himself.[55]

Bowes writes to Burghley once more on 12 November:

The King has conceived great offence against Edward Spenser publishing in print in the second part of the *Fairy Queen* and 9th chapter som dishonourable effects (as the King deems thereof) against himself and his mother deceased. He alleged that this book was passed with privilege of Her Majesty's Commissioners for the view and allowance of all writings to be received into print. But therein I have (I think) satisfied him that it is not given out with such privilege. Yet he still desires that Edward Spenser for his fault may be duly tried and punished.[56]

This Anglo-Scottish exchange answers two questions. Firstly, it explains the immediate suppression of the *View*. I shall cite further plausible reasons for that particular action shortly, reasons which pertain to the politics of the *View* with special reference to the long-standing Scottish claim to Ulster. Secondly, the continuing confinement of the *View* to manuscript form is more easily understood when set against this public show of disapproval directed at Spenser by the future king of England. What patron could reasonably undertake the publication of the *View* before 1625?

On the other hand, *The Faerie Queene* went through three further editions during the reign of James in 1609, 1611 and 1617. But in contrast to the persisting political sensitivity of the opinions expressed by Spenser in the *View*, the representation of Mary's trial in Book V of *The Faerie Queene* ceased to be politically sensitive once James ascended to the English throne, and the filial reaction to Spenser's defamation of his mother's character therefore receded. One could go further, and suggest that the issue in the first place had been rather more political than personal for James. The succession controversy was behind James's adverse response to the Mary/Duessa identification. Richard McCabe has argued that the claims of the Scottish monarch to the English throne governed his objections to the allegorical depiction of his mother in *The Faerie Queene*, concluding that Spenser's literary representation of the trial and execution of Mary Queen of Scots became an 'official embarrassment' in both kingdoms by the late 1590s.[57] Graham Hough writes that in the Radigund episode: 'Some political reference to the prepotency of Mary Queen of Scots may be intended, and Spenser may be reinforcing the arguments of Knox's *Monstrous Regiment of Women*.'[58] Knox was a controversial character, and Elizabeth bore him no love for his ill-timed diatribe against female rulers. Hough goes on to say that: 'The trial of Duessa or Mary Queen of Scots (ix. 38–50) is an exceptionally fair and plausible piece of dialectic; and here the political atmosphere did not forbid the humanity of divided sympathies.'[59] Evidently this fairness was lost on Mary's son.

With Spenser's death, followed four years later by that of Elizabeth, it is not hard to imagine the King's earlier, studied outrage dissipating in the face of more pressing matters. Before the passing of Spenser and Elizabeth, though, there ensued a further instalment of the saga. On 25 February 1598, a servant of Bowes, George Nicholson, wrote to Burleigh's son, Robert Cecil, informing him that James had commissioned Robert Walgrave, the royal printer, to publish a book by Walter Quin, 'the Irishman', stating the King's title to England. Quin 'is also answering Spencer's book whereat the King was offended'.[60]

Two months later, on 14 April 1598, the *View* was entered in the Stationers' Register on behalf of the bookseller Matthew Lownes 'Uppon condicion that hee get further aucthoritie before yt be prynted'.[61] No such authority was granted, and my contention is that this refusal to publish on the part of the English crown – I am presuming that 'further aucthoritie' implies high level interference – was prompted in the first instance by the recent correspondence between Edinburgh and London. I say 'in the first instance' because I believe there to be textual as well as contextual reasons for this decision.

Jonathan Goldberg's suggestion that the *View* was suppressed because it was too blatant a statement of royal intent with regard to Ireland is, I think, too simplistic, and for three reasons.[62] Firstly, because it assumes an unproblematic relation between royal policy and New English actions, contrary to what we know of the deep ideological divisions between the court and its colonial communities. Secondly, because it implies that the *View* exposed 'sovereign power', a fairly abstract, not to mention incorrect, hypothesis, where more concrete issues such as the wisdom of despatching an army of the size Spenser was recommending, at such an incredible cost, in the midst of a decade of dearth might have been considered. Thirdly, it treats a diffuse document as an integral statement. Nor is David Baker's claim that 'the government suppressed a work that stated its case' because the *View* too flagrantly revealed the limits of English law, and, by extension, royal authority in Ireland any more convincing.[63]

Both Baker and Goldberg assume that the *View* too eloquently and openly stated a coherent official policy. No such policy existed, and if it had, the *View* would not have concurred with it. Such a reading depends on the old canard of the assumed intimacy of Colin Clout and Gloriana, as though the poet's creation was an accurate representation of Elizabeth in her ardent imperialist attitudes, rather than a covert cultural critique. A stronger argument would be that the *View* too readily offered to confer absolute power upon the next viceroy, whom many expected to be Essex, a courtier Elizabeth was understandably reluctant to endow with unrestrained authority.[64]

There are two interrelated features of the *View* that would have offended James: its approval of George Buchanan and its dismissal of the Scottish claim to Ulster.[65] John Derricke records a speech by Turlough Luineach O'Neill which is presented as the Ulster chieftain's proposal to Lord Deputy Sidney:

Few Scottes in North (if Quene will have it so)
Shall there abide, the grounde for to manure,
Excepte that thei, their homage yeeld her to:
Avowynge eke, their fealtie to endure,
Conjoyning it, with compliments most sure.
Not one, I saie, (if Queene will me supporte)
Shall there possesse, one castell toune or forte.[66]

We recall that in the *View* Irenius had insisted that 'the chiefest caveat and provision in reformation of the north, must be to keep out those *Scottes*'. How could the English Privy Council sanction a text which was so unequivocally anti-Scottish at a time when relations between the two nations were entering their most sensitive stages in living memory? Ulster had been a bone of contention throughout the period. Hugh O'Neill claimed the province, and later all Ireland, as his kingdom. His father, Shane, in the early 1560s, fought off the attentions of Lord Deputy Sussex, who desired 'to be styled Earl of Ulster'.[67] Bacon later recommended that the young Prince Henry be endowed with that title.[68]

Significantly, the Scottish right to Ulster was the only point on which Spenser departed from the thinker he acknowledged as his most abiding intellectual influence, George Buchanan. Buchanan had been a tyrannical tutor to the young King James. He contributed to the trial and execution of Mary. After his death, he remained an unpopular figure in the eyes of both Elizabeth and James due to his republican theories. Those theories made him popular with the Sidney circle, and, later, with John Milton. Buchanan had links with members of Henry Sidney's viceregal administration as early as 1570. In his emphatic expression of resistance to the one component of Buchanan's politics

likely to appeal to James, Spenser may have been committing a tactical
error in submitting the *View* for publication when he did – assuming
that he did submit it. He provoked the wrath of a man who would
be king of a united kingdom Elizabethans only dreamed of.[69]

The reference to 'Easterland' in *FQ*.II.10.41 is a key point where
Ireland and Scotland are linked, according to James Vink:

> Spenser's coinages 'Easterland' and 'Easterlings' have long been
> recognized as anomalous, for they are among Spenser's rare
> intrusions on his source material by Spenser himself ... This anomaly
> is explained by Spenser's need to create a millennial event which
> would join Ireland, or 'Easterland', to England under a single
> crown – prefiguring and authorizing, around 467 B.C., the strong
> union to be founded again in A.D. 533 and A.D. 1533. Holinshed's
> *Chronicles*, Spenser's main source for British history, employs the
> word 'Ostemani', but not 'Easterland'.[70]

Vink explains the thinking behind Spenser's use of 'Easterland':

> Ireland in its northern reaches, as well as the northern fringe of
> Scotland, is considered by Bede to have been settled by 'Redshanks',
> whom he defines as Picts from Scandinavia, the 'eastland' of the
> Norse. Bede distinguishes between these and the Celts, whom they
> drove south: 'Britons being spoiled of the Scots and Redshanks
> sought aid of the Romans' (Bede I.17). This last Briton group,
> Spenser's heroes, are despised for cowardice by Bede. South Irish
> tribes were closely related to the Welsh Celtic or 'Trojan' Briton
> groups, the supposed ancestors of Artegall and, hence, Elizabeth
> I. For her, Spenser must claim descent by the earliest authorized
> lineage.[71]

Vink argues that Spenser's 'Easterland' is an amalgam of Ireland and
Scotland:

> Ireland and Scotland, taken as a single unit as in ancient times, could
> be called by the term 'Easterland'. Such a rebellious Easterland had
> also included, geographically, that very North of England that had
> remained faithful to Rome in the time of Henry VIII and Queen
> Elizabeth I, causing painful rebellions in favour of the old religion.[72]

'Easterland' thus becomes a term that embraces all of the sites of resistance to English metropolitan rule. Spenser's twinning of Ireland and Scotland, most evident in Book V, is something to which critics of the poet should attend.

IV SCATTERING SPENSER

This chapter has been a scattering, an attempt to open up the closed coupling of 'Spenser and Ireland' to a third term. What I have tried to salvage is something that I firmly believe is worth saving. In the *View* Irenius speaks of the excessive mourning of the Irish, and discusses the origins of their keening and wakes, finally concluding:

> For it is the manner of all *Pagans* and *Infidels* to be intemperate in their waylings of their dead, for that they had no faith nor hope of salvation. And this custome also is specially noted by *Diodorus Siculus*, to have beene in the *Scythians*, and is yet amongst the Northerne *Scots* at this day, as you may reade in their Chronicles. (p. 40)

As a descendant of the 'Northern *Scots*', as well as the Western Irish, I feel a sense of loss that has resulted from the focus on Ireland in Spenser studies to the exclusion of the matter of Britain, generally, and the Scottish dimension particular.

'Anglo-Irish' history is also, culturally and politically, 'British' history, the history of the British state, and as such it has to include Scotland. Neither early modern nor modern Irish history can be understood or explained solely by reference to *English* colonialism, no matter how fractured that Englishness is shown to be. Remember that for four hundred years there was English control of Ireland while Scotland enjoyed relative autonomy. The *View*, too often seen as an anti-Irish tract pure and simple, is a complex meditation on race, culture, and national identity. *The Faerie Queene* is not 'all about Ireland'. Book V is not 'all about Ireland'. Scotland matters. (So too does Wales, of course, as Arthur and the Tudors attest.)

In Sir James Perrott's *The Chronicle of Ireland* , the author records a diplomatic mission to St Andrews in Scotland by Captain Nicholas Dawtrey in August 1585, in which Dawtrey represented the Lord Deputy, Sir John Perrott:

Whilst the Lord Deputie was in this second Northerne expedition, percevinge that the inhabitantes of the Out Isles of Scotland continewed theyr course to make incursions into Ulster, he sent one Captayne Dawtry unto the Kinge of Scotland to intreate his Majestie that none of the Islanders should be suffered to come over to invade the North partes of Ireland, as formerly they had don; assuringe hym that if he would be pleased to take order for this, and for the freedom of some Irish marchantes goods stayed in some partes of Scotland, there should be the like mutuall correspondence of justice to the people of that nation within the realme of Ireland whilste he governed there.[73]

The King 'returned a princely answer'. As well as pledging to keep the 'Out Islanders':

from coming over to molest the Queenes good subjectes, the Kinge allsoe promised immediately to direct his letters to inhibite them to make any roades upon the kingdom of Ireland on payne of treason; and if they nevertheles should attempt the contrary, his highnes would use them as his rebells, and geive commission unto MacAllen and the contrie thereaboutes to rise and prosecute them accordingly.[74]

In the 1550s the increased influx of Highland 'redshanks' into Ulster raised the spectre of a Franco-Scottish invasion.[75] A Franco-Scottish invasion in the North and a Spanish force backing Irish rebels in the South was not an attractive prospect for the English. It was the Anglo-Scottish Treaty of 1560, the victory over the Spanish at Kinsale in 1601, and the Anglo-Scottish Union of 1603 that prevented this scenario.

One final question: Was Spenser in Scotland? Are those the 'north parts' to which Colin repaired before heading for Ireland? There was a Spenser mentioned in a letter by James VI in 1583, writing to Elizabeth from St Andrews: 'I have staied Maister Spenser upon the letter quhilk is written with my ain hand quhilk sall be readie within tua daies.'[76] We know that in May of this year Spenser was appointed a commissioner for musters in Co. Kildare, that he paid rent on New Abbey in August, and that he received payment from Lodowick Bryskett in December, possibly for carrying letters. Whether or not he ever made it to Scotland, Spenser was clearly influenced by Scotland, and it plays a part in his work and life that I have tried to sketch out here.

8

Spensership: A Judicial Review

I know it will be said by many, that I might have been more pleasing
to the Reader, if I had written the story of mine owne times; having
been permitted to draw water as near the well-head as another. To
this I answere, that who-so-ever in writing a modern historie, shall
follow truth too neare the heeles, it may happelie strike out his teeth.
(Sir Walter Raleigh, *The History of the World*)

I CENSORSHIP

My last act of salvaging brings me to the very brink of the present.
The present is a dangerous place to live, and present views of Ireland
are notoriously vexed. In this chapter I want to tackle the question of
censorship as it impinges upon a key text in Spenser's corpus. It is
significant that Spenser's prose dialogue, entered in the Stationers'
Register in April 1598 as 'A viewe of the *present* state of Ireland', was
first published, thirty-five years later, by an Irish antiquarian as *A View
of the State of Ireland*. Against Ware's editorial intentions, it was viewed
with ire, not as ancient history but as all-too-topical, and as a text it
continues to be haunted by the present.

One of the most decisive interventions in Spenser studies in recent
years must surely be Jean Brink's painstaking review of the evidence
for Spenser's authorship of the *View*.[1] Brink's work, which has already
provoked considerable debate, is important enough to merit a chapter
to itself, and I want here to address some of the vexed issues raised
by her exemplary textual scholarship. The assumption that the *View*
was censored in 1598 has been commonly held for so long that it has
become orthodox and dogmatic. While critics may disagree as to
why it was suppressed, they are united in their belief that it did
suffer an act of official censorship. According to Nicholas Canny the
View 'failed to obtain official approval for publication'.[2] Ciarán Brady
concludes that 'after years of redrafting his text was refused

publication by the Master Stationers in 1598, to remain unpublished for the next thirty-five years'.[3] John Breen maintains that: 'Permission to publish was not granted and the *View* was first published in 1633.'[4] Jonathan Goldberg's contention is that Spenser went too far: 'Why should the government suppress a work that states its case? The answer can only be that it is a case that cannot be stated.'[5] Goldberg cites the defence of Grey as a crux of controversy: 'the official position on Lord Grey was censorship, recall, humiliation'.[6] Goldberg's claim that Spenser was too faithfully representing the views of the government is countered by those critics who maintain that it was his defence of Lord Grey that prompted the suppression of his treatise. Thus Elizabeth Porges Watson insists:

> The correlative to Spenser's endorsement of a discredited administration is his undisguised contempt for Grey's successors in office. The *Veue* was ... not surprisingly rejected for publication.[7]

Ciarán Brady is convinced that it was Spenser's exposure of the shortcomings of English law that lay at the heart of official objections to the *View*.[8] Other critics see Spenser's tract as being generally critical of what they imagine to be a coherent official policy. Tracey Hill contends that Spenser's *View* was refused a licence 'because he was criticising English governmental policy for being insufficiently firm on the unruly Irish; any such critique would have been unacceptable to the authorities'.[9] Tom Healy argues that Spenser wrote the *View* 'not as a vindication of Elizabethan policy towards Ireland but as a document highly critical of it under a necessarily respectful guise'.[10] But what was Elizabethan policy towards Ireland? Certainly not something that remained constant between 1558 and 1603. Multiple strategies were employed, from plantation, sword and famine, to surrender and regrant.

Kenneth Gross shares Brady's view that it was Spenser's critique of law that underpinned the suppression of his treatise, but sees this as part of a fundamental and far-reaching critique of political culture: 'There runs through the dialogue a deep strain of scepticism about the place and power of such structures of order as myth, custom and law.'[11] Since that section of the *View* was 'perhaps the most pungent, if not the most original, portion of the dialogue; one wonders', writes Gross, 'if its ominous suggestions were not the sole reason why the dialogue was never published in Spenser's lifetime, no matter how seriously the court advisors may have read it'.[12] Thus there is a strain of Spenser criticism that holds to the view that Spenser's prose dialogue was penalized for its boldness – 'Be bold, be not too bold'. This is a well-established position. Some forty years ago Constantia Maxwell remarked that 'Spenser's book was too outspoken to please the Government, and publication was refused, so that it was not until 1633, when Sir James Ware discovered the Dublin copy in the library of Archbishop Ussher, that it was actually printed.'[13] This act of discovery, of course, came in the wake of a long manuscript history, with copies of the *View* circulating for some thirty-five years among an informed readership who arguably recognized its importance.

Side by side with arguments over content have gone arguments over form. Some critics see the text as inconsistent or incomplete, while others admire its coherence. Brady sees in the dialogue's apparent breaking off a kind of self-censorship:

> The silencing of Spenser's *View*, and his own self-censorship in abandoning the manuscript in an incomplete form, represented therefore more than a mere concession to political expediency or propagandist sensitivities, but a recognition that his way of explaining England's failure to govern Ireland was by definition untenable.[14]

By contrast, Raymond Jenkins is not struck by the document's incompleteness at all:

> The *Veue*'s completeness and systematic development, qualities which make it the most significant Elizabethan document on Ireland, were possible because it is the product of the poet's varied labours and associations with English leaders as secretary, Clerk of the Council of Munster, landowner, and traveller.[15]

Whatever the individual disagreements, the critical consensus on the *View* is summed up in David Baker's assertion that 'Elizabeth's Council did not want the treatise published.'[16] Yet Baker himself acknowledges another consensus, that of the colonial milieu in which Spenser moved:

> Wretchedly cruel as colonial policy seems, to Spenser it was not repugnant, simply because according to the political consensus within which he moved and had his being it was justified, or more precisely, needed no justification at all ... His views never

encompassed the brutal realities of English colonization because
for him they were neither brutal nor real.[17]

That is the story thus far. Now, in a compelling essay Jean Brink has
fused questions of censorship with issues of authorship and has in
the process made a major contribution to our understanding of
Spenser's relation to the *View*.

Brink begins by alerting us to the fact that this is a controversial
text, in terms of politics, if not, at least hitherto, a contested one in
terms of authorship. The *View*,

> because of its advocacy of the complete subjugation of the Irish by
> famine and military conquest, has long been a focal point for anti-
> colonial and anti-English discourse.[18]

It is important that Brink sets out the debate in this frank manner. The
View has indeed become a focal point for anti-colonial criticism. Less
convincing is her suggestion that:

> Until the twentieth century the *View* was largely ignored by literary
> scholars except for sporadic attempts to use it as a vehicle for
> attacking or defending England's policies in Ireland. Irish school
> books, to be sure, did not ignore the *View*; its highly quotable
> passages sp!endidly illustrated the brutality of the English and
> insured that Spenser was vilified as the archetypal English
> colonialist, a characterization of Spenser that has the merit, at least,
> of being simple. (p. 203)

This is a text, after all, that went through several editions prior to this
century, and that had been read by Milton, Edgeworth and
Wordsworth, and that caused a sensation when it first appeared
in print.

Brink notes with distaste that 'it has become increasingly fashionable
to use the *View* to interpret Spenser's biography and to explicate *The
Faerie Queene*' (p. 203). She reminds us that the *View* is a text 'first
attributed to Spenser thirty-five years after his death and one for
which there is no holograph manuscript' (p. 204). She might have
added that we have none of Spenser's poetry in his own hand, and
that *The Shepheardes Calender* was published anonymously, as were
the translations of epigrams and sonnets in *A Theatre for Worldlings*
(1569), and that a fragment of Book VII of *The Faerie Queene* – 'Two

Cantos of Mutabilitie' – was appended to the poem posthumously.[19] How certain can we be that Spenser was sole author of the letters signed by him in the published correspondence between himself and Harvey? These were, after all, as his former tutor attests, 'Patcheries, and fragments'. Let us be plain. Spenser's corpus is and always has been in a state of flux.

Having established that the *View* is controversial and is used by critics in dubious ways, that it was posthumously attributed and posthumously published, and that no copies survive in Spenser's hand, Brink proceeds to the main body of her essay, in which she asks three key questions, the answers to which the remainder of the argument is devoted. The first query is: 'Was the *View* suppressed?' Brink's marshalling of evidence is impressive, and her premise that Spenser has been unfairly scapegoated is one I share. I am also sympathetic to the standpoint that sees the Irish angle as coming to dominate studies of Spenser to a worrying extent. (This might jar with the contents of this book, but it is in order both to salvage and savage that I choose Ireland as my text.) Brink's initial strategy here is to undermine the authority of the cautionary note in the Stationers' Register concerning the *View*, and to thus advance the proposition that its alleged suppression lacks documentary evidence: 'No documentary evidence, however, has been cited to demonstrate that either the Privy Council or the bishop of London suppressed it' (p. 204). This is a moot point. It depends on how one interprets the words 'uppon Condicion that hee gett further aucthoritie before yt be prynted'. Brink maintains that 'speculation that the *View* was suppressed by the government derives from an uncritical reading of a cautionary note in the Stationers' Register', and that 'the cautionary note in the entry for the *View* could just as well signal a disagreement over publication rights as government censorship' (p. 207). Brink goes on: 'If the entry concerning the *View* is compared with similar entries in April 1598, we have insufficient evidence to conclude that the government suppressed the publication of the *View*' (p. 208). It is the nature of evidence to always be insufficient.

The *View* was registered in 1598. It was not printed until 1633. The evidence, from this distance, is conclusive. A closer look, such as the one Brink forces us to take, is revealing and informative, but ultimately, in my own view, as problematic as the blithe assumptions that it seeks rigorously to oppose. Brink refers to a number of other works that were registered in 1598, but none of them are Irish texts by an author who was officially upbraided two years earlier by the King of Scotland, so the comparison is insufficient. One could cite the dialogue between Sylvanus and Peregrine, which has a title page, a dedication (to Essex) and an index, yet remains unpublished, or the 'Supplication', a text that waited 400 years to see the light of day in print.[20] Brink refers to the former treatise in a footnote and remarks that 'the reference to his sons merits further attention' (p. 227, n. 42).

I am surprised that Brink, normally so sceptical, should assume that Sylvanus and Peregrine, the names of the two speakers in this dialogue, are 'Spenser's two sons', since the names were common enough at the time. Gottfried, too, believed that the author 'must have been a friend of the poet's family: two names like Peregrine and Sylvane do not fall together by chance, and these interlocutors are brothers'.[21] I am not so sure about this. I find it easier to believe that Spenser authored the *View* than that he had copyright on these names. Whatever its precise date, this treatise is a hotch-potch of material, parts of which may have predated the birth of Spenser's sons. Perhaps he named them after it, or some other dialogue that employed the same device. It is interesting that Brink should relegate reference to this text to a footnote, since as a contemporary tract with a dedication and an index it is obviously a document that can be read alongside the *View* in terms of its failure to appear in print. It is also relevant as a text that is dedicated to Essex. Rudolph Gottfried notes that Irenius proposes that the anonymous candidate mooted as the next viceroy 'is to be honoured with the title of Lord Lieutenant, usually reserved for a member of the royal family, and is to reside in England at the court'.[22] Gottfried contend that 'the *View* is not only a defence of Lord Grey ... but also a subtle means of flattering Essex'.[23] How then could it fail to stir controversy?

Brink is clearly troubled by the cautionary note in the Stationers' Register. For example: 'It is conceivable that the Privy Council suppressed the *View*, but the entry in the Stationers' Register, by itself, does not warrant that assumption.' Or again: 'Before any conclusions can be drawn about government censorship, a cautionary note in the Stationers' Register has to be contextualized.' Or, finally: 'Unless evidence other than the entry in the Stationers' Register is forthcoming, it is only prudent to assume that no official effort was made to suppress the *View*' (p. 209). Three disclaimers on a single page are evidence of a profound anxiety. I'll have grounds more relative than this for amputating the *View* from Spenser's corpus.

Brink notes in passing that 'the printing of any English history was forbidden unless it was authorized by a member of the Privy Council', but she appears not to consider the *View*, a provocative Irish history by a controversial English poet, to be worthy of such censorship (p. 205). Brink points out that 'efforts to prevent the circulation of seditious, libellous, or obscene books were usually ineffective' (p. 205). This was clearly the case with *The Faerie Queene*, which James objected to because it slandered his mother, and all copies of which he asked be destroyed.[24] The objections of James VI to Spenser's poem, and his request to Elizabeth that it be seized and destroyed and the poet punished, may have had some bearing on the failure of the *View* to find its way from manuscript to print for forty years. Brink chooses to ignore the attempted suppression of Book V of Spenser's epic poem as a possible context for the censorship of the *View*, yet it was plausibly a factor when it came to granting 'further aucthoritie'.

Brink asks: 'What evidence do we have that the *View* was suppressed? Even if we were to accept the notion of effective censorship, the suppression of the *View* is unsupported by documentary evidence in either the *Acts of the Privy Council* or the state papers' (pp. 205–6). Leaving aside the matter of the documentary evidence of the cautionary note in the Stationers' Register, the claim that censorship was ineffective, borne out by the failure of James VI to have *The Faerie Queene* suppressed south of the border, does not prove that the *View* was not censored. In fact, it might prove the opposite. The net may have tightened on Spenser as a result of earlier encounters with authority, such as *Mother Hubberds Tale* and Book V. Jonathan Goldberg points to the way in which the punishment of Malfont in Book V anticipates the Scottish king's reaction: 'James's desire for justice, we could say, is firmly inscribed in the text he condemns, as is his demand that the poet be subject to royal authority.'[25] Ireland is no stranger to censorship. Roland Smith points to an astonishing nine instances of persons named 'Malfont' pardoned in Ireland between 1573 and 1601, and further indicates that in 'each instance the name appears to belong to the neighbourhood of Kilcolman'.[26] It would be a cruel twist of fate that made Spenser the tenth Malfont, and refused him a pardon. Annabel Patterson proposes that:

Spenser's Legend of Justice and his *View* were participating in a contemporary struggle for control over the idea of Justice that went far beyond Ireland in its implications. At the centre of that struggle was the question ... what could be thought, spoken, and published in early modern England, and especially in the last, increasingly tense years of Elizabeth's reign?[27]

Thus Spenser, always ahead of his time and his critics, can be seen to have anticipated exactly the kind of debate that is currently raging around the *View*.

Brink observes that 'James Ware, who first attributed the authorship of the *View* to Spenser, does not mention any attempts to suppress its publication' (p. 206). Again, Brink ignores the fact that Ware was not only the first – *in print*, that we know of – to attribute the *View* to Spenser, but was the first to edit it for publication, and effectively a censor of sorts. Indeed Ware admits in his preface that he would rather it had been a less provocative document. We know by the impact it had that even Ware's doctored version proved too potent for many readers. Brink notes that:

> Not one of the seventeenth or eighteenth-century biographies of Spenser suggests that the *View* was suppressed by the government or even regarded as suspect. Later biographies are silent or tentative about the suppression of the *View*. (p. 206)

Brink cites further cases of Spenser scholars who have left open or undecided the issue of censorship of the *View*, and concludes: 'Grosart thus sees Spenser as the courageous and disinterested defender of Lord Grey; Henley thinks that the government may have rewarded him for writing his dialogue; and Judson begs the question' (p. 206). Other critics have been less circumspect. Brink is selective here. One could cite, for example, John W. Hales, who, in his 'Memoir' prefixed to the Globe edition of 1910, written in 1869, and revised in 1896, remarks that the *View*, completed in 1596, 'was not registered till April 1598, and then only conditionally'.[28] Hales does give space to James's efforts at censorship of Book V, but does not link this to the putative conditional status of the *View*. It is worth noting, as part of the wonderful history of anachronisms, that Hales, like Ware and many others, writes of the 'present state of Ireland' as much happier than it was in Spenser's day, as though Spenser's day was history: 'He was far from anticipating that policy of conciliation whose triumphant application it may perhaps be the signal honour of our own day to achieve.'[29] These words, written a century ago, are as untimely, and as timely, 'today'. Hales mentions 'some fragments' of poetry that 'may have perished in the flames at Kilcolman'. A rebellion, in other words, is, in its own way, an act of suppression.

Ware dropped the 'present' from the title of the *View*, his Greek Gift to Wentworth, yet it is the presentness of the text that is so disturbing, its anachronistic power to unsettle generations of readers, as though that 'state of present time' alluded to in the proem to Book V (pro.1.1) is still with us. The editor of the Globe edition of Spenser's works wrote:

> The *title* itself as given by Ware is incorrectly stated. All the manuscripts, as well as the entry on the books of the Stationers' Company, read 'A View of the PRESENT State of Ireland', but, curiously enough, the word 'present' is omitted in all the editions that I have seen.[30]

In dropping the present, Ware elevated the past, but as something of interest only to antiquarians. Indeed, he replaced the 'present' with the past, with antiquity. As Andrew Hadfield has observed:

> Ware's use of the term 'Ancient' in the title of his anthology suggests a certain nervousness about the legitimacy of his project and a desire to neutralize any attempt to read the histories in terms of contemporary Irish history ... The reader is invited to read the *View* purely as an antiquarian work, or as an example of an ancient (dead) historical tradition.[31]

Hadfield cites Ware's preface – 'we may wish that in some passages it had bin tempered with more moderation' – as evidence, together with Gottfried's list of excisions in the *Variorum*, that Ware cut the text.[32] But was it Ware's custom to excise? Or did he in fact censure rather than censor? Hadfield also suggests that the non-antiquarian section of Campion's contribution to Ware's anthology was a 'rather sketchy and slightly inoffensive book which would have cut little ice in the 1630s'.[33] It was not inoffensive to John Lynch, who included Campion in his list of 'calumniators' of Ireland in *Cambrenis Eversus*. Campion inspired Stanyhurst's provocative Irish history in Holinshed's *Chronicles* (1577), and died a Jesuit martyr at Tyburn in 1581. He was hardly a character free from controversy.

Ciarán Brady shares with Gottfried, Brink and Hadfield the belief that Ware's text is a bowdlerized one:

Ware silently but systematically purged Spenser's text of all its more offensive blemishes, omitting whole sections in places and changing the sense of argument in others. The cumulative effect of this extensive bowdlerization was to rob the *View* of much of its polemical and rebarbative character, leaving it to be read as an interesting account by a famous man of desperate times long past. For Ware had complacently but prematurely concluded that the social and political divisions of Spenser's day had all been resolved: 'and now we may truly say "iam cuncti gens una sumus" [now we are one whole people]'. Thus even if the *View* had been conceived of as an aggressive and exclusive New English tract and even if it had been read as such by a small circle who shared the manuscript copies, this was not the guise it assumed when it first appeared in print, and this was not, consequently, how it was generally perceived.[34]

But how then did Ware's copy prove to be such a bombshell when it was published in 1633? Critics have to attend to how the published version of the *View* was read, and they have to read it for themselves, instead of engaging in some futile paper chase for a missing original. If Ware really was the censor we have inherited then he was an exceptionally incompetent one. Moreover, the guise of antiquarianism could not conceal the polemical import of Spenser's text. Ware may have taken out the word 'present', but it was a naive reader who failed to see the treatise as anything other than volatile.

Yet the myth of a neutered text persists. Patricia Coughlan writes of Ware:

His version of the *View* makes systematic and highly significant textual modifications to the original, all tending to a considerable softening of Spenser's harsh judgements about the native Irish and particularly the Old English. He further affects readers' reception of the *View* by reprinting along with it the rivers passage from *Faerie Queene* IV and the Mutabilitie Cantos, the two passages of Spenser's text which most idealise and offer a benign transformation of the Irish landscape. Ware also adds an eirenic preface which expresses (optimistically) his sense of an Irish unity now achieved. A major shift of emphasis has occurred between Spenser's unbending condemnation of Irish actuality – delivered in the context of rebellion and confiscation – and Ware's foregrounding of the *View*'s historical and antiquarian aspect, which can hardly have been in the 1590s the most salient part of the text.[35]

After Brink, one must ask, what 'original'? Ware's copy-text is in doubt, and there is no holograph, therefore the claim that Ware censored the *View* is hard to sustain. Ware certainly did not cut out the Scottish component. That particular act of censorship was executed by subsequent scholars. In fact, Spenser's text may have been read in manuscript as an antiquarian text, but once in print it was a stick of dynamite. Whatever Ware's subjective intentions in his 'eirenic preface', the objective effect of his edition was to put a match to the powder keg of Anglo-Irish relations in the 1630s and beyond. Even the antiquarianism is fraught. Those readers who see Ware's insistence on the *View* as a history as a way of depoliticizing it have a rather naive view of history, and of the politically charged nature of antiquarianism.

Brink highlights an apparent contradiction in the writings of those who see the *View* as a position paper gone awry: 'Underpinning many of these arguments are two suppositions difficult to reconcile: Spenser wrote the *View* to promote his career, and the government intervened to prohibit its publication' (p. 206). Is it really so difficult to reconcile these suppositions? Is not the message of so much Renaissance literature, including *Virgil's Gnat* , that vaulting ambition can lead to a downfall? Brink presses further: 'If Spenser wrote the *View* to win the patronage of powerful people in the government, then we have to envision a singularly inept Spenser, if he failed so ignominiously that the government actually suppressed his work' (p. 207). Once more it is a question of emphasis. The 'government' has never been a unified entity. Spenser's patrons – Harvey, Sidney, Leicester, Grey, Raleigh and Essex – were never universally popular with the authorities that they represented, but that did not stop them from serving as they saw fit. Brink's argument here presupposes a self-assured author and a coherent authority.

Andrew Hadfield has reminded us that 'the purpose of entering books into *The Stationers' Registers* was not primarily to have them checked by censors; rather, it was to register them as the property of the individual printer, in other words, an early form of copyright law'.[36] But Hadfield points to the uniqueness of the *View* in a sense quite different from that claimed by critics such as Bradshaw, Brady and Canny who argue about its representativeness: 'An inspection of the records of *The Stationers' Registers* should alert us to the fact that hardly anything dealing with Ireland was entered, let alone published, during Elizabeth's reign.'[37] Only in the archives would one be aware of this, not from a study of the Stationers' Register. Hadfield goes on to say: 'What is clear from this list is that Spenser's tract was the only analytic, exhortationary work on Ireland entered into *The Stationers' Registers* during Elizabeth's reign.'[38] Hadfield rehearses the reasons why the *View* might have been considered too hot to handle by the authorities: 'possibly for just being about Ireland in the first place; or even, for mentioning Ireland in its title, as we have no reason to assume that censors were any more assiduous and careful readers than they are now'.[39] Hadfield argues that we should not be surprised that the *View* was not published until 1633. Rather, we should wonder that it was submitted for consideration in 1598.

While I accept that there are problems with Judith Anderson's assertion that Ware's version of Spenser's dialogue, as 'the first printed edition of the *View* (1633), justifiably claims manuscript authority', I nonetheless grant it an authority as the copy to which Milton and other seventeenth-century writers and readers had access.[40] It may well be the case today that the authoritative edition for modern readers is the *Variorum*, while the most widely read and quoted copy is the 1970 Renwick edition, but I remain attached to the first printed edition as the one that early modern readers knew. Anne Fogarty reminds us of Ware's uneasiness about the text: 'Ware notes the disjunctive nature of the *View* and attributes this impression to the stark contrast between the writer's circumspect erudition and the stridency of his political opinion.'[41] Thus for Ware it was the polemical content of Spenser's treatise that dictated its form.

Patricia Coughlan sums up the argument that Spenser was appropriated by the antiquarian Ware as an Anglo-Irish historian rather than a New English political commentator:

In spite of the rebarbatively negative tone of Spenser's version of Ireland in the *View*, it was nevertheless already being naturalised or refunctioned as distinctively Anglo-Irish discourse when it was first published in Sir James Ware's version ... Ware, a Protestant of English stock, embodies in his own repertoire of social roles the doubleness or multiplicity of perspectives often entailed upon those publicly active in colonial situations. He was, on the one hand, a trusted office-holder in Strafford's divisive and autocratic regime, and on the other an extremely important antiquarian, historian and collector of ancient Irish manuscripts, who maintained cordial communications with contemporary Gaelic poets and was responsible for the survival of precious early works.[42]

The exemplary colonial role of Ware – as editor, censor, and antiquarian – is crucial. It is a role that Spenser critics have unwittingly been playing for some time.

II SCHOLARSHIP

Having impugned the authority of the entry in the Stationers' Register, Brink proceeds to the question of the text itself, its status as an unfinished document. The second part of her argument is headed: 'Is the *View* a finished work?' If in the preceding section it was a question of 'evidence', in this section it is a matter of 'textual scholarship'. For example: 'In many instances, textual scholarship might offer a reliable means of determining when the manuscripts of the *View* were copied, that is, before or after Ware's edition.' Or again: 'Although interpretative commentary on Spenser is voluminous, much of it of high quality, textual scholarship is unreliable, particularly in the case of the *View*.' Or, finally: 'Both literary and historical interpretation depends upon accurate and thorough textual scholarship' (p. 206). I lay no claims to 'textual scholarship', though I am drawn to the expression. Its talismanic incantation certainly has a mesmerizing effect. Indeed, its appearance three times on the same page lulls one into a false sense of security, as though one was in safe hands, awaiting further authority. The old debate about close versus contextual reading always ignores the profound complicity between the two approaches. It is a question of con-text. Jacques Derrida points up this interface:

Everything comes down to one of those reading exercises with magnifying glass which calmly claim to lay down the law, in police fashion indeed. – ['close reading'] can always ... become police-like ... It can also arm you against that other (secret) police which, on the pretext of delivering you from the chains of writing and reading (chains which are always, illiterately, reduced to the alphabet), hastily lock you up in a supposed outside of the text: the pre-text of perception, of living speech, of bare hands, of living creation, of real history, etc. Pretext indeed to bash on with the most hackneyed, crude, and tired of discourses. And it's also with supposed nontext, naked pre-text, the immediate, that they try to intimidate you, to subject you to the oldest, most dogmatic, most sinisterly authoritarian of programs, to the most massive mediatizing machines.[43]

There is no doubt that Brink is absolutely right to rebuke readers of the *View* for adopting an overly contextual approach that overlooks the text itself, in this case a disparate, divided, and apparently incomplete text, but she has arguably gone too far in the opposite direction – which comes down to the same thing. The *View*'s unfinished state, its unevenness, the many manuscript variations, the uncertainty surrounding Ware's copy-text, Ware's editorial excisions, and the fact that the text itself, in its multifarious forms, begins *in media res* and ends rather abruptly, all point to an 'unperfite' work, but one no less unfinished than *The Faerie Queene*.

Brink feels that the *View* is insufficiently royalist for a text ostensibly composed by the founder of the myth of Gloriana. She states that 'both Beacon and Herbert are critical of English policies in Ireland and advocate reforms, but their critical stances do not prevent them from celebrating the queen' (p. 206). Again, it's a question of reading and emphasis. One could interpret the opening of *Solon his follie* as very critical of royal parsimony. Moreover, as a Machiavellian discourse it can hardly be regarded as unequivocally celebrating Elizabeth. As Andrew Hadfield suggests: 'It is probably the case that *Solon His Follie* escaped censorship by default, having been published through the back door quite deliberately.'[44] Again, Brink is clearly uncomfortable with the unpublished status of Herbert's tract, commenting that 'his own death on March 4, 1593 may have prevented him from publishing *Croftus*' (p. 215). What stopped it from being published posthumously? It may be that the completion of the *View* and the incomplete nature of *The Faerie Queene* are linked. Yeats conjectured that the Irish who overthrew Kilcolman did so with 'some rumours of *The Present State of Ireland* sticking in their stomachs'.[45]

Brink's case for the unfinished nature of the Spenser's dialogue is forcefully made:

> We have several kinds of textual evidence that the *View* should not be treated as a finished text. First, we have the authoritative testimony of the modern editors who have worked most closely with the manuscripts. Renwick stated that another revision must have been intended in a passage that Gottfried took care to include in the *Spenser Variorum* ... Second we have clumsy examples of

repetition ... which would probably have been revised in a finished text. Third, we have the problem that editorial practices used to construct early twentieth-century standard editions were based on theories developed to produce conflated editions of printed works. (p. 212)

While it suits Brink's case to wed Renwick and Gottfried it should be noted that Gottfried held a very low opinion of Renwick's authority as an editor. Is there any evidence that is not 'textual'? Are clumsiness and repetition uncommon in texts, whether literary or critical? Brink asserts: 'In spite of these significant textual problems, most interpretive commentary on the *View* has assumed that it was finished and that its finished state is represented by these edited texts' (pp. 212–13). I am not entirely convinced that most readers have seen it as a finished text. In any case, surely the crucial question must be: Is a text's unfinishedness a reason to stop reading, or is it, rather, an incitement to discourse? It is precisely the openness and contradictory nature of Spenser's text, partly a result of its dialogue form, partly the product of its fraught production, that make it so widely read and hotly disputed. It is an 'incomplete fiction', both in the sense that Katherine Wilson speaks of the Renaissance dialogue form, and in the sense of a text with which we are still coming to terms.[46]

There is another aspect of the form of the *View* that may have some bearing upon the issue of censorship. It is, remember, a dialogue. John Breen reminds us that Philip Sidney, in his *Apology for Poetry*, claimed that Plato was a poet because of his use of dialogue: 'Sidney suggests that dialogue is an indeterminate genre as to feign a speaker is a poetic strategy that belongs to discourses other than the poetical.'[47] Like allegory and anonymity, patronage and distance from the metropolis, dialogue may be a way of evading censorship.

My own feeling is that Spenser's work has undergone another kind of censorship, not official, but informal. Again it is a question of a repressive hypothesis complicit with an incitement to discourse. On the one hand, Book V is bad poetry, on the other hand, Ireland is a highly marketable commodity. The extremity of Spenser's views account for the reluctance of some critics to address the Irish context of his work, while those same views, giving rise to a political *frisson*, incite others. Speaking of the reception of Book V, Richard McCabe notes that:

Readers of the 1940s and 1950s were disturbed by unpleasant similarities to the methods and attitudes of modern fascism. Even critics such as Graham Hough who laboured to defend Spenser from these associations, found in his apparent lack of compassion one of the inherent 'corruptions of imperialism'.[48]

Yet McCabe is unhappy about this analogy: 'As applied to *The Faerie Queene* Hough's concept of "imperialism" is at least as anachronistic as the popular recourse to "fascism".'[49] McCabe appears not to appreciate that anachrony is the condition of *The Faerie Queene*, a complex negotiation between eternity and mutability. What, after all, is the time of literature? How can literary texts be fixed in a period when they are read, not for an age, but for all time? This is an especially fraught area when it comes to the Renaissance, a time when authors were self-consciously reinventing history. Moreover, what is the time of fascism? Is it safely consigned to history? McCabe is as reluctant as Hough to supply any definition of 'fascism', it merely hovers in the air as an absolute evil, an evil that is of itself evil. Michel Foucault, in his preface to Deleuze and Guattari's *Anti-Oedipus*, warns us to beware 'not only historical fascism, the fascism of Hitler and Mussolini – which was able to mobilize and use the desire of the masses so effectively – but also the fascism in us all, in our heads and in our everyday behaviour, the fascism that causes us to love power, to desire the very thing that dominates and exploits us'. Foucault asks:

> How does one keep from being fascist, even (especially) when one believes oneself to be a revolutionary militant? How do we rid our speech and our acts, our hearts and our pleasures, of fascism? How do we ferret out the fascism that is ingrained in our behaviour?[50]

Lest we think that Foucault's opening up of fascism is perverse and anachronistic, let us recall that the word 'fascist' comes from the Latin 'fascis', or 'bundle', and that Spenser's man of iron, Talus, wields an instrument for flailing not dissimilar to the classic *fascis*.

As I have noted, critics disagree about the incompleteness of the *View*. Many are less unequivocal than Brink. Anne Fogarty, for instance, sees in the abrupt opening of the *View* a deliberate rhetorical strategy:

> Irenius describes his speech as 'a remembrance' and in this light his dialogue with Eudoxus may be viewed as an eternal retrospective on a predetermined structure of order which it can

never fully encompass. Even the formal frame of their discussion stresses its iterative nature. The text begins *in media res*. The opening statement delivered by Eudoxus points backwards to previous comments made by Irenius about Ireland ... The discourse about to commence is thereby divested of its uniqueness and situated within a chain of similar encounters between these two interlocutors.[51]

The method of a poet historical, we recall from the 'Letter to Raleigh', differs from that of an historiographer in that the latter recounts events orderly, as they were done, whilst the former 'thrusteth into the middest'. Thus the immediacy of the dialogue's opening is quite in keeping with Spenser's historical approach. After all, *The Faerie Queene* itself opens *in media res*, with the Redcrosse Knight in mid-stride. Fogarty reinforces her argument by reminding us that the treatise ends as abruptly as it begins, but with a similar sense of occasion or context: 'A comparable feeling of infinite regress is elicited by the ending of the dialogue when Irenius and Eudoxus promise to circle back on terrain covered, in order to make good deferrals and omissions necessitated by the rigour of the talk which they have just concluded.'[52] For Andrew Hadfield, the abrupt opening of the *View* is not a sign of haste or fragmentary nature, as it is for Brink, but rather is an indication of the gravity of the discourse: 'The dialogue wastes no time with formalities or presenting a fictionalized setting, but plunges straight into the argument, which may serve to highlight its seriousness and connote a desired verisimilitude.'[53]

In addition to those readers who have no difficulty with what they see as the staged improvisatory nature of the text, there are critics who, like Helena Shire, find the text coherent, and who in fact see it as 'a carefully marshalled exposition of the distressed and deeply disturbing state of Ireland'.[54] Kenneth Gross appreciates the *View* as a text which is not read for its literary virtues, but which does raise larger questions of culture and politics:

> Spenser's dialogue, when it is considered at all, is usually treated as a rather elegant piece of journalism, a firsthand account of the abuses in an English colony together with some comments on the possibility of reform. Nonetheless, the *View* is a quite shrewd piece of literary work. There is, admittedly, little real drama in the exchanges between the informant Irenius ... and his questioner Eudoxus ... But this formal fiction, set in England (at a reflective

distance from its subject), becomes the frame for an intricate analysis of other fictions in both life and literature.[55]

How far does the absence of a dedication suggest an unfinished project? What of the 'Dialogue of Sylvanus and Peregrine', dedicated to Essex, indexed, yet never published? Might it be that a dedication to Essex was removed, or that Spenser was erring on the side of caution? Does the absence of explicit praise of the monarch really cast doubt on Spenser's authorship? Does it, as Brink suggests, support her argument that the treatise is unfinished: 'That the *View* departs from the politic conventions observed in the finished political treatises of Beacon and Herbert, and Spenser's own practice, supports Renwick's and Gottfried's editorial judgments that its text is unfinished' (p. 216). But what was Spenser's own practice? Let us take two examples. He dedicated *The Shepheardes Calender* to Sidney and appended a letter to Raleigh to *The Faerie Queene*. Both of these figures offended royal authority during their careers. If we recall that Grey was recalled, and assume that Essex is the figure coasting on the seas in the *View*, and thus the implicit or covert dedicatee of the dialogue, then it begins to look like Spenser's own practice, as far as patrons were concerned, was to live dangerously.

Nicholas Canny has speculated that Beacon escaped censorship because of his mode of representation:

> Perhaps his fear of government retaliation for such specific criticism explains why *Solon his follie* is presented in allegorical form, and perhaps it also explains why he succeeded in having his work published in 1594, whereas Spenser's *Vewe*, which was entered in the Stationers' Register in 1596, was not published until 1633, and even then only in a truncated form.[56]

Now, one can understand why Brink gets impatient with such assertions. The *View* was registered not in 1596 but in 1598, and it is difficult to confirm the extent to which Ware's edition was a 'truncated form', since we have no certain proof that Ware's copy-text was an 'original'.

Brink makes much of the fact that 'the manuscripts of the *View* lack both a dedication and a preface', saying that this 'also suggests that it is an unfinished work'. The point is reinforced: 'I am unaware of any sixteenth-century manuscript intended for presentation or any printed text that lacks both a dedication and a preface.' And again:

'that no contemporary dedication, or preface, for the *View* has ever been identified further substantiates Renwick's and Gottfried's conclusion that the *View* is an unfinished text, *an unstable foundation upon which to construct interpretations of Spenser and his work*' (p. 216; my emphasis). Again, three references, this time to the lack of the formal textual apparatus one expects to find in a Renaissance text. But having a dedication or a preface is no guarantee of publication. *The Supplication of the blood of the English* (1598) is dedicated to Elizabeth but spent four centuries consigned to the archives. The reference to a 'contemporary dedication' is clearly prompted by the fact that the *View* was dedicated by Ware to Wentworth. Ware had to be pretty sure of his source before he risked such a dedication, either that or he meant Wentworth harm.

Spenser had of course mocked such formal scholarship in *The Shepheardes Calender*, with the elaborate editorial hoax epitomized in the mysterious figure of 'E. K.' Like E. K., we are suppliers of glosses. Indeed, it cannot be overemphasized that Spenser's entire corpus is 'unperfite'. *The Shepheardes Calender* is anonymous. *The Faerie Queene*, intended as twelve books, only made it as far as seven. As Andrew Hadfield reminds us, '*The Faerie Queene* itself remains a fragment.'[57] In Sonnet 32 of *Amoretti* (1595) Spenser writes:

> Great wrong I doe, I can it not deny,
> to that most sacred Empresse my dear dred,
> not finishing here Queene of faery,
> that mote enlarge her living prayses dead. (lines 1–4)

Christ and Faustus can say 'Consummatum est', but not Spenser. He says: 'But yet the end is not'.

To be 'unperfite' is not necessarily a bad thing. In fact, it fits in with Spenser's idea of eternity in mutability, and of permanent reformation, uninterrupted reading, interminable interpretation. *The Faerie Queene* is unfinished. The 'Two cantos of Mutability' are posthumous. The authorship of *Axiochus* and *A Briefe Note of Ireland* is in doubt. The correspondence with Harvey may have been co-authored with Harvey. Spenser was in Ireland and some of his work may have gone to press not in the form he desired. The only material we have in Spenser's hand are letters dictated to him by his superiors in Ireland.

Editors have always been selective. Ware wished that Spenser had been less controversial in the *View*. Renwick included a verse alleged by Ware to have been written on a lute belonging to the Earl of Cork,

Richard Boyle, but refused to incorporate *A Briefe Note*. Ironically, Brink
mentions two poems attributed by Ware to Spenser in 1633 which have
not generally been acknowledged by Spenserians, something that she
says David Lee Miller is going to correct (p. 226, n. 28). Writing in the
wake of the *Variorum* edition of Spenser's works, Roland Smith
declared: 'Gottfried argues so eloquently and convincingly for the
inclusion of the *Axiochus* and the *Brief Note*, which according to certain
critics are not Spenser's, that it may be doubted whether the question
of Spenser's authorship will again be raised.'[58] Yet Smith concluded
his review of *The Prose Works* with these words:

> we may never know exactly what Spenser wrote ... Much of our
> explanation of Spenser's prose – as of his poetry – is still incorrect
> or incomplete. On many points we can resort only to conjecture.[59]

Conjecture will never satisfy the 'textual scholar' or the censor.

Among many questions raised by Brink's careful analysis are the
vexed issues of genre and discipline. Do historians approach the
View in a different way from literary critics? According to Nicholas
Canny:

> For the literary scholars the offensive nature of the text is apparent
> from its very language and especially from the language employed
> by Spenser in that infamous passage where he describes the
> starvation of the population in Munster that followed upon the
> military actions of Lord Grey. Historians, who are more familiar
> with such gory descriptions in the every-day correspondence of the
> time, recognize that the use of such language in itself would not
> have condemned Spenser's *View* to oblivion.[60]

This is an important point. It pertains to the question of the example,
and of exemplarity. Spenser has been made an example of, and the
View has been read as an exemplary text, yet it is implicated within
a larger colonial and cultural discourse. Canny goes on to argue that:

> historians, while impressed with the polished prose in particular
> passages of Spenser's *View*, come away from it with the impression
> that it is an incomplete and hastily fashioned text. This is suggested
> to them by the fact that the discussion appears to have been well
> underway when the reader is introduced to it, and also because the

two parties to the debate digress regularly from their main thread of argument.[61]

Thus the *View*, the work of a poet historical, appropriately enough, falls between two stools.

III AUTHORSHIP

Brink's third and final section asks: 'Did Spenser write the *View*?' Here, Brink takes the rather unusual step of asking why Spenser didn't write about Ireland. This passage contains a rare allusion to Book V, which Brink prefers to leave out of the discussion because of its inconvenient treatment of Ireland, and because Irena does tend inevitably to lead to Irenius. Brink states that:

> The massive collection of state papers relating to Ireland attests to the fact that nearly every state servant at some point or another advised the government on the Irish question. Spenser, however, wrote no letters of advice that have survived. Geoffrey Fenton, Lodowick Bryskett, Barnabe Googe, Sir John Davies, Sir Philip Sidney, Sir John Harington, and Barnaby Barnes – all literary men – wrote letters or tracts on Ireland. Many of Spenser's letters written in the capacity of secretary to Lord Grey have survived, but we have no letters stating his personal views. Prior to 1633, nothing, other than Book V of *The Faerie Queene*, suggests that Spenser aspired to be regarded as an expert on the Irish question. (p. 217)

Nothing, that is, other than the fact that he spent almost his entire creative life in Ireland, that he had served in a variety of posts, as secretary to the Lord Deputy, as a Master of Musters for Munster, as Deputy Clerk of the Faculties, as an undertaker in the Munster plantation. Nothing, other than the fact that in October 1598, six months after the *View* was entered in the Stationers' Register, Spenser was recommended by the Privy Council for the post of Sheriff of Cork as a man skilled and knowledgeable in Irish affairs. That subordinate clause – 'other than Book V of *The Faerie Queene*' – speaks volumes. Nothing, in other words, other than one-sixth of an epic poem. I am not so sure that Book V is 'all about Ireland', but its treatment of the 'Irish question' in relation to the *View* cannot be so lightly dismissed. Nor does Brink's claim that 'we have no letters stating his personal views' fit in with Roland Smith's analysis of Spenser's Irish correspondence. The role of secretary was not necessarily as uncreative as Brink implies. In fact, Brink's argument, that Spenser did not present himself as an expert on Irish affairs unlike his contemporaries rings false, and could be advanced contrariwise as an argument in favour of his authorship of the *View*. In other words, Spenser ought to have written the *View*. Nothing should surprise us less than that one of the most articulate members of the New English community should commit his opinions to paper, if not to print.

In fact, Brink's claim that 'we have no letters stating his personal views' does not quite ring true. Once we disregard the possibility that Spenser had some creative input into the state correspondence he was employed to carry and compose, and assume that he was merely a slavish scribe in relation to the letters dictated to him by Grey and the Norris brothers, then yes, we have no letters stating his 'personal' views on Ireland – if we discount here the poetry – but we do have the 'Letter to Raleigh' annexed to *The Faerie Queene*. This letter speaks of the difference between the poet historical and the historiographer, and insists that the former does not discourse orderly of affairs as they were done, but 'thrusteth into the middest'. On the evidence of this text, one whose authorship is undisputed, Spenser advocated a disorderly order, and thus the fact that the View starts *in media res* is inadmissible as evidence against his authorship, and may in fact suggest the converse.

Brink cites a marginal attribution in a manuscript copy of the *View* referring to 'Edward [crossed out] Edmund Spenser' Clarke of the Counsell of the Province of Mounster in Ireland in ano 1596', which she suspects post-dates Ware's edition (p. 218). Brink states that: 'A knowledgeable contemporary would have been unlikely to have identified Spenser as the Clerk of the Council of Munster because Lodowick Bryskett held the patent for that office until several years after Spenser's death. Grosart seems to have been the first of Spenser's biographers to mention that he may have served in this capacity, but this possibility was not widely discussed until the twentieth century' (pp. 218–19). But if we look at the State Papers for Ireland in February 1599, within two months of Spenser's death, we find that a Nicholas Curtis is complaining to Cecil, through Sir Thomas Norris, of his maltreatment at the hands of Lodowick Bryskett. Curtis had long served 'in that poor and troublesome place of Clerk of the Council in Munster', and held this office 'upon the trust of Lodowick Bryskett and Edmund Spenser (men not unknown to your Honour)'. Curtis puts his case thus:

> Now, by this rebellion I have had all burned, and taken from me. The said Lodowick Bryskett, to press me down to the lowest degree of misery (Edmund Spenser being lately deceased, the mean and witness of our mutual trust and confidence), goeth about to take away the said place also; which if he be suffered to do by reason of my weakness and hard fortune, I having framed myself wholly, and those poor parts God hath given more, unto that service, I shall remain the most distressed man that liveth.[62]

Thus a 'knowledgeable contemporary' would have been likely to know that Spenser served as Clerk of the Council of Munster, or at least Curtis, Norris and Cecil knew that Bryskett and Spenser had farmed that office out to Curtis.

Brink is right to draw attention to the way in which establishing the corpus of a canonical author 'most frequently requires the rejection of spurious attributions' (p. 219). She questions the incorporation of *A Briefe Note of Ireland*, first attributed to Spenser by Grosart a century ago. Brink promises in a future article to prove that not even the third of the three pieces that make up *A Briefe Note*, the one that Brady insists is solely by Spenser, belongs in his corpus. She notes too that *Britains Ida*, printed in the 1679 folio of Spenser's works together with the *View*, was dislodged from his corpus in 1923 as the work of Phineas Fletcher. Brink further attests that *Axiochus* did not appear as a Spenser text until the publication of the *Variorum* edition of his works in 1949. Brink incisively points out that *Axiochus* and *A Briefe Note* were thus ironically attributed to Spenser on the grounds that they conformed in style to the *View*, itself a dubious attribution in her judgement.

Brink elaborates the relationship between Spenser and Arland Ussher, who succeeded Spenser in the office of Registrar or Clerk in the Chancery of the Faculties in Dublin. Arland was father of James Ussher, bishop of Armagh, an antiquarian like Ware. Bishop Ussher's mother was Margaret Stanyhurst, sister of Richard. Ware claimed to have edited the *View* from a copy in Bishop Ussher's library. Brink is right to call for further study in order to clarify the question of Ware's copy-text, but her reasons for doing so seem to me to be almost wholly negative: 'if the manuscript copy text for Ware's printed edition can be identified and it can be proved that Ware did in fact

radically tamper with the text of the *View*, then the reliability of his
attribution to Spenser cannot be taken for granted' (p. 221). In other
words, if Ware, an associate of Ussher, 'tampered with' – that is,
'edited' – the *View*, then his attribution is suspect. I cannot accept this
as a logical argument. Brink is absolutely justified in her reproach of
Gottfried for speaking lightly about Ware's 'doctored' text without
proving beyond doubt that this was the case (pp. 220–1). But
throughout her essay one has the feeling that Brink does not want the
View to be by Spenser and that this colours her argument. One
illustration of this tendency is her astute observation that Humphrey
Lownes, brother of Matthew, failed to include the *View* in his three
folio editions of Spenser's works between 1611 and 1617. Brink offers
two possible explanations for this omission: '(1) By 1611 Lownes had
lost or disposed of his manuscript of the *View* and could not obtain
another copy; (2) Lownes did not think that Spenser was the author
of the *View*' (p. 222). A third reason, that the *View* had been censored
and Lownes was reluctant to include a controversial document in
prose in a canon that was exclusively poetic, is not offered by Brink.
This makes her conclusion harder to swallow: 'From a purely bibliographical perspective, Lownes's exclusion of the *View* from his 1611,
1613, and 1617 folio editions of Spenser's complete works would
seem to offset Ware's attribution of this work to him in 1633' (p. 222).
Since we know of many examples of texts being added over time to
an author's corpus, the existence of early editions of 'complete' works
that exclude the *View*, especially in the wake of the cautionary note
that greeted its attempted publication, cannot be taken as evidence
of the spuriousness of Ware's attribution.

Rudolf Gottfried, in an article on the debt of Fynes Moryson's
Itinerary (1617) to the *View*, argues that Moryson's allusion to Spenser
as 'Master Spencer' in a list of names that are given in full suggests
that 'Moryson was able to identify the author of the *View*.'[63] Gottfried
reasons, and his logic is by no means flawless, that since Moryson
knew the poet Spenser dwelt in Cork, he would have assumed him
to be the author of a text attributed to 'Edmund Spenser'. This does
not prove the attribution, but the familiar reference to Spenser by an
author who clearly valued a *View* is intriguing.

Gottfried retained an open mind on the question of the interval
between the *View*'s registration and its publication:

The history of the *View* between its composition in 1596 and its first
publication in 1633 has never been wholly explained. Permission

to publish the dialogue was apparently refused in 1598, perhaps from fear of offending certain Anglo-Irish nobles, perhaps to clip the wings of certain flattering allusions there made to the Earl of Essex; and yet the existence of more than a dozen manuscripts of the *View* seems to show that while still unprinted it was occasionally read.[64]

Yet we still know too little about this interval between submission and publication. Jean Brink has performed a vital service in drawing our attention to this gap in Spenser scholarship.

Paradoxically, although she is advancing a case based on textual scholarship, Brink is sharpest when her argument touches on matters of politics and context. Thus she questions Ware's motives, not simply in publishing the *View*, but in attributing it to such an established figure in the Elizabethan colonial community as Spenser:

> Tempting though it may be to scapegoat the author of *The Faerie Queene* for England's colonial policies, politics is not a Post-colonial invention. Did James Ware know that the *View* was written by Spenser or did he attribute the work of an unidentified E. S. to the distinguished author of *The Faerie Queene*? What motivated Ware to publish the *View* in 1633 shortly after Wentworth took office: eagerness to illustrate the success of James's policies 'in these our halcyon days' (Dedication to Wentworth, 2R), antiquarian zeal to preserve records of Irish history (Ware's Preface to the *View*, 3V), interest in publishing a work written by a famous author (conjecture?) Is it possible that Ware's attribution of the *View* to Edmund Spenser was politically motivated? Could Spenser's name have been appropriated to promote the political agenda of Anglo-Irish Protestants in the 1630s? (p. 222)

Brink's telling questions invite others. Is Ware, like Spenser, either disingenuous in terms of his alleged loyalty, or is he incompetent? Was Ware the first to scapegoat Spenser by using him as a take-the-blame for the *View*? Did the gullible antiquarian know that he was dealing with dynamite, and that a text dedicated to Strafford would contribute to his downfall?

It is because I agree with Brink's underlying argument that Spenser has been scapegoated, and because I desire to salvage something from the wreckage of Kilcolman, that I have spent so long reviewing her immensely important article. I do not wish to rule out the *View* in order to save Spenser's neck, either from the halter or the sword. Brink's conjecture that Ware may have wanted the *View* to be by Spenser because of his renown is telling. There is no doubt in my mind that Irish historians – such as Bradshaw, Brady and Canny, to give three prominent examples – have revelled in the fact that they can confront an English colonist who also happens to be a key figure in the English literary canon. Having staked out their territory in fine detail, they will not appreciate having Spenser's authorship of one of the most controversial documents on early modern Ireland thrown into doubt. There is nothing unusual about the fact that canonical authorship lends weight and gravitas to a text. Stephen Booth observed that 'we care about *Holinshed's Chronicles* because Shakespeare read them', and, while this is debatable, one could equally assert that we care about the *View* because Spenser wrote it.[65] Spenser is a big scalp. He will not be readily relinquished.[66]

Brink sums up the evidence against the attribution to Spenser thus:

> Since the manuscript copy text for Ware's edition has not yet been identified, his attribution is not confirmed by an independent witness ... There is no substantive evidence that the *View* is a finished work ... Comparison of the *View* with similar, more finished, political commentaries underscores its failure to offer a conventional praise of the reigning monarch. No dedication or preface for the *View*, written prior to Spenser's death in 1599, has ever been identified. Based on the cumulative weight of this evidence, we must conclude that the text of the *View* is unfinished and thus problematical, if not unsuitable, for close literary or historical analysis. (p. 223)

Again, there are *non sequiturs* here. Does it follow, if no holograph survives, that contradictions, gaps and repetitions, and no dedication, constitutes unfinishedness, or that unfinishedness precludes 'close literary or historical analysis'? Brink is emphatic:

> The conjectured suppression of the *View* by the Elizabethan government conveniently explains why the *View* was never published during Spenser's lifetime, but this suppression is a fiction for which there is no documentary evidence. Censorship occurred after publication in cases that can be documented. Of course, Spenser, if he wrote the *View* (and if he was in England in 1598),

may have intervened to prevent the publication of an unfinished text, but this, too, is pure speculation. (p. 223)

Brink is correct in her assertion that while 'Scholarship abhors a vacuum' we should fill it with facts rather than speculation, but wrong, I think, to make the links she makes. There is no 'documentary evidence' only if we set aside the cautionary note in the Stationers' Register. We know that censorship occurred after publication, as in the case of James VI's response to Book V of *The Faerie Queene*, and in the case of the outrage provoked by Ware's edition of the *View*, but does this rule out official censorship? And Brink, in casting doubt on Spenser's presence in England in 1598 is surely being disingenuous, since we know for a fact that he left Cork on 9 December of that year carrying letters to London from Thomas Norris: 'This despatched by the hand of Edmund Spenser, the poet.' He was again mentioned in despatches by Norris on 21 December: 'Since my last of the 9th of this month, and sent by Mr. Spenser.' Finally, we know that he was paid £8 at Whitehall on 30 December 1598.[67]

The controversy aroused by Ware's edition is arguably evidence in itself of the explosive nature of the text. Whoever wrote the *View* meant business. As John Gilbert wrote in his *History of the Irish Confederation*:

> Serious apprehensions were excited amongst the Irish, in 1633, at the publication, for the first time, of Spenser's tractate on Ireland, under the editorial care of a high official of the Government of Dublin, with the patronage of the newly appointed Deputy, Viscount Wentworth, and accompanied by a suggestion that the remedies proposed in the work for 'reformation of the natives' were, 'for the most part, excellent'.[68]

Richard Bellings, writing two years after Ware's edition appeared in print, spoke of the *View* in terms that again suggest that it was a time bomb waiting to go off:

> In a book intituled 'A View of the state of Ireland' written dialogue-wise between Eudoxus and Irenaeus by an ill-wisher of Ireland, Edmund Spenser, Esquire, in anno salutis 1596, and ever sithence kept dormant, as a destructive platform laid for the utter subversion of this kingdom, and their aims thereby almost finished, it was printed and published at Dublin, anno 1633.[69]

There is also evidence to suggest that Spenser's family accepted the attribution. In a petition to Cromwell William Spenser pleaded for assistance on the grounds that his grandfather had written a text against the Irish that was the reason for the unpopularity of his descendants.[70] In the petition itself, William is referred to as one 'whose grandfather, Edmund Spenser, by his book, entituled, *A View of Ireland*, modled the settlement of that kingdom, and these lands were given him by Queen Elizabeth, of blessed memory, for his services to the crown'.[71] If William Spenser considered his grandfather to be the author of a *View* then that would appear to be fairly important. Yet Brink chooses to regard all posthumous and post-publication attributions with suspicion.

There is a great deal of confusion still surrounding the various editions of the *View*, let alone the various manuscript versions. A recent account states:

> The delay in publication is explained by the outspoken nature of the text and this is probably why Ware saw the need to truncate the original. Yet although it was not published until 1633, several manuscript copies were in circulation before that date and they appear to have come into the hands of many who had responsibility for governing Ireland. Thereafter the Ware text held sway until 1934 and the publication by Oxford University Press of a modernized edition prepared by W. L. Renwick; this was followed by the variorum text in 1949.[72]

Once again, what original? Moreover, Renwick's modernized text did not appear of course until 1970. His edition of 1934 is in the old-style spelling.

Ray Heffner notes: 'Although the Gough manuscript is incomplete and breaks off abruptly, it was obviously prepared for publication.'[73] Heffner compares the title page of the Gough manuscript with its praise of the 'Authors opinion out of long employment and experience there how that Realme may be reduced to Obedience and Civility' with the letter of 30 September 1598 proposing Spenser as Sheriff of Cork, recommending him as 'a man endowed with good knowledge in learning and not unskilful as wthout experience in the service of the warrs'.[74]

It is possible to refute the idea that the *View* was censored without questioning Spenser's authorship. Over fifty years ago Roland Smith did just that, while reviewing Renwick's 1934 edition. Having suggested that Spenser may never have considered his *View of the Present State of Ireland* ready for publication during his lifetime, Smith goes on to say: 'Renwick (p. 250) assumes, in connection with the entry of the *View* for publication in 1598, that the authorities "apparently forbade its printing". But there is no evidence that publication was forbidden.' Thus far this is in keeping with Brink's rigorous demand for proof of the text's suppression. However, Smith continues:

> It is not at all impossible that Spenser was more interested in publishing *The Faerie Queene* and his other poems ... than in going through the red tape of getting 'further aucthoritee' for printing the *View*. Spenser, upon re-perusal of the manuscript, may have felt that it was not yet ready for publication, which he decided either to postpone or drop.[75]

Of course, Spenser may not have been the sole author of the *View*, and it may have passed through other hands, including those of Ware. It may be a dialogue in fact as well as form, one of those formal debates like the one in which he took part in Bryskett's house in the 1580s, or that in which his tutor, Gabriel Harvey participated at the house of Sir Thomas Smith. Roland Smith has reminded us of the role of the 'discomposing compositor', and informed us that 'the "tyranny of the typesetter" and "freedom of the press" flourished long before the phrases were born'.[76] Thus to the possibility of editorial interference, and co-authorship or multi-authorship, one could add an inventive and creative compositor.

IV BRINKMANSHIP

Brink's case, made with much wit and good sense, remains, to use a Scottish legal ruling unavailable in England, 'Not Proven'. What is proven is that this bold intervention by a distinguished textual scholar, through the patient elaboration of questions of authorship, censorship and publication, has given a fresh edge to studies of Spenser and Ireland. As an exercise in brinkmanship it is worthy of our admiration. My concern remains that in questioning, with some justification, the suppression and attribution of the *View*, there is a risk of enacting a second sort of censorship. Spenser does not need our protection, only our caution.[77] The *View* is a double-edged sword. It casts a shadow

over Spenser's poetry, but at the same time ensures that he continues
to be read.

No discussion of the censorship of the *View* would be complete
without some reference to the *Briefe Note* of 1598. Ciarán Brady has
set out the evidence in his entry in *The Spenser Encyclopedia*.

> A set of three state papers (PRO, SP 63/202/4/59) known
> collectively after the title of the first. The group remains among the
> most doubtful of writings attributed to Spenser. Though known to
> scholars for some time, *Brief Note* became officially considered part
> of Spenser's works only with its publication in Grosart's complete
> edition (1882–84). Since then its status has been vigorously
> challenged by some scholars, trenchantly defended by others, and
> tacitly ignored by a majority unsure of its value and unwilling to
> enter into controversy on its behalf.[78]

Brady's remarks concerning this text anticipate Brink's iconoclastic
treatment of the *View*:

> The difficulties presented by *Brief Note* are twofold. First, the
> collection is quite heterogeneous, each of the items being wholly
> distinct from its fellows in tone, style, content, and objective. Second,
> no original or contemporary copy has survived.[79]

Brady notes that Viola Hulbert has convincingly argued that the first
two items are not by Spenser, but insists that the third item is by the
author of the *View*:

> There can, however, be little doubt concerning Spenser's authorship
> of the third and final item in the collection: 'Certaine pointes to be
> considered of in the recovery of the Realme of Ireland'. This is not
> only the only piece in *Brief Note* that has been doubly attributed to
> him: it is also the one that is closest in emphasis and argument to
> *Vewe*. Tersely written in a schematic deductive form, it essays in
> about 800 words to prove that attempts to recover Ireland either
> by peaceful reform or by piecemeal conquest will inevitably fail,
> and to argue that 'great force must be the instrument [and] famine
> ... the meane' of subjugation.[80]

Heffner had complained of Renwick's exclusion of the *Briefe Note* from
his 1934 edition. Renwick had done so on the grounds that it was

endorsed 'by Spenser' in a later hand. Renwick draws attention to a copy of the first part of the documents that make up this text in the British Museum (Harl. Ms. 3787, 21, 184) headed 'Spenser's discourse briefly of Ireland', subtitled 'certain p[re]mises to be considered in the recovery of Ireland'. There is a verse that is appended to this part of this copy that reads:

> Mark Irish when this doth fall
> Tirone and Tire all
> A peere out of Ingland shall come
> The Irish shall tire all and some
> St Patrick and St George a horseboy shalbe sene
> And this shall happen in ninetye nyne.

The pun on Tyrone alone does not make this by Spenser, as such puns were common enough – the dialogue of Sylvanus and Peregrine, for example, speaks of Tyrone being 'Therowne over the barre for forgery' – but as Heffner says:

> These verses obviously refer to Essex and give the date of the document, then, as early in 1599 or late in 1598. Mr Renwick may arbitrarily dismiss one ascription of the 'Brief Note' to Spenser, but he cannot so easily dismiss two.[81]

Now critics must contend with a question mark hovering over the authorship of the *View*.

Having long held that Book V of *The Faerie Queene* was bad poetry, and that *A Briefe Note of Irelande*, if it was by Spenser at all, was only partially his, it was inevitable that scholars should proceed to cast a shadow on his authorship of the *View*. Having exhausted the ambiguities of this prose dialogue, the convenient fact that there is no authoritative manuscript, and that it was published posthumously, offers an escape hatch, just as the foxholes around Kilcolman may have furnished Spenser with his way out in the wake of the overthrow of the Munster plantation. Spenser called Kilcolman 'Hap Hazard', and it proved appropriate.[82]

There are times when one must reconcile oneself to loss, even to originary loss, to a loss of originals. The story persists that Spenser lost manuscripts in the flight from Kilcolman in October 1598, or in the passage from Cork to London two months later.[83] We have no evidence that such manuscripts were lost, but as a writer we can safely assume that Spenser did lose documentation, and that those who overthrew his estate did not think to give him time to gather his papers together. Like most bodies of work, Spenser's is a *corpus interruptus*. Spensership is 'unperfite'. We must salvage what we can, but we can never successfully summon, through 'textual scholarship', or any other conjuration, an imaginary whole from the shipwreck of history.

Notes

INTRODUCTION

1. See Michel Foucault, *The History of Sexuality, Volume One: An Introduction*, trans. Robert Hurley (London: Allen Lane, 1979), Chapter One: 'We "Other" Victorians'. For a flawed critique of Foucault's perspective in this text, specifically his 'history of bodies' in relation to questions of gender and class, see my 'Undermining Archaeology: From Reconstruction to Deconstruction', in Ian Bapty and Tim Yates (eds), *Archaeology After Structuralism: Post-Structuralism and the Practice of Archaeology* (Routledge: London, 1990), pp. 62–77.
2. Declan Kiberd, *Inventing Ireland: The Literature of the Modern Nation* (London: Jonathan Cape, 1995), p. 656, n. 7.
3. Cited in J. H Andrews, 'Appendix: The beginnings of the surveying profession in Ireland – Abstract', in Sarah Tyacke (ed.), *English Map-Making, 1500–1650* (London: British Library, 1983), p. 20.
4. See Seamus Deane, 'Introduction', *Nationalism, Colonialism, and Literature: Terry Eagleton, Fredric Jameson, Edward Said* (Minneapolis: University of Minnesota Press, 1990; 1992), p. 8.
5. Colin MacCabe, 'Broken English', *Critical Inquiry* 28, 1&2 (1986), pp. 3–14; p. 11.
6. Thomas Healy, 'Civilisation and its discontents: the case of Edmund Spenser', in *New Latitudes: Theory and English Renaissance Literature* (London: Edward Arnold, 1992), p. 92.
7. Andrew Hadfield, 'Review essay', *Textual Practice* 8, 1 (1994), p. 158.
8. Edward W. Said, *Culture and Imperialism* (London: Vintage, 1993), p. 5.
9. Said, *Culture and Imperialism*, p. 266.
10. Said, *Culture and Imperialism*, p. 268.
11. See Christopher Hill, 'Seventeenth-Century English Radicals and Ireland', in Patrick Corish (ed.), *Radicals, Rebels and Establishments, Historical Studies* 15 (Belfast: Appletree Press, 1985), pp. 33–49.
12. See Ray Heffner, 'Spenser's acquisition of Kilcolman', *Modern Language Notes* 46, 8 (1931), p. 496.
13. Heffner, 'Spenser's acquisition of Kilcolman', p. 498.
14. Said, *Culture and Imperialism*, pp. 284–5.
15. M. M. Gray, 'The influence of Spenser's Irish experiences on *The Faerie Queene*', *RES* 6, 24 (1930), p. 421.
16. Gray, 'The influence of Spenser's Irish experiences on *The Faerie Queene*', p. 421, n. 1.
17. David J. Baker, '"Some Quirk, Some Subtle Evasion": Legal Subversion in Spenser's *A View of the Present State of Ireland*', *Spenser Studies* 6 (1986), p. 155.
18. See Steven G. Ellis, *Tudor Ireland: Crown, Community and the Conflict of Cultures, 1470–1603* (London: Longman, 1985).

19. Andrew Hadfield, 'Review essay', *Textual Practice* 8, 1 (1994), pp. 158–9.
20. *Spenser Newsletter* 24, 1 (1993), p. 27.
21. Brink's sterling scholarship has uncovered a crucial deposit of Chancery Bills (Salved) in the National Archives of Ireland, located in Dublin. See Jean Brink, 'Documenting Edmund Spenser: A New Life Record', *ANQ* 7 (1994), pp. 201–8.
22. Patricia Coughlan, '"Cheap and common animals": the English anatomy of Ireland in the seventeenth century', in Thomas Healy and Jonathan Sawday (eds), *Literature and the English Civil War* (Cambridge: Cambridge University Press, 1990), p. 207.
23. Coughlan, '"Cheap and common animals"', p. 207.
24. Healy, 'Civilisation and its discontents', p. 103.
25. Kenneth Borris, 'Salvage Man', in A. C. Hamilton (gen. ed.), *The Spenser Encyclopedia* (London and Toronto: Routledge, 1990), p. 624.
26. Andrew Hadfield, 'The "sacred hunger of ambitious minds": Spenser's savage religion', in Donna B. Hamilton and Richard Strier (eds), *Religion, Literature, and Politics in Post-Reformation England, 1540–1688* (Cambridge: Cambridge University Press, 1995), p. 30.
27. See for example Henry F. Hore, 'Woods and fastnesses in ancient Ireland', *Ulster Journal of Archaeology* 6 (1858), pp. 145–61: 'The author of *The Faerie Queene* loved the woods with a poet's love for the beautiful, the wild, and free.'
28. Roland M. Smith, 'Spenser's tale of the two sons of Milesio', *Modern Language Quarterly* 3, 4 (1942), pp. 547–57.
29. Pauline Henley, *Spenser in Ireland* (Cork: Cork University Press, 1928). There is also of course the important collection of essays edited by Patricia Coughlan. See *Spenser and Ireland: An Interdisciplinary Perspective* (Cork: Cork University Press, 1989).
30. *TLS* (1928), p. 423.
31. Richard Rambuss, *Spenser's Secret Career* (Cambridge: Cambridge University Press, 1993), p. 3.
32. See Patricia Coughlan, '"Some secret scourge which shall by her come unto England": Ireland and Incivility in Spenser', in Coughlan (ed.), *Spenser and Ireland*, pp. 46–74.

CHAPTER 1: *THE SHEPHEARDES CALENDAR* AS COLONIAL TEXT

1. See L. T. Cooper, 'Spenser's *Veue of the Present State of Ireland*: An Introduction with Notes on the first 55 pages in Grosart's Edition' (Cornell University, unpublished MA thesis, 1913), p. 5; Raymond Jenkins, 'Spenser and the Clerkship in Munster', *PMLA* 47 (1932), pp. 109–10; William Cliff Martin, 'Edmund Spenser, *A View of the Present State of Ireland*; An Annotated Edition' (Cornell University, unpublished PhD thesis, 1925), pp. 18–24; Roland M. Smith, 'Spenser's Scholarly Script and "Right Writing"', in D. C. Allen (ed.), *Studies in Honor of T. W. Baldwin* (Urbana, Illinois: University of Illinois Press, 1958), pp. 102–3;

J. C. Smith and E. de Selincourt, *Spenser: Poetical Works* (Oxford: Oxford University Press, 1912; 1985), p. xii.

2. A. C. Judson, (1945), *The Works of Edmund Spenser: A Variorum Edition*, 11 vols (Baltimore: Johns Hopkins University Press, 1932–49), 11, *The Life of Edmund Spenser*, p. 46; Andrew J. Magill, 'Spenser and Ireland: a synthesis and revaluation of twentieth century scholarship' (University of Texas at Austin, unpublished PhD thesis, 1967), p. 547.

3. Raymond Jenkins, 'Spenser at Smerwick', *TLS* 32 (11 May, 1933), p. 331.

4. Paul E. McLane, 'Was Spenser in Ireland in Early November 1579?', *Notes and Queries* 204 (1959), pp. 99–101; W. H. Welply, 'Spenser in Ireland', *Times Literary Supplement* 32 (18 May, 1933), p. 348.

5. T. C. Curtis and R. B. McDowell (eds), *Irish Historical Documents, 1172–1922*, 2nd edn (London: Methuen, 1977), p. 104.

6. Richard Helgerson, 'The new poet presents himself: Spenser and the idea of a literary career', *PMLA* 93, 5 (1978), pp. 893–911; Ruth Samson Luborsky, 'The allusive presentation of *The Shepheardes Calender*', *Spenser Studies* 1 (1980), pp. 29–67; 'The illustrations to *The Shepheardes Calender*', *Spenser Studies* 2 (1981), pp. 3–53; Michael McCanles, '*The Shepheardes Calender* as document and monument', *SEL* 22, 1 (1982), p. 5; Richard Mallette, 'Spenser's portrait of the artist in *The Shepheardes Calender* and *Colin Clouts Come Home Againe*', *SEL* 19, 1 (1979), pp. 19–41; David Lee Miller, 'Spenser's vocation, Spenser's career', *ELH* 50, 2 (1983), p. 198; Roscoe E. Parker, 'Spenser's language and the pastoral tradition', *Language* 1, 3 (1925), p. 87; Marie Røstvig, '*The Shepheardes Calender*: a structural analysis', *Renaissance and Modern Studies* 13 (1969), p. 49; Bruce R. Smith, 'On reading *The Shepheardes Calender*', *Spenser Studies* 1 (1980), p. 69.

7. Paul Alpers, 'Pastoral and the domain of lyric in Spenser's *Shepheardes Calender*', *Representations* 12 (1985), p. 95.

8. Spenser, *View*, pp. 28–9.

9. Harry Berger, 'The aging boy: paradise and parricide in Spenser's *Shepheardes Calender*', in Maynard Mack and George de Forest Lord (eds), *Poetic Traditions of the English Renaissance* (New Haven: Yale University Press, 1982), pp. 25–46; Louis Adrian Montrose, 'Interpreting Spenser's February Eclogue: some contexts and implications', *Spenser Studies* 2 (1981), pp. 67–74; Steven R. Marx, *Youth Against Age: Generational Strife in Renaissance Poetry, with special reference to Edmund Spenser's* 'The Shepheardes Calender', *American University Studies*, ser. 4, *English Language and Literature* 21 (New York, Berne and Frankfurt am Main: Peter Lang, 1985).

10. A. Esler, *The Aspiring Mind of the Elizabethan Younger Generation* (Durham, North Carolina: University of North Carolina Press, 1966); Joan Thirsk, 'Younger sons in the seventeenth century', *History* 54, 182 (1969), pp. 358–77.

11. Keith V. Thomas, 'Age and authority in early modern England', *Proceedings of the British Academy* 62 (1976), p. 205.

12. D. C. Allen, 'The degeneration of Man and Renaissance pessimism', *Studies in Philology* 35, 2 (1938), pp. 202–27.

13. Simon Adams, 'Eliza enthroned?: the court and its politics', in Christopher Haigh (ed.), *The Reign of Elizabeth* (London: Macmillan, 1984), pp. 55–77; Ronald B. Bond, 'Supplantation in the Elizabethan court: the theme of Spenser's February Eclogue', *Spenser Studies* 2 (1981), pp. 55–65; Muriel Bradbrook, 'No room at the top: Spenser's pursuit of fame', in *The Artist and Society in Shakespeare's England: The Collected Papers of Muriel Bradbrook*, I (Brighton: Harvester Press, 1982), pp. 19–36; Wallace McCaffrey, 'Place and patronage in Elizabethan politics', in S. T. Bindoff, J. Hurstfield and C. H. Williams (eds), *Elizabethan Government and Society: essays presented to Sir John Neale* (London: Athlone Press, 1961), pp. 95–126.

14. Louis Adrian Montrose, '"The Perfecte Paterne of a Poete" the poetics of courtship in *The Shepheardes Calender*', *TSLL* 21, 1 (1979), p. 37.

15. J. H. P. Pafford (ed.), *Lodowick Bryskett: Literary Works* (Farnborough: Gregg International, 1972), p. 160.

16. Bradbrook, 'No room at the top'; Esler, *The Aspiring Mind of the Elizabethan Younger Generation*; *SC*, gloss to February Eclogue.

17. Raphael Holinshed (ed.), *Chronicles of England, Scotland and Ireland*, 6 vols, VI, Ireland, (London: J. Johnson, 1807–1808), p. 69.

18. G. Hill, *The MacDonnells of Antrim* (Belfast, 1873; 1976), p. 406.

19. Brendan Bradshaw, 'A treatise for the reformation of Ireland, 1554–5', *Irish Jurist*, n.s., 16, 2 (1981), p. 310.

20. See for example Dennis J. Kennedy, 'The Presidency of Munster under Elizabeth and James I' (MA thesis, University College, Cork, 1973), p. 30. Richard Rambuss has argued forcefully for a serious consideration of Spenser's 'secret career' against those who wish to see his various administrative roles as necessities or poor substitutes for the 'real task' of poetry. See Richard Rambuss, *Spenser's Secret Career* (Cambridge: Cambridge University Press, 1993).

21. Cooper, 'Spenser's *Veue of the Present State of Ireland*', p. 13; C. L. Falkiner, 'Spenser in Ireland', in *Essays Relating to Ireland: Biographical, Historical, and Topographical* (London: Longman, 1909), p. 16.

22. W. Pinkerton, 'Barnaby Googe', *N&Q* 3rd ser., 3 (1883), p. 141.

23. M. D. O'Sullivan, 'Barnabe Googe: Provost-Marshal of Connaught, 1582–1585', *JGAHS* 18, 1&2 (1938), p. 6.

24. P. E. Parnell, 'Barnabe Googe: a Puritan in Arcadia', *JEGP* 60, 2 (1961), p. 281.

25. Mark Eccles, 'Barnabe Googe in England, Spain, and Ireland', *ELR* 15, 3 (1985), p. 357.

26. Eccles, 'Barnabe Googe in England, Spain, and Ireland', p. 365.

27. E. M. Hinton (ed.) (1940), 'Rych's *Anothomy of Ireland*, with an account of the author', *PMLA* 55 (1940), p. 91.

28. R. C. Hope (ed.), *The Popishe Kingdome* (1570), by Barnaby Googe (London, 1880), p. vii.

29. Eccles, 'Barnabe Googe in England, Spain, and Ireland', p. 364.

30. Barnaby Googe, *Foure Bookes of Husbandrie* (London, 1577), 1, p. 4.

31. See Peter Lindenbaum, *Changing Landscapes: Anti-Pastoral sentiment in the English Renaissance* (Atlanta, Georgia: The University of Georgia Press, 1986), p. 121; Julia Lupton, 'Home-making in Ireland: Virgil's

Eclogue I and Book VI of *The Faerie Queene'*, *Spenser Studies* 8 (1990), pp. 119–45; Raymond Williams, *The Country and the City* (London: The Hogarth Press, 1985), pp. 133–4.

32. Barnaby Googe, *Eglogs, Epytaphes and Sonettes* (London, 1563), p. 142.

33. J. Small (ed.), *The Image of Irelande, with A Discoverie of Woodkarne*, by John Derricke (London, 1581; Edinburgh, 1883), p. 64, p. 72.

34. John Davies, *A Discoverie of the True Causes why Ireland was never entirely Subdued, nor brought under Obedience of the Crowne of England, untill the Beginning of his Majesties happie Raigne* (London, 1612), p. 284.

35. 'Dialogue between Peregryne and Sylvanus, c.1598', *State Papers, Ireland*, 63/203/119, ff. 283–357 (London: Public Record Office), f. 285.

36. On this episode see James Hogan, 'Shane O'Neill comes to the Court of Elizabeth', in S. Pender (ed.), *Feil-scribhinn Torna: Essays and studies presented to Professor Tadhg ua Donnchadha on the occasion of his seventieth birthday* (Cork: Cork University Press, 1947), pp. 154–70.

37. Lisa Jardine, 'Encountering Ireland: Gabriel Harvey, Edmund Spenser, and English colonial ventures', in Brendan Bradshaw, Andrew Hadfield and Willy Maley (eds), *Representing Ireland: Literature and the Origins of Conflict* (Cambridge: Cambridge University Press, 1993), pp. 60–75; Hiram Morgan, 'The colonial venture of Sir Thomas Smith in Ulster, 1571–5', *Historical Journal* 28 (1985), pp. 261–78; D. B. Quinn, 'Sir Thomas Smith (1513–1577) and the beginnings of English colonial theory', *Proceedings of the American Philosophical Society* 89 (1945), pp. 543–60.

38. Two further contemporary texts from the Bynneman press deserve to be noted, as they reinforce the impression of a radical protestant publisher with a particular penchant for colonial pamphlets and travel literature. Bynneman was responsible for G. Best, *A True discourse of the late voyage of Discoverie* (1578), and John Florio, *A Short and Briefe Narration of the two Navigations and Discoveries to the North-west partes called New Fraunce* (1580). There is unfortunately no separate entry for Bynneman in *The Spenser Encyclopedia*, though there is one for William Ponsonby, whose imprint is found on the 1590 and 1596 editions of *The Faerie Queene*, and on several other works by Spenser published in the latter part of his career, and another for Hugh Singleton, the printer of the first edition of the *Calender*.

39. Hill, *The MacDonnells of Antrim*, p. 409.

40. Mary Dewar, *Sir Thomas Smith – A Tudor Intellectual in Office* (London: Athlone Press, 1964), p. 156.

41. Nicholas Canny, *The Elizabethan Conquest of Ireland: a pattern established, 1565–76* (Hassocks, Sussex: The Harvester Press, 1976), pp. 70–6.

42. Quinn, 'Sir Thomas Smith', p. 546.

43. On Harvey, see Anthony Grafton and Lisa Jardine, *From Humanism to the Humanities* (Princeton: Princeton University Press, 1986), pp. 184–96. See also V. F. Stern, *Gabriel Harvey: His Life, Marginalia and Library* (Oxford: Clarendon Press, 1979). On Boyle, see Nicholas Canny, *The Upstart Earl: a study of the social and mental world of Richard Boyle, first earl of Cork, 1566–1643* (Cambridge: Cambridge University Press, 1982); *DNB*; Terence Ranger, 'Richard Boyle and the Making of an Irish Fortune' *IHS* 10 (1957), pp. 257–97.

44. See Jardine, 'Encountering Ireland'. In Harvey's *Foure Letters* (1592), he alludes to 'my Cosen, M. Thomas Smith ... Colonel of the Ards in Ireland', suggesting that he reflected with pride upon his earlier association with that fateful colonial expedition. Cited Stern, *Gabriel Harvey*, pp. 65–6.

45. Cited in Jardine, 'Encountering Ireland', p. 63.

46. See F. J. Furnivall (ed.), *Queen Elizabethes Achademy*, by Humphrey Gilbert (London, 1869), p. 12; see also D. B. Quinn, *The Voyages and Colonizing Enterprises of Sir Humphrey Gilbert*, 2 vols (London: Hakluyt Society, 1940).

47. Hill, *The MacDonnells of Antrim*, p. 409.

48. Furnivall (ed.), *Queen Elizabethes Achademy*, p. 3.

49. F. J. Levy, 'Hayward, Daniel, and the beginnings of politic history in England', *HLQ* 50 (1987), pp. 1–34; N. Orsini, '"Policy", or the language of Elizabethan Machiavellianism', *JWCI* 9 (1946), pp. 122–34.

50. Steven G. Ellis, *Tudor Ireland: Crown, Community and the Conflict of Cultures, 1470–1603* (London: Longman, 1985), p. 69.

51. Canny, *The Elizabethan Conquest of Ireland*.

52. See Ciarán Brady, 'The government of Ireland, c.1540–1583' (PhD thesis, Trinity College, Dublin, 1980), p. 164; *DNB*; Nicholas Canny, *From Reformation to Restoration: Ireland, 1534–1660* (Dublin: Helicon, 1987), p. 72.

53. See A. F. Vossen (ed.), *Two Bokes of the Histories of Ireland*, by Edmund Campion (Assen, Netherlands: Van Gorcum, 1963), p. 151.

54. See *DNB*; R. B. Gottfried (ed.), *A Historie of Ireland (1571) by Edmund Campion* (New York, 1940); Edmund Hogan, 'The blessed Edmund Campion's *History of Ireland* and its critics', *IER* 3rd ser., 12 (1891), pp. 629–41, 725–35; Evelyn Waugh, *Edmund Campion* (Harmondsworth: Penguin, 1954).

55. Vossen (ed.), *Two Bokes of the Histories of Ireland*, p. 2.

56. Kenneth Ferguson, 'The development of a standing army in Ireland', *The Irish Sword* 15, 60 (1983), p. 157.

57. Vossen (ed.), *Two Bokes of the Histories of Ireland*, pp. 147–50.

58. See Willy Maley (ed.), 'The Supplication of the blood of the English, most lamentably murdred in Ireland, Cryeng out of the Yearth for Revenge (1598)', introduced and transcribed, *Analecta Hibernica*, 36 (1994), p. 39.

59. See J. O'Mahoney (ed.), *The History of Ireland*, by Geoffrey Keating (New York, 1886), p. xix. See also Bernadette Cunningham, 'Seventeenth-century interpretations of the past: the case of Geoffrey Keating', *IHS* 25, 98 (1986), pp. 116–28.

60. Following his beatification in the nineteenth century, a sympathetic scholar refuted Keating's charges, referring to them as 'misplaced'. See Hogan, 'The blessed Edmund Campion's *History of Ireland* and its critics', pp. 631–8; Colm Lennon, *Richard Stanyhurst: The Dubliner, 1547–1618* (Dublin: Irish Academic Press, 1981), pp. 88–98.

61. D. B. Quinn, *The Elizabethans and the Irish* (Ithaca: Cornell University Press, 1966), pp. 99–100.

62. Quinn, *The Elizabethans and the Irish*, p. 100.

63. Small (ed.), *The Image of Irelande*, p. 11.
64. E. M. Hinton, *Ireland Through Tudor Eyes* (Philadelphia: University of Pennsylvania Press, 1935), p. 39; Small (ed.), *The Image of Irelande*, p. 14.
65. Hinton, *Ireland Through Tudor Eyes*, pp. 38–41; Quinn, *The Elizabethans and the Irish*, pp. 99–105.
66. Henry F. Hore (ed.), 'Sir Henry Sidney's memoir of his government of Ireland, 1583', *UJA* 5 (1857), p. 314.
67. Philip Sidney, 'Discourse of Irish Affairs', in K. Duncan-Jones and J. Van Dorsten, *Miscellaneous Prose of Sir Philip Sidney* (Oxford: Clarendon Press, 1973), pp. 3–12.
68. C. McNeill (ed.), 'Lord Chancellor Gerrard's "Notes on Ireland" (1577–8)', *Analecta Hibernica* 2 (1931), p. 103.
69. Sidney, 'Discourse of Irish Affairs', p. 11.
70. Sidney, 'Discourse of Irish Affairs', p. 10.
71. Spenser, *View*, p. 67.
72. Sidney, 'Discourse of Irish Affairs', pp. 10, 12; Michael MacCarthy-Morrogh, *The Munster Plantation: English Migration to Southern Ireland, 1583–1641* (Oxford: Clarendon Press, 1986), p. 26.
73. Maureen Quilligan, 'Sidney and his Queen', in Heather Dubrow and Richard Strier (eds), *The Historical Renaissance: New Essays on Tudor and Stuart Literature and Culture* (Chicago and London: Chicago University Press, 1988), p. 189.
74. Arthur F. Kinney, 'Sir Philip Sidney and the uses of history', in Dubrow and Richard Strier (eds), *The Historical Renaissance*, pp. 293–314.
75. Edward Berry, 'The poet as warrior in Sidney's *Defence of Poetry*', *SEL* 29, 1 (1989), p. 32.
76. For example, Barnaby Rich, *Allarme to Englande* (London, 1578).
77. Berry, 'The poet as warrior in Sidney's *Defence of Poetry*', p. 33.
78. See for example Percy W. Long, 'Spenser's Rosalind', *Anglia* 31 (January 1908), pp. 72–104; Theodore H. Banks, 'Spenser's Rosalind: A Conjecture', *PMLA* 52, (1937), pp. 335–7; Richard Mallette, 'Rosalind', in A. C. Hamilton (ed.), *The Spenser Encyclopedia* (London: Routledge, 1990), p. 622. I am aware of the fact that one-to-one correspondences are the graveyard of Spenser criticism. One thinks here of W. L. Renwick's claim that Galathea and Naera in *Colin Clouts Come Home Againe* are Lady Katherine Wallop and the Countess of Ormond respectively. See Renwick, 'Spenser's Galathea and Naera', *TLS* (14 March, 1929), pp. 206–7.
79. See Arthur F. Marotti, '"Love is not love": Elizabethan sonnet sequences and the social order', *ELH* 49 (1982), pp. 396–428.
80. Andrew Hadfield, '"Who knowes not Colin Clout?" The permanent exile of Edmund Spenser', in *Literature, Politics and National Identity: Reformation to Renaissance* (Cambridge: Cambridge University Press, 1994), p. 188.
81. Hadfield, '"Who knowes not Colin Clout?"', p. 189.
82. Smith, 'Spenser's Scholarly Script and "Right Writing"', pp. 102–3.
83. Barbara J. Bono, 'Dido', in A. C. Hamilton (gen. ed.), *The Spenser Encyclopedia* (London and Toronto: Routledge, 1990), p. 218.

84. Paul E. McLane, 'Was Spenser in Ireland in Early November 1579?', *NQ* 204 (1959), 99–101.

85. Jardine, 'Encountering Ireland'.

86. Smith, 'Spenser's Scholarly Script and "Right Writing"', pp. 102–3.

87. Mary Parmenter, 'Spenser's "Twelve Eglogues Proportionable to the Twelve Monethes"', *ELH* 3 (1936), p. 210. Richard Rambuss, in his wonderful book on Spenser and secrecy, writes: 'While the setting of *The Shepheardes Calender* its fields, streams, high and low places – is essentially a lexicon of generic pastoral topoi', *Colin Clouts Come Home Againe* 'is markedly Irish in topography'. See Richard Rambuss, *Spenser's Secret Career*, p. 97. I am arguing here that the categories of *genre* and *topoi* require stretching, and that the *Calender* itself secretes an Irish context.

88. On Kildare see Vincent P. Carey, 'Collaborator *and* Survivor? Gerald the eleventh Earl of Kildare and Tudor Rule in Ireland', *History Ireland* 2, 2 (1994), pp. 13–17. Lord Grey 'celebrated the Christmas of 1580 by imprisoning two of his collaborators, the Earl of Kildare and his son-in-law Lord Devlin, for their slackness in coercing the insurgents of Wicklow'. See Donald Bruce, 'Edmund Spenser and the Irish Wars', *Contemporary Review* 266 (1995), p. 133.

89. Liam Miller and Eileen Power (eds), *Holinshed's Irish Chronicle (1577): The Historie of Ireland from the first inhabitation thereof, unto the yeare 1509. Collected by Raphael Holinshed, & continued till the yeare 1547, by Richard Stanyhurst* (North America: Dolmen Editions, Humanities Press Inc., 1979). I have argued Spenser's familiarity with Stanyhurst in 'Spenser's Irish English: Language and Identity in Early Modern Ireland', *Studies in Philology* 91, 4 (1994), pp. 417–31.

90. Stanyhurst, *Description*, pp. 54–8.

91. See Lennon, *Richard Stanyhurst, The Dubliner*, pp. 86, 120; St. John D. Seymour, *Anglo-Irish Literature, 1200–1582* (Cambridge: Cambridge University Press, 1929), pp. 45–65; Herbert F. Hore and James Graves, *Social State of South-East Ireland, The Annuary of the Royal Historical and Archaeological Society of Ireland for the years 1868 and 1869* (Dublin: printed at the University Press for the Association, 1870), p. 28.

92. Stanyhurst, *Description*, p. 98.

93. Edmund Hogan (ed.), *The Description of Ireland and The State thereof as it is at this present* ([London] Dublin, 1878), p. 60. On Scurlock, see Ellis, *Tudor Ireland*, pp. 273, 282, 285.

94. Hore and Graves, *Social State of South-East Ireland*, p. 269.

95. See Ciarán Brady, 'Faction and the Origins of the Desmond Rebellion', *Irish Historical Studies* 22 (1981), pp. 289–312; Michael MacCarthy-Morrogh, *The Munster Plantation: English Migration to Southern Ireland, 1583–1641* (Oxford: Clarendon Press, 1986), pp. 1–4.

96. Stanyhurst, *Description*, p. 13.

97. Stanyhurst, *Description*, pp. 7–8.

98. Stanyhurst, *Description*, p. 8.

99. Stanyhurst, *Description*, p. 54.

CHAPTER 2: LANGUAGE AND IDENTITY
IN EARLY MODERN IRELAND

* An earlier version of this chapter was published in *Studies in Philology* 91, 4 (1994), pp. 417–31.

1. *DNB*; Colm Lennon, 'Richard Stanyhurst (1547–1618) and Old English Identity', *Irish Historical Studies* 21 (1978), pp. 121–43; *Richard Stanyhurst: The Dubliner, 1547–1618* (Dublin: Irish Academic Press, 1981), pp. 13–34; A. F. Vossen (ed.), *Two Bokes of the Histories of Ireland*, by Edmund Campion (Assen, Netherlands: Van Gorcum, 1963), pp. 41–7.

2. Richard Stanyhurst, 'Description of Ireland', in Raphael Holinshed (ed.), *Chronicles of England, Scotland and Ireland*, 6 vols, VI, Ireland (London: J. Johnson, 1807–8), p. 4.

3. Stanyhurst, 'Description of Ireland', p. 4.

4. Stanyhurst, 'Description of Ireland', p. 4.

5. Stanyhurst, 'Description of Ireland', p. 67.

6. Vossen, *Two Bokes*, 67. See Stanyhurst, 'Description of Ireland', p. 6.

7. *View*, lines 2101–33. All references to the *View* are to the Variorum edition, ix, ed. R. B. Gottfried, 1949.

8. Stanyhurst, 'Description of Ireland', p. 4.

9. Alan Bliss, 'The Development of the English Language', in T. W. Moody, F. X. Martin and F. J. Byrne (eds), *A New History of Ireland*, 3, *Early Modern Ireland, 1534–1691* (Oxford: Clarendon Press, 1976), p. 550.

10. Edmund Spenser, *The Shepheardes Calender*, in *Poetical Works*, J. C. Smith and E. De Selincourt (eds), (Oxford: Clarendon Press, 1912), p. 422.

11. Stanyhurst, 'Description of Ireland', p. 6.

12. Spenser, *Shepheardes Calender*, in Smith and De Selincourt, *Poetical Works*, pp. 416–17.

13. Edmund Spenser and Gabriel Harvey, *Three Proper, and wittie, familiar Letters* (London: Bynneman, 1580), in Smith and De Selincourt, *Poetical Works*, p. 612. Spenser is telling Harvey of his work on English rivers for *Epithalamion*: 'A worke beleeve me, of much labour, wherein notwithstanding Master *Holinshed* hath muche furthered and advantaged me, who therein hath bestowed singular paines, in searching oute their first heades, and sourses: and also in tracing, and dogging out all their Course, til they fall into the Sea.' It is worth noting that there is a critical tradition that has viewed Spenser's archaisms as features of contemporary dialect, but of the north of England rather than the south of Ireland. John Hales, for example, wrote over a century ago: 'It may be suggested that what are called the archaisms of Spenser's style may be *in part* due to the author's long residence in the country with one of the older forms of the language spoken all around him and spoken by him, in fact his vernacular. I say *in part*, because of course his much study of Chaucer must be taken into account. But, as Mr Richard Morris [the editor of the Globe edition] has remarked to me, he could not have drawn from Chaucer those forms and words of a *northern* dialect which appear in the *Calendar*.' See John

W. Hales, 'Edmund Spenser', in R. Morris (ed.), *The Works of Edmund Spenser: The Globe Edition* (London: Macmillan, 1910), p. xviii.

14. Bliss, 'The Development of the English Language', p. 548.
15. Bliss, 'The Development of the English Language', p. 548.
16. Bliss, 'The Development of the English Language', p. 549.
17. T. W. Moody, F. X. Martin and F. J. Byrne (eds), *Early Modern Ireland,* p. 44.
18. Spenser, *The Shepheardes Calender*, in Smith and De Selincourt, *Poetical Works*, p. 417.
19. Stanyhurst, 'Description of Ireland', p. 5; Spenser, *Shepheardes Calender*, p. 417.
20. Philip Sidney, *An Apology for Poetry* (London, 1595), ed. Geoffrey Shepherd (London: J. M. Dent, 1973), p. 133.
21. *View*, lines 1387–98.
22. George O'Brien (ed.), *Advertisements for Ireland: Being a Description of the State of Ireland in the reign of James I* (Dublin: Irish Academic Press, 1923), p. 1.
23. R. M. Smith, 'Spenser's scholarly script and "right writing"', in D. C. Allen (ed.), *Studies in Honor of T. W. Baldwin* (Urbana, Illinois: University of Illinois Press, 1958), p. 89. Smith observes: 'Writers at the turn of our century were prone to believe that words then considered obsolete were, when found in Spenser's poetry, archaisms consciously introduced by the poet' (p. 98). Ironically, this is exactly E. K.'s complaint in the preface to *The Shepheardes Calender*. After I had written this paper, and published a version, I re-read my Spenser archive and came across two notes that must have lodged in my mind during the preparation of my thesis. In the conclusion to the chapter on Ireland in her excellent *A Preface to Spenser*, Helena Shire writes:

> the language he heard about him every day was the English of the Pale, antiquated in usage and affected by Celtic idiom. The way a word sounded and the spread of its possible meanings must often have diverged markedly from English as spoken in courtly circles in London. A poet's ear would not be deaf to this 'Doric' speech. (p. 64)

In his essay on the Desmond Rebellion in *Ireland Through Tudor Eyes* Edward Hinton, recalling Richard Stanyhurst's claim that Wexford preserved a 'Chaucerian English', speculates thus:

> It is pleasant to play with the thought that Spenser may here have been brought into contact with the vital, everyday use of an archaic idiom to which already his academic Chaucer-worship inclined him. (p. 45)

My re-discovery of these passages proves E. K.'s punning dictum that being 'throughly redd, how could it be ... but that walking in the sonne although for other cause he walked, yet needes he mought be sunburnt'. This argument is thus belatedly indebted to these suggestive comments.

24. R. M. Smith, 'Spenser's Scholarly Script,' pp. 102–3. As with Stephen's tundish, a word deemed Irish can turn out to be English. The word 'churl', as it happens, comes from Old English 'ceorl'. Spenser does not distinguish between words like 'glen', which are Gaelic in origin, and those like 'churl', which are Old English, although Stanyhurst would have recognized Chaucer's influence. I am grateful to Katie Wales for this point.

25. G. Hill, *The MacDonnells of Antrim* (Belfast, 1873), p. 410.

26. *View*, lines 729–30, 3201.

27. Stanyhurst, 'Description of Ireland', p. 68.

28. *View*, lines 1937–42. For a speculative note on a possible visit to Ireland prior to Grey's appointment as Lord Deputy in 1580, see Paul E. McLane, 'Was Spenser in Ireland in Early November 1579?' *N&Q* 204 (1959), pp. 99–101.

29. In one of the more far-fetched observations on Spenser's Irish influences, one critic claimed that the land peopled by wolves in the September Eclogue is 'Ireland, whence Sir Henry Sidney had lately returned in bitterness.' See Mary Parmenter, 'Spenser's "Twelve Eglogues Proportionable to the Twelve Monethes"', *ELH* 3 (1936), p. 210.

30. Charles L. Barber, *Early Modern English* (London: Deutsch, 1976), p. 181.

31. Francis Bacon, 'Certain Considerations Touching the Plantations in Ireland (1606)', in *Francis Bacon: Works*, 5 vols (London, 1778), vol. 1, p. 195.

32. James Joyce, *A Portrait of the Artist as a Young Man*, in *The Essential James Joyce*, ed. Harry Levin (St Albans: Granada, 1983), p. 315.

33. Joyce, *Portrait*, p. 364.

34. Richard Mallette, 'Spenser's Portrait of the Artist in *The Shepheardes Calendar* and *Colin Clouts Come Home Againe*', *SEL* 19 (1979), pp. 19–41.

35. Edward Arber (ed.), *Richard Stanyhurst. 'Translation of The first Four Books of the Aneis,'* Leiden, 1582 (London, 1880), p. xxi. This brings to mind Karl Bottigheimer's question: 'if Englishness was to be defined as a virtue in Ireland, who could be more English than the English-born newcomers?' Who but the Old English, who were drinking from the 'well of English undefyled'? (*FQ*.IV.ii.32.8). See Karl Bottigheimer, 'Kingdom and colony: Ireland in the westward enterprise, 1536–1660', in K. R. Andrews, N. P. Canny and P. E. Hair (eds), *The Westward Enterprise: English activities in Ireland, the Atlantic and America, 1480–1650* (Liverpool: Liverpool University Press, 1978), p. 49.

36. Lennon, 'Richard Stanyhurst and Old English Identity'; *Richard Stanyhurst: The Dubliner*. On the relationship between Spenser and Stanyhurst, see R. B. Gottfried, 'Spenser and Stanyhurst', *TLS* 35 (October 31, 1936), p. 887; R. M. Smith, 'Spenser, Holinshed, and the *Leabhar Gabhala*', *JEGP* 42 (1944), pp. 390–401.

37. G. G. Smith, *Elizabethan Critical Essays* (London: Oxford University Press, 1904), II, p. 240.

38. G. G. Smith, *Elizabethan Critical Essays*, II, p. 320.

39. Arber, *Richard Stanyhurst. 'Translation of the first Four Books of the Aneis'*, viii; Barnaby Rich, *The Irish Hubbub or, The English Hue and Crie* (London, 1617), p. 2.

40. Arber, *Richard Stanyhurst. 'Translation of The first Four Books of the Aneis'*, p. 17.
41. Gillian Brennan, 'Patriotism, Language and Power: English Translations of the Bible, 1520–1580', *History Workshop* 27 (1989): pp. 18–36, p. 32.
42. N. F. Blake, *Non-Standard Language in English Literature* (London: Macmillan, 1981), p. 59.
43. H. W. Sugden, *The Grammar of Spenser's Faerie Queene* (New York: Kraus Reprint Corp., 1966), p. 9.
44. Stanyhurst, 'Description of Ireland', p. 5.
45. Stephen J. Greenblatt, 'Preface', *Renaissance Self-Fashioning: From More to Shakespeare* (Chicago: Chicago University Press, 1980), n.p. See also Elizabeth Porges Watson, 'A note on the text', in *Spenser: Selected Writings* (London: Routledge, 1992), p. ix: 'The importance of archaisms, colloquialisms and even of coinages in Spenser's writing makes any modernization of the text impossible.'
46. John Hollander, 'Dallying Nicely with Words', *The Linguistics of Writing: Arguments Between Language and Literature*, Nigel Fabb, Derek Attridge, Alan Durant and Colin MacCabe (eds), (Manchester: Manchester University Press, 1987), p. 125.
47. Jeffrey Knapp, 'Error as a means of Empire in *The Faerie Queene*', *ELH* 54 (1987), p. 820.
48. Vernam Hull, 'Edmund Spenser's *Mona-shul*', *PMLA* 56, 2 (1941), p. 578.
49. Patricia Ingham, 'dialect', in A. C. Hamilton (gen. ed.), *The Spenser Encyclopedia* (London and Toronto: Routledge, 1990), pp. 215, 216.
50. For a fascinating discussion of this phrase see Richard Helgerson, 'Barbarous Tongues: The Ideology of Poetic Form in Renaissance England', in H. Dubrow and R. Strier (eds), *The Historical Renaissance: New Essays on Tudor and Stuart Literature and Culture* (Chicago and London: Chicago University Press, 1988), pp. 273–4.

CHAPTER 3: PLANTING A NEW CULTURE BEYOND THE PALE

1. Nicholas Canny, 'Introduction: Spenser and the Reform of Ireland', in Patricia Coughlan (ed.), *Spenser and Ireland: An Interdisciplinary Perspective* (Cork: Cork University Press, 1989), p. 9.
2. Rudolf Gottfried, 'Irish geography in Spenser's *View*', *ELH* 6, 2 (1939), p. 137.
3. Ciarán Brady, 'The Road to the *View*: On the Decline of Reform Thought in Tudor Ireland', in Patricia Coughlan (ed.), *Spenser and Ireland: An Interdisciplinary Perspective* (Cork: Cork University Press, 1989), p. 37.
4. Roland M. Smith, 'The Irish background of Spenser's *View*', *JEGP* 42, 4 (1943), p. 515.
5. Ciarán Brady, 'Spenser's Irish Crisis: Humanism and Experience in the 1590s', *Past and Present* 111 (1986), p. 43.
6. Michael MacCarthy-Morrogh, *The Munster Plantation: English Migration to Southern Ireland, 1583–1641* (Oxford: Clarendon Press, 1986).

7. Spenser, *View*, pp. 114–15.
8. Michael MacCarthy-Morrogh, 'The Munster Plantation, 1583–1641', PhD thesis, University of London, 1983, App. 2; MacCarthy-Morrogh, *The Munster Plantation*, p. viii. Other theses furnish us with information on the composition of the Irish Privy Council in the crucial period leading up to the plantation, analysis of the crucial decade of the 1590s, and a detailed breakdown of the Munster presidency. See John Gregory Crawford, 'The privy council in Ireland, 1556–1578: expansion and change in the English government of Ireland', PhD thesis, (The University of North Carolina at Chapel Hill, 1975) pp. 407–56; Dennis J. Kennedy, 'The Presidency of Munster under Elizabeth and James I' (MA thesis, University College, Cork, 1973); Anthony J. Sheehan, 'Provincial grievance and national revolt: Munster in the Nine Years War' (MA thesis, University College, Dublin, 1981).
9. Lawrence Stone, *The Past and the Present Revisited* (London and New York: Routledge, 1987), p. 45.
10. A major new biography by Jean Brink, an exemplary scholar, will no doubt fill this gap in Spenser studies. I have made a modest attempt at sketching a 'Spenser circle' in *A Spenser Chronology*, pp. 85–108.
11. MacCarthy-Morrogh, *The Munster Plantation*, p. 284.
12. MacCarthy-Morrogh, *The Munster Plantation*, p. viii.
13. Patrick O'Connor, 'The Munster Plantation era: rebellion, survey and land transfer in North County Kerry', *JKAHS* 15 (1982), p. 18. See also Edward M. Hinton, 'The Munster Plantation, 1586–1599', in *Ireland Through Tudor Eyes* (Philadelphia: University of Pennsylvania Press, 1935), pp. 49–50.
14. Robert Dunlop, 'The plantation of Munster, 1584–1589', *EHR* 3, 10 (1888), p. 250.
15. See Elizabeth Heale, *'The Faerie Queene': A Reader's Guide* (Cambridge: Cambridge University Press, 1987), p. 2.
16. J. Lodge (ed.), *Desiderata Curiosa Hibernica* (Dublin, 1772), pp. 24–8, 33.
17. John Davies, *A Discoverie of the True Causes why Ireland was never entirely Subdued, nor brought under Obedience of the Crowne of England, untill the Beginning of his Majesties happie Raigne* (London, 1612), p. 285; Howard Mumford Jones, 'Origins of the colonial idea in England', *Proceedings of the American Philosophical Society* 85, 5 (1942), p. 455; D. B. Quinn, '"A Discourse of Ireland" (Circa 1599): a sidelight on English colonial policy', *Proceedings of the Royal Irish Academy* 47 (1942), p. 166.
18. See Kenneth Gross, *Spenserian Poetics: Idolatry, Iconoclasm, and Magic* (Ithaca and London: Cornell University Press, 1985), p. 20; Elizabeth Heale, *'The Faerie Queene': A Reader's Guide*, pp. 4, 143.
19. Marx and Engels, *Ireland and the Irish Question* (London: Lawrence and Wishart, 1978), p. 264.
20. Brendan Bradshaw, *The Irish Constitutional Revolution of the Sixteenth Century* (Cambridge: Cambridge University Press, 1979); Ciarán Brady, 'Conservative subversives: the community of the Pale and the Dublin administration', in P. J. Corish (ed.), *Radicals, Rebels and Establishments, Historical Studies* 15 (Belfast: Appletree Press, 1985), pp. 11–32; Nicholas Canny, 'The formation of the Old English elite in Ireland', *18th O'Donnell*

Lecture (Dublin: NUI, 1975); Aidan Clarke, *The Old English in Ireland, 1625–42* (Worcester and London, 1966); F. R. M. Hitchcock, *The Midland Septs and the Pale: An account of the early septs and later settlers of the King's county and of life in the English Pale* (Dublin, 1908); Colm Lennon, 'Richard Stanyhurst (1547–1618) and Old English Identity', *IHS* 21, 82 (1978), pp. 121–43; *Richard Stanyhurst: The Dubliner, 1547–1618* (Dublin: Irish Academic Press, 1981); James Lydon, 'The Middle Nation', in Lydon (ed.), *The English in Medieval Ireland* (Dublin: Irish Academic Press, 1984), pp. 1–26.

21. Spenser, *View*, (Ware edition), p. 106.
22. Spenser, *View*, p. 21.
23. Spenser, *View*, pp. 21–2.
24. Raymond Jenkins, 'Spenser: The Uncertain Years 1584–1589', *PMLA* 53 (1938), p. 359.
25. Spenser, *View*, p. 13.
26. J. W. Draper, 'Spenser's Linguistics in *The Present State of Ireland*', *Modern Philology* 17, 8 (1919), pp. 474–5.
27. William Camden, *Britannia, or a Chorographical Description of Great Britain and Ireland*, ed. E. Gibson (London, 1722), pp. 1327–8.
28. See D. G. White, 'The Tudor plantations in Ireland, pre-1571', (PhD thesis, University of Dublin, 1967), p. 120.
29. Gottfried, 'Irish geography in Spenser's *View*', p. 120.
30. James Buckley, 'Munster in A. D. 1597', *JCHAS* 12 (1906), pp. 53–68.
31. Brendan Bradshaw, 'A Treatise for the Reformation of Ireland, 1554–5', *The Irish Jurist* 16 n.s. (1981), pp. 309–10.
32. D. J. Dickson, 'Property and social structure in eighteenth-century south Munster', in L. M. Cullen and F. Furet (eds), *Ireland and France, 17th–20th Centuries: Towards a comparative study of rural history* (Paris, 1980), p. 129.
33. Brendan Bradshaw, 'Cromwellian reform and the origins of the Kildare rebellion', *TRHS* 5th ser., 27 (1977), pp. 69–93; Ciarán Brady, 'Faction and the origins of the Desmond rebellion', *IHS* 22, 88 (1981), pp. 289–312; Steven G. Ellis, 'The Kildare rebellion and the early Henrican Reformation', *HJ* 19, 4 (1976), pp. 807–30; Margaret MacCurtain, 'The fall of the house of Desmond', *JKAHS* 8 (1975), pp. 28–44; J. J. N. McGurk, 'The fall of the noble house of Desmond, 1579–83', *History Today* 29 (1979), pp. 578–85, 670–5.
34. Steven G. Ellis, *Tudor Ireland: Crown, Community and the Conflict of Cultures, 1470–1603* (London: Longman, 1985).
35. Vincent Gookin, *The great case of transplantation in Ireland discussed* (London, 1655), p. 2.
36. C. McNeill (ed.), 'Report on Fitzwilliam manuscripts at Milton, England', *Analecta Hibernica* 4 (1932), p. 315; D. B. Quinn, 'The Munster Plantation: problems and opportunities', *JCHAS* 71 (1966), p. 24.
37. M. M. Gray, 'The influence of Spenser's Irish experiences on *The Faerie Queene*', *RES* 6, 24 (1930), p. 425.
38. Karl Bottigheimer, *English Money and Irish Land: The 'Adventurers' in the Cromwellian Settlement of Ireland* (Oxford: Clarendon Press, 1971), pp. 9–10; Nicholas Canny, *The Upstart Earl: a study of the social and*

mental world of Richard Boyle, first Earl of Cork, 1566–1643 (Cambridge: Cambridge University Press, 1982); Ellis, *Tudor Ireland*, p. 253; MacCarthy-Morrogh, *The Munster Plantation*, pp. 33–8; M. Mac Lir, 'Spenser as high sheriff of Cork county', *JCHAS* 7, 52 (1901), pp. 249–50; P. J. Piveronus, 'Sir Warham St Leger and the first Munster plantation', *Éire-Ireland* 14, 2 (1979), pp. 15–36.

39. Gray, 'The influence of Spenser's Irish experiences on *The Faerie Queene*', p. 426.

40. Richard A. McCabe, 'The Fate of Irena: Spenser and Political Violence', in Patricia Coughlan (ed.), *Spenser and Ireland: An Interdisciplinary Perspective* (Cork: Cork University Press, 1989), p. 117.

41. McCabe, 'The Fate of Irena', pp. 117–18.

42. D. B. Quinn, *The Voyages and Colonizing Enterprises of Sir Humphrey Gilbert*, 2 vols (London: Hakluyt Society, 1940), p. 493.

43. See MacCarthy-Morrogh, *The Munster Plantation*, pp. 38–45. See also James Hogan and N. M. O'Farrell (eds), *The Walsingham Letter-book or Register of Ireland, May, 1578 to December, 1579* (Dublin: Irish Manuscripts Commission, 1959).

44. Robert Dunlop, 'Sixteenth-century schemes for the plantation of Ulster', *SHR* 22, 86 (1924–25), p. 120.

45. *Cal. S. P. Ire.* 27 Jan. 1582; MacCarthy-Morrogh, *The Munster Plantation*, pp. 291–2; Anthony Sheehan, 'The killing of the Earl of Desmond', *JCHAS* 88, 247 (1983), pp. 106–10.

46. Spenser, *View*, p. 72.

47. Brady, 'Faction and the origins of the Desmond rebellion'; MacCurtain, 'The fall of the house of Desmond'; McGurk, 'The fall of the noble house of Desmond, 1579–83'.

48. Dunlop, 'The plantation of Munster'; MacCarthy-Morrogh *The Munster Plantation*, pp. 108–19; Quinn, 'The Munster plantation'; Anthony Sheehan, 'The population of the plantation of Munster: Quinn reconsidered', *JCHAS* 87, 246 (1982), pp. 107–17.

49. Brady, 'Spenser's Irish crisis', p. 17.

50. Bradshaw, 'Native reaction to the westward enterprise: a case-study in Gaelic ideology', in K. R. Andrews, Nicholas Canny and P. E. Hair (eds), *The Westward Enterprise: English activities in Ireland, the Atlantic and America, 1480–1650* (Liverpool: Liverpool University Press, 1978), pp. 65–80; Bernadette Cunningham, 'Native culture and political change in Ireland, 1580–1640', in Ciarán Brady and Raymond Gillespie (eds), *Natives and Newcomers: Essays on the making of Irish Colonial Society, 1534–1641* (Dublin: Irish Academic Press, 1986), p. 170; Tom Dunne, 'The Gaelic response to conquest and colonisation: the evidence of the poetry', *Studia Hibernica* 19 (1979), pp. 7–30.

51. Marianne Moore, 'Spenser's Ireland', in *The Complete Poems of Marianne Moore* (New York, 1981), p. 113.

52. MacCurtain, 'The fall of the house of Desmond'; McGurk, 'The fall of the noble house of Desmond, 1579–83'.

53. Ellis, *Tudor Ireland*, p. 252; MacCarthy-Morrogh, *The Munster Plantation*, p. 14; Sheehan, 'The killing of the Earl of Desmond'.

54. Brady, 'Faction and the origins of the Desmond rebellion', p. 312.

55. O'Connor, 'The Munster plantation era', p. 18.

56. Piveronus, 'Sir Warham St Leger', pp. 17–18.

57. Bottigheimer, 'The restoration land settlement in Ireland: a structural view', *IHS* 18, 69 (1972), pp. 9–10; Ellis, *Tudor Ireland*, p. 252.

58. *Cal. S. P. Ire.*, 27 Jan. 1582; C. L. Falkiner, *Illustrations of Irish History and Topography, Mainly of the Seventeenth Century* (London, 1904), pp. 23–56; Judson, *The Life of Edmund Spenser*, pp. 101–2.

59. Dunlop, 'The plantation of Munster', p. 250.

60. Brady, 'Spenser's Irish crisis', p. 17.

61. J. H. P. Pafford (ed.), *Lodowick Bryskett: Literary Works* (Farnborough: Gregg International, 1972), p. 158.

62. Holinshed, *Chronicles* 6, p. 439.

63. See Susan Brigden, 'Youth and the English Reformation', in Paul Slack (ed.), *Rebellion, Popular Protest and the Social Order in Early Modern England* (Cambridge: Cambridge University Press, 1984), pp. 77–107; *DNB*.

64. Spenser, *View*, p. 72.

65. Spenser, *View*, p. 73.

66. Spenser, *View*, pp. 73–5.

67. See Dunlop, 'The depositions relating to the Irish massacres of 1641', *EHR* 1, 4 (1886), pp. 740–4, *EHR* 2, 6 (1887), pp. 338–40; Mary Hickson, 'The depositions relating to the Irish massacres of 1641', *EHR* 2, 5 (1887), pp. 133–7; James Hogan (ed.), *Letters and Papers relating to the Irish Rebellion between 1642–46* (Dublin: Irish Manuscripts Commission, 1936); Robert M. Kingdon, *Myths about the St Bartholomew's Day Massacres, 1572–1576* (Cambridge, Massachusetts: Harvard University Press, 1988); Maley (ed.), *Supplication*, pp. 7–8.

68. Jonathan Dollimore and Alan Sinfield, 'History and ideology: the instance of *Henry V*', in John Drakakis (ed.), *Alternative Shakespeares* (London: Methuen, 1986), p. 226.

69. Gookin, *The great case of transplantation in Ireland*, pp. 30–1.

70. Herbert F. Hore (ed.), 'Sir Henry Sidney's Memoir of his Government of Ireland, 1583', *UJA* 3 (1856), p. 344.

71. Moore, 'Spenser's Ireland', p. 112.

72. See E. Legouis, *Spenser* (London and Toronto, 1926), p. 126; H. R. Plomer and T. P. Cross (eds), *The Life and Correspondence of Lodowick Bryskett* (Chicago: Chicago University Press, 1927), pp. 80–3.

73. Frederic Ives Carpenter, 'Spenser in Ireland', *Modern Philology* 19, 4 (1922), p. 417.

74. Plomer and Cross (eds), *The Life and Correspondence of Lodowick Bryskett* (Chicago: Chicago University Press, 1927), p. 23.

75. *DNB*; D. Jones, 'Lodowick Bryskett and his family', in C. J. Sisson (ed.), *Thomas Lodge and other Elizabethans* (London, 1966), pp. 243–61.

76. Christopher Carleil, *A discourse upon the entended voyage to the nethermoste partes of America* (London, 1583); *DNB*; Richard Hakluyt, *The principal navigations, voyages, traffiques & discoveries of the English nation* 2nd edn, 3 vols (1598–1600), III, p. 182; Plomer and Cross (eds), *The Life and Correspondence of Lodowick Bryskett*, pp. 81–2; H. Wood (ed.), *The Chronicle*

of Ireland, 1584–1608, by J. Perrot (Dublin: Irish Manuscripts Commission, 1933), p. 77; J. Dawtrey, *The Falstaff Saga* (London, 1927).

77. Hiram Morgan (ed.), 'A Booke of questions and answars', *Analecta Hibernica* 36 (1994), pp. 93–153.
78. Henry Billingsley, *The elements of geometrie: translated by Henry Billingsley with a very fruitful preface made by M. J. Dee* (London, 1570); *DNB*.
79. Crawford, 'The privy council in Ireland, 1556–1578', pp. 422–3; *DNB*.
80. Holinshed, *Chronicles*, 6, pp. 30–3, 59; Lennon, *Richard Stanyhurst: The Dubliner*, p. 86; Plomer and Cross (eds), *The Life and Correspondence of Lodowick Bryskett*, p. 81; St J. D. Seymour, *Anglo-Irish Literature, 1200–1582* (Cambridge: Cambridge University Press, 1929), pp. 22–30.
81. *DNB*; Ellis, *Tudor Ireland*, p. 336; Plomer and Cross (eds), *The Life and Correspondence of Lodowick Bryskett*, p. 81.
82. *DNB*; Ellis, *Tudor Ireland*, p. 9.
83. Falkiner, *Illustrations of Irish History and Topography*, p. 311; Holinshed, *Chronicles* VI, p. 7; Plomer and Cross (eds), *The Life and Correspondence of Lodowick Bryskett*, p. 82; T. A. O'Rahilly, 'Irish poets, historians, and judges in English documents, 1538–1615', *RIA Proc.* 36 (1922), pp. 86–120; Spenser, *View*, p. 51.
84. *DNB*; Crawford, 'The privy council in Ireland, 1556–1578', pp. 44–67; Ellis, *Tudor Ireland*, pp. 328–9; Plomer and Cross (eds), *The Life and Correspondence of Lodowick Bryskett*, p. 82.
85. Foster, 'Varieties of Irishness'; Kiberd, *Inventing Ireland*. See also Bradshaw, Hadfield and Maley (eds), *Representing Ireland*. Each of these texts contains valuable material on images of Ireland, but there is in all of them the absence of a concomitant analysis of Englishness.
86. Bruce Avery, 'Mapping the Irish Other: Spenser's *A View of the Present State of Ireland*', *ELH* 57, 2 (1990), p. 273.
87. Andrew Hadfield, 'English colonialism and national identity in early modern Ireland', *Éire-Ireland* 28, 1 (1993), p. 86.
88. Brady, 'Spenser's Irish crisis', p. 24.
89. Ciarán Brady, 'Reply to Nicholas Canny', *Past and Present* 120 (1988), p. 212.
90. Walter J. Ong, 'Spenser's View and the tradition of the "wild" Irish', *Modern Language Quarterly* 3, 4 (1942), p. 569.
91. Brady, 'The Road to the *View*', p. 39.
92. Brady, 'The Road to the *View*', p. 39.
93. Nicholas Canny, 'Introduction: Spenser and the Reform of Ireland', p. 17.
94. Nicholas Canny, 'Introduction: Spenser and the Reform of Ireland', p. 19.
95. Nicholas Canny, 'Introduction: Spenser and the Reform of Ireland', p. 20.
96. Brady, 'The Road to the *View*', p. 25.
97. Brady, 'The Road to the *View*', p. 25.
98. Nicholas Canny, 'Debate: Spenser's Irish Crisis: Humanism and Experience in the 1590s', *Past and Present* 120 (1988), p. 203, n. 9.
99. Patricia Coughlan, '"Cheap and common animals": the English anatomy of Ireland in the seventeenth century', in Thomas Healy and Jonathan

Sawday (eds), *Literature and the English Civil War* (Cambridge: Cambridge University Press, 1990), p. 205.

100. Stephen Greenblatt, 'To fashion a gentleman: Spenser and the destruction of the Bower of Bliss', in *Renaissance Self-Fashioning: From More to Shakespeare* (Chicago: Chicago University Press, 1980), p. 188.

101. Edmund Campion, *Two Bokes of the Histories of Ireland*, ed. A. F. Vossen (Assen: Van Gorcum, 1963), p. 20.

102. Eva Gold, 'Spenser the borderer: boundary, property, identity in *A View of the Present State of Ireland* and Book 6 of *The Faerie Queene*', *Journal of the Rocky Mountain Medieval and Renaissance Association* 14 (1993), p. 103.

103. Gold, 'Spenser the borderer', p. 104.

CHAPTER 4: CHANGING PLACES IN *THE FAERIE QUEENE*

1. The phrase is from Jeffrey Fruen, '"True Glorious Type": the place of Gloriana in *The Faerie Queene*', *Spenser Studies* 6 (1986), p. 147.

2. Courtenay Moore, 'Spenser's knowledge of the neighbourhood of Mitchelstown', *JCHAS* 10, 61 (1904), p. 33.

3. Geoffrey Elton, *England under the Tudors*, 2nd edn (London: Longman, 1969), p. 386.

4. M. M. Gray, 'The influence of Spenser's Irish experiences on *The Faerie Queene*', *RES* 6, 24 (1930), p. 414.

5. Pauline Henley, 'Spenser's "Stony Aubrian"', *TLS* 35 (28 November 1936), p. 996; P. W. Joyce, 'Spenser's Irish rivers', *Fraser's Magazine* 97 (1878), pp. 315–33; T. Keightley, 'Irish rivers named in *The Faerie Queene*', *N&Q* 4th ser., 4 (1869), pp. 169–70; Courteney Moore, 'The Bregoge', *JCHAS* 10, 61 (1913), pp. 40–2; R. M. Smith, 'Spenser's Irish river stories', *PMLA* 50, 4 (1935), pp. 1047-56; R. M. Smith, 'Spenser's "stony Aubrian"', *Modern Language Notes* 59, 1 (1944), pp. 1–5.

6. Smith, 'Spenser's Irish river stories', p. 1056.

7. Spenser, *View*, p. 10.

8. Maureen Quilligan, *Milton's Spenser* (Ithaca and London: Cornell University Press, 1983), pp. 160–5.

9. Spenser, *View*, p. 68.

10. See George E. McLean, 'Spenser's Territorial History: Book V of *The Faerie Queene* and *A View of the Present State of Ireland*' (The University of Arizona, unpublished PhD thesis, 1986).

11. R. B. Gottfried, 'Irish geography in Spenser's *View*', *ELH* 6, 2 (1939), p. 114.

12. BL Add. Ms. 44738, f. 86.

13. Anne Fogarty, 'The Colonization of Language: Narrative Strategy in *A View of the Present State of Ireland* and *The Faerie Queene*, Book VI', in Patricia Coughlan (ed.), *Spenser and Ireland: An Interdisciplinary Perspective* (Cork: Cork University Press, 1989), p. 91. See also Merritt Y. Hughes, 'Spenser and Utopia', *Studies in Philology* 17, 2 (1920), pp. 132–46.

14. Lewis, *Studies in Medieval and Renaissance Literature* (Cambridge: Cambridge University Press, 1966), p. 126.

15. Richard Helgerson, 'The new poet presents himself: Spenser and the idea of a literary career', *PMLA* 93, 5 (1978), pp. 893–911; Richard Mallette, 'Spenser's portrait of the artist in *The Shepheardes Calender* and *Colin Clouts Come Home Againe*', *SEL* 19, 1 (1979), pp. 19–41; David Lee Miller, 'Authorship, anonymity, and *The Shepheardes Calender*', *MLQ* 40, 3 (1979), pp. 219–36; 'Spenser's vocation, Spenser's career', *ELH* 50, 2 (1983), pp. 197–231.
16. Stephen Greenblatt, 'To fashion a gentleman: Spenser and the destruction of the Bower of Bliss', *Renaissance Self-Fashioning: From More to Shakespeare* (Chicago: Chicago University Press, 1980), p. 179.
17. Greenblatt, 'To fashion a gentleman', pp. 186–7.
18. Greenblatt, 'To fashion a gentleman', p. 288, n. 62.
19. Spenser, *View*, p. 53.
20. See Tracey Hill, 'Humanism and homicide: Spenser's *A View of the Present State of Ireland*', *Irish Studies Review* 4 (1993), pp. 2–4; Lisa Jardine, 'Encountering Ireland: Gabriel Harvey, Edmund Spenser, and English colonial ventures', in Brendan Bradshaw, Andrew Hadfield and Willy Maley (eds), *Representing Ireland: Literature and the Origins of Conflict* (Cambridge: Cambridge University Press, 1993), pp. 60–75; Hiram Morgan, 'Faith and fatherland in sixteenth-century Ireland', *History Ireland* 3, 2 (1995), pp. 13–20; John N. King, 'Was Spenser a Puritan?', *Spenser Studies* 6 (1986), pp. 1–31; Katherine Walsh, 'The Reformation and education – humanist theory and sectarian practice', *Studies* (Autumn, 1975), pp. 215–29; Terence Ranger, 'From humanism to the science of Man: colonialism and the understanding of alien societies', *TRHS* 5th ser., 26 (1976), pp. 115–41; Steven Ellis, *Tudor Ireland: Crown, Community and the Conflict of Cultures, 1470–1603* (London: Longman, 1985), p. 292.
21. J. Coleman, 'Biographical sketches of persons remarkable in local history: Edmund Spenser', *JCHAS* 3, 29 (1894), p. 92.
22. Nicholas Canny and Andrew Carpenter (eds), 'The early planters: Spenser and his contemporaries', in Seamus Deane (ed.), *The Field Day Anthology of Irish Writing* (Derry: Field Day, 1991), I, p. 225.
23. R. M. Smith, 'Origines Arthurianae: the two crosses of Spenser's Red Cross Knight', *JEGP* 54, 4 (1955), p. 673.
24. Paul E. McLane, 'Was Spenser in Ireland in early November 1579?', *N&Q* 204 (1959), pp. 99–101.
25. T. C. Curtis and R. B. McDowell (eds), *Irish Historical Documents, 1172–1922*, 2nd edn (London: Methuen, 1977), p. 104.
26. Smith, 'Origines Arthurianae', p. 674.
27. Smith, 'Origines Arthurianae', p. 675, n. 34, citing *Notes & Queries*, 3rd ser., 3 (1863), p. 182b.
28. Smith, 'Origines Arthurianae', p. 676.
29. Smith, 'Origines Arthurianae', p. 676, n. 37. 'Spenser's Redcrosse Knight may even have fathered Rosicrucianism', according to Frances Yates. See Frances Yates, *Ideas and Ideals in the North European Renaissance* (London: Routledge, 1984), cited in James Vink, 'Spenser's "Easterland" as the Columban Church of ancient Ireland', *Éire-Ireland* 25, 3 (1990), p. 104.

30. Kenneth Ferguson, 'The development of a standing army in Ireland', *The Irish Sword* 15, 60 (1983), p. 155.

31. Ellis, *Tudor Ireland*, p. 292.

32. Elizabeth Heale, *'The Faerie Queene': A Reader's Guide* (Cambridge: Cambridge University Press, 1987), p. 7.

33. K. R. Andrews, 'Elizabethan privateering', in Joyce Youings (ed.), *Raleigh in Exeter 1985: Privateering and Colonisation in the reign of Elizabeth I* (Exeter: University of Exeter, 1985), p. 9.

34. Paul Alpers, 'Pastoral and the domain of lyric in Spenser's *Shepheardes Calender'*, *Representations* 12 (1985), p. 95.

35. See Linda Gregerson, *The Reformation of the Subject: Spenser, Milton and the English Protestant Epic* (Cambridge: Cambridge University Press, 1995), p. 230; Andrew Hadfield, 'The trials of Jove: Spenser's allegory and the mastery of the Irish', *Bullán* 4 (1996), pp. 8–9.

36. John Breen, 'The Empirical Eye: Edmund Spenser's *A View of the Present State of Ireland'*, *The Irish Review* (1995), p. 50.

37. Donald Bruce, 'Edmund Spenser and the Irish Wars', *Contemporary Review* 266 (1995), p. 136.

38. Clare Carroll, 'The construction of gender and the cultural and political Other in *The Faerie Queene* and *A View of the Present State of Ireland*: the critics, the context, and the case of Radigund', *Criticism* 32, 2 (1990), p. 163.

39. Thomas Healy, 'Civilisation and its discontents: the case of Edmund Spenser', in *New Latitudes: Theory and English Renaissance Literature* (London: Edward Arnold, 1992), p. 95.

40. Healy, 'Civilisation and its discontents', p. 95.

41. Carroll, 'The construction of gender', p. 171.

42. Carroll, 'The construction of gender', p. 172, citing Margaret Waller, 'Academic Tootsie: the denial of difference and the difference it makes', *Diacritics* 17, 1 (1987), p. 3.

43. Greenblatt, 'To fashion a gentleman', p. 185.

44. John T. Gilbert, *History of the Irish Confederation, and The War in Ireland, 1641–1643* (Dublin: M. H. Gill, 1882), p. xiii.

45. Edwin A. Greenlaw, 'Spenser and British imperialism', *Modern Philology* 9, 3 (1912), p. 7.

46. Sheila Cavanagh, '"Such was Irena's countenance": Ireland in Spenser's prose and poetry', *TSLL* 28, 1 (1986), p. 47.

47. See Jane Dawson, 'William Cecil and the British dimension of early Elizabethan foreign policy', *History* 74, 241 (1989), pp. 196–216; Rigby Graham, *Edmund Spenser's Kilcolman* (Leicester: Brewhouse Private Press, 1975); Sidney Lysaght, 'Kilcolman castle', *The Antiquary* 5, 28 (1882), pp. 153–6; Michael MacCarthy-Morrogh, 'The Munster Plantation, 1583–1641' (PhD thesis, University of London, 1983), pp. 367–8; R. B. Outhwaite, 'Dearth, the English crown, and the "Crisis of the 1590s"', in Peter Clark (ed.), *The European Crisis of the 1590s: essays in comparative history* (London: Allen and Unwin, 1985), pp. 23–43; Spenser, *View*, p. 97.

48. Ciarán Brady, 'Spenser's Irish crisis: humanism and experience in the 1590s', *P&P* 111 (1986), pp. 17–49; Lewis, *Studies in Medieval and Renaissance Literature*, p. 126.

49. Kenneth Gross, 'Mythmaking in Hibernia (*A View of the Present State of Ireland*)', in *Spenserian Poetics: Idolatry, Iconoclasm, and Magic* (Ithaca and London: Cornell University Press, 1985), p. 79.

50. R. B. Gottfried, 'Spenser and the Italian myth of locality', *Studies in Philology* 34, 1 (1937), pp. 107–25.

51. Jacqueline T. Miller, 'The status of Faeryland: Spenser's "unjust possession"', *Spenser Studies* 5 (1984), p. 33.

52. Miller 1984, 'The status of Faeryland', p. 33.

53. Jane Dawson, 'Anglo-Scottish protestant culture and integration in sixteenth-century Britain', in Steven G. Ellis and Sarah Barber (eds), *Conquest and Union: Fashioning a British State, 1485–1725* (London: Longman, 1995), pp. 87–114; Steven G. Ellis, '"Not Mere English": The British Perspective, Perspective, 1400–1650', *History Today* 38, 12 (1988), pp. 41–8; Conrad Russell, 'John Bull's Other Nations', *TLS* (March 12, 1993), pp. 3–4; David Stevenson, 'The Century of the Three Kingdoms', in Jenny Wormald (ed.), *Scotland Revisited* (London: Collins and Brown, 1991), pp. 107–18; Jenny Wormald, 'The Creation of Britain: Multiple Kingdoms or Core and Colonies?', *Transactions of the Royal Historical Society* 6, 2 (1992), pp. 175–94.

54. Greenlaw, 'Spenser and British imperialism'.

55. Judith Anderson, 'The antiquities of Fairyland and Ireland', *JEGP* 86, 2 (1987), p. 204.

56. Spenser, *View*, p. 29.

57. R. M. Smith, 'Spenser, Holinshed, and the *Leabhar Gabhala*', *JEGP* 43, 4 (1944), pp. 390–401.

58. Clare O'Halloran, 'Irish re-creations of the past: the challenge of MacPherson's *Ossian*', *P&P* 124 (1989), p. 73.

59. Bernadette Cunningham, 'Seventeenth-century interpretations of the past: the case of Geoffrey Keating', *IHS* 25, 98 (1986), pp. 116–28; O'Halloran, 'Irish re-creations of the past', p. 72; Hughes, 'Spenser and Utopia'; R. H. Pearce, 'Primitivistic ideas in *The Faerie Queene*', *JEGP* 44, 2 (1945), pp. 139–51.

60. Jeffrey Knapp, 'Error as a means of Empire in *The Faerie Queene*', *ELH* 54, 4 (1987), p. 820.

61. See Nicholas Canny, 'Dominant minorities: English settlers in Ireland and Virginia, 1550–1650', in A. C. Hepburn (ed.), *Minorities in History: Historical Studies* 12 (London: Arnold, 1978), pp. 51–69.

62. A. B. Giamatti, 'Hippolytus among the exiles: the romance of early humanism', in Maynard Mack and George de Forest Lord (eds), *Poetic Traditions of the English Renaissance* (New Haven: Yale University Press, 1982), pp. 1–23.

63. Jane Tylus, 'Spenser, Virgil, and the politics of poetic labour', *ELH* 55, 1 (1988), p. 72.

64. Julia Lupton, 'Home-making in Ireland: Virgil's Eclogue I and Book VI of *The Faerie Queene*', *Spenser Studies*, 8 (1990), pp. 119–45.

65. Cited in David Cairns and Shaun Richards, *Writing Ireland: Nationalism, colonialism and culture* (Manchester: Manchester University Press, 1988), p. 8.
66. See J. H. Andrews, *A Paper Landscape: The Ordnance Survey in Ireland* (Oxford: Clarendon Press, 1976); Mary Hamer, 'Putting Ireland on the map', *Textual Practice* 3, 2 (1989), pp. 184–201.
67. J. C. Smith and E. de Selincourt, *Spenser: Poetical Works* (Oxford: Oxford University Press, 1912; 1985), p. 509.
68. David Norbrook, *Poetry and Politics in the English Renaissance* (London: Routledge, 1984), p. 109.
69. Alastair Fowler, *A History of English Literature: Forms and Kinds from the Middle Ages to the Present* (Oxford: Blackwell, 1987), p. 63.
70. Greenblatt, 'To fashion a gentleman'; Smith, 'Origines Arthurianae'; Clarence Steinberg, 'Atin, Pyrochles, Cymochles: on Irish emblems in *The Faerie Queene*', *Neuphilologische Mitteilungen* 72, 4 (1971), pp. 749–61.
71. Steinberg, 'Atin, Pyrochles, Cymochles', p. 750.
72. Steinberg, 'Atin, Pyrochles, Cymochles', p. 760.
73. Roland M. Smith, 'A further note on Una and Duessa', *PMLA* 61, 2 (1946), pp. 592–93, n. 4.
74. Greenblatt, 'To fashion a gentleman', p. 186.
75. A. C. Hamilton (ed.), *The Faerie Queene: an annotated edition*, 2nd edn (London: Longman, 1984), p. 526.
76. Sean Kane, *Spenser's Moral Allegory* (Toronto, Buffalo and London: Routledge, 1989), p. 140.
77. Graham Hough, *A Preface to the 'Faerie Queene'* (London: Duckworth, 1962; 1983), p. 191.
78. Kane, *Spenser's Moral Allegory*, p. x.
79. R. L. Entzminger, 'Courtesy: the cultural imperative', *PQ* 53, 3 (1974), p. 389.
80. See Robert M. Kingdon, *Myths about the St. Bartholomew's Day Massacres, 1572–1576* (Cambridge, Massachusetts: Harvard University Press, 1988).
81. For a compelling discussion of Spenser's attitude to sword and word, see Andrew Hadfield, 'The "sacred hunger of ambitious minds": Spenser's savage religion', in Donna B. Hamilton and Richard Strier (eds), *Religion, Literature, and Politics in Post-Reformation England, 1540–1688* (Cambridge: Cambridge University Press, 1995), pp. 27–45.
82. A. B. Giamatti, 'Primitivism and the process of civility in Spenser's *Faerie Queene*', in F. Chiapelli (ed.), *First Images of America: The Impact of the New World on the Old* (Berkeley: University of California Press, 1976), p. 80.
83. Hugh MacLachlan, 'The "carelesse heavens": a study of revenge and atonement in *The Faerie Queene*', *Spenser Studies* 1 (1980), pp. 135–61.
84. C. S. Lewis, *The Allegory of Love* (Oxford: Oxford University Press, 1966); Norbrook, *Poetry and Politics in the English Renaissance*, pp. 85–7, 92; Kevin Sharpe, *Criticism and Compliment: The Politics of Literature in the England of Charles I* (Cambridge: Cambridge University Press, 1987), p. 270.

85. J. H. Andrews, 'Geography and government in Elizabethan Ireland', in N. Stephen and R. E. Glasscock (eds), *Irish Geographical Studies in Honour of E. Estyn Evans* (Belfast: Queen's University of Belfast, 1970), pp. 183–4.
86. Cited in Andrews, 'Geography and government in Elizabethan Ireland', p. 184.
87. Richard Bagwell, *Ireland under the Tudors*, 3 vols (London: Longman, 1885–90), 3, p. 458.

CHAPTER 5: ROYAL ABSENTEEISM AND VICEREGAL VERSES

1. A deficiency partially remedied by the recent publication of Ciarán Brady, *The Chief Governors: The rise and fall of reform government in Tudor Ireland 1536–1588* (Cambridge: Cambridge University Press, 1994).
2. J. Small (ed.), *The Image of Irelande, with A Discoverie of Woodkarne*, by John Derricke (London, 1581; Edinburgh, 1883), Plate 12.
3. Ellis, *Tudor Ireland*, p. 260.
4. Simon Adams, 'Eliza enthroned?: the court and its politics', in Christopher Haigh (ed.), *The Reign of Elizabeth* (London: Macmillan, 1984), p. 67.
5. Maureen Quilligan, *Milton's Spenser: The Politics of Reading* (Ithaca and London: Cornell University Press, 1983), p. 172.
6. David Norbrook, *Poetry and Politics in the English Renaissance*, (London: Routledge, 1985), p. 118.
7. Andrew Hadfield, 'Spenser, Ireland, and sixteenth-century political theory', *Modern Language Review* 9, 1 (1994), p. 16.
8. Cited A. C. Hamilton (ed.), *Spenser: 'The Faerie Queene': An annotated edition* (London: Longman, 1984), p. 712.
9. Aidan Clarke, 'Review of N. P. Canny and A. Pagden (eds), *Colonial Identity in the Atlantic World, 1500–1800'*, *IHS* 26, 101 (1988), pp. 117–18.
10. Jeffrey Fruen, '"True Glorious type": the place of Gloriana in *The Faerie Queene'*, *Spenser Studies* 7 (1986), p. 147.
11. Marie Axton, *The Queen's Two Bodies: Drama and the Elizabethan Succession* (Cambridge: Cambridge University Press, 1977), pp. 17–18. See also N. L. Jones, 'Elizabeth's first year: the conception and birth of the Elizabethan political world', in Haigh (ed.), *The Reign of Elizabeth I*, pp. 27–53.
12. Axton, *The Queen's Two Bodies*, p. 75; Michael Leslie, *Spenser's 'Fierce Warres and Faithfull Loves'* (Woodbridge: Boydell and Brewer, 1983), pp. 186–95.
13. Spenser, *View*, p. 33.
14. James Vink, 'Spenser's "Easterland" as the Columban Church of ancient Ireland', *Éire-Ireland* 25, 3 (1990), p. 103.
15. Spenser, *View*, p. 33.
16. Peter Walsh, *A Prospect of the State of Ireland, from the year of the world 1750, to the year of Christ 1652* (London, 1682), p. 396.
17. Walsh, *A Prospect of the State of Ireland*, pp. 396–400.
18. Spenser, *View*, p. 123.

19. Clare Carroll, 'The construction of gender and the cultural and political Other in *The Faerie Queene* and *A View of the Present State of Ireland*: the critics, the context, and the case of Radigund', *Criticism* 32, 2 (1990), p. 177.

20. D. L. Miller, 'Spenser's poetics: the poem's two bodies', *PMLA* 101, 2 (1986), pp. 170–85.

21. Axton, *The Queen's Two Bodies*, p. x.

22. Miller, 'Spenser's poetics', p. 170.

23. Fruen, '"True Glorious type"', pp. 148–9; Miller, 'Spenser's poetics', p. 170.

24. See Judith H. Anderson, *Biographical Truth: The Representation of Historical Persons in Tudor–Stuart Writing* (New Haven and London: Yale University Press, 1984), p. 54. See also, by the same author, '"In living colours and right hew": the Queen in Spenser's central books', in Maynard Mack and G. de Forest Lord (eds), *Poetic Traditions of the English Renaissance* (New Haven: Yale University Press, 1982), pp. 47–66.

25. See Robin Headlam Wells, *Spenser's 'Faerie Queene' and the Cult of Elizabeth* (London: Macmillan, 1983).

26. Louis Adrian Montrose, 'The Elizabethan subject and the Spenserian text', in Patricia Parker and David Quint (eds), *Literary Theory/Renaissance Texts* (Baltimore: Johns Hopkins University Press, 1986), p. 303.

27. Leonard Tennenhouse, *Power on Display: The Politics of Shakespeare's Genres* (New York and London: Methuen, 1986), pp. 102–46.

28. Brian Levack, *The Formation of the British State: England, Scotland, and the Union, 1603–1707* (Oxford: Clarendon Press, 1987), p. 2; Miller, 'Spenser's poetics', p. 170.

29. See Peter Lindenbaum, *Changing Landscapes: Anti-pastoral sentiment in the English Renaissance* (Georgia: The University of Georgia Press, 1986).

30. Helena Shire, *A Preface to Spenser*, p. 64.

31. Maureen Quilligan, *Milton's Spenser*, p. 172.

32. Diane Parkin-Speer, 'Allegorical trials in Spenser's *The Faerie Queene*', *Sixteenth Century Journal* 23, 3 (1992), p. 500.

33. See Thomas H. Cain, 'The strategy of praise in Spenser's "April"', *SEL* 8, 1 (1968), pp. 45–58; S. L. Johnson, 'Elizabeth, bride and queen: a study of Spenser's April Eclogue and the metaphors of English Protestantism', *Spenser Studies* 2 (1981), pp. 75–91; Louis Adrian Montrose, '"Eliza, Queene of Shepheardes", and the pastoral of power', *ELR* 10, 2 (1980), pp. 153–82.

34. Lisa Jardine, 'Mastering the uncouth', p. 70.

35. Stevie Davies and Douglas Brooks-Davies, 'monarchy', in A. C. Hamilton (ed.), *The Spenser Encyclopedia* (London and Toronto: Routledge, 1990), p. 478.

36. Davies and Brooks-Davies, 'monarchy', p. 478.

37. T. C. Curtis and R. B. McDowell (eds), *Irish Historical Documents, 1172–1922* (London: Methuen, 1943; 1977), p. 77.

38. Karl Bottigheimer, 'Kingdom and colony: Ireland in the westward enterprise, 1536–1660', in K. R. Andrews, N. P. Canny and P. E. Hair

(eds), *The Westward Enterprise: English activities in Ireland, the Atlantic and America* (Liverpool: Liverpool University Press, 1978), p. 46.

39. Brendan Bradshaw, *The Irish constitutional revolution of the sixteenth century* (Cambridge: Cambridge University Press, 1979).

40. Ciarán Brady, 'Court, castle and country: the framework of government in Tudor Ireland', in Ciarán Brady and Raymond Gillespie (eds), *Natives and Newcomers: Essays on the making of Irish Colonial Society, 1534–1641* (Dublin: Irish Academic Press, 1986), pp. 28–9.

41. Brady, 'Court, castle and country', p. 30.

42. Brady, 'Court, castle and country', p. 49.

43. Anon., *The Present State of Ireland Together with Some Remarks upon the Ancient State Thereof* (London, 1673), p. 165.

44. F. J. Furnivall (ed.), *The Fyrst Boke of the Introduction of Knowledge (1548)*, by Andrew Boorde, *Early English Text Society*, extra ser., 10 (London, 1870), p. 132.

45. John Bale, *The vocacyon of Johan Bale to the bishoprick of Ossorie in Irela[n]de his persecucio[n]s in y* same & finall delyveraunce* ('Rome' [Wesel], 1553), ff. 18–19.

46. Spenser, *View*, p. 7.

47. Spenser, *View*, p. 7.

48. Anon., *The Present State of Ireland*, pp. 170–1.

49. Richard Cox, *Hibernia Anglicana: or, The History of Ireland from the Conquest thereof by the English, To this Present Time*, 2 vols (London, 1689–90), I, p. d.

50. Elizabeth Bellamy, 'The vocative and the vocational: the unreadability of Elizabeth in *The Faerie Queene*', *ELH* 54, 1 (1987), p. 1.

51. Bellamy, 'The vocative and the vocational', p. 12.

52. Bellamy, 'The vocative and the vocational', pp. 22–3; Quilligan, *Milton's Spenser*, pp. 171–4.

53. T. C. Barnard, 'Planters and policies in Cromwellian Ireland', *P&P* 61 (1973), pp. 31–69; *Cromwellian Ireland: English government and reform in Ireland, 1649–60* (Oxford: Clarendon Press, 1975); Hamilton (ed.), *Spenser: 'The Faerie Queene'*, p. 735.

54. T. W. Moody, F. X. Martin and F. J. Byrne (eds), *A New History of Ireland, 8, A Chronology of Irish History to 1976* (Oxford: Clarendon Press, 1982), pp. 237, 242. Milton, in *Paradise Lost* X. 56–7 describes the Son as 'Viceregent', in keeping with his theory that only God and the Son merited royal titles.

55. Spenser, *View*, p. 66.

56. Ciarán Brady, 'Spenser's Irish crisis: reply to Canny', *P&P* 120 (1988), pp. 214–15; Nicholas P. Canny, '"Spenser's Irish crisis": a comment', *P&P* 120 (1988), p. 202; Eamonn Grennan, 'Language and politics: a note on some metaphors in Spenser's *A View of the Present State of Ireland*', *Spenser Studies*, 3 (1982), pp. 105–6.

57. Robin Frame, *Colonial Ireland, 1169–1369* (Dublin: Helicon, 1982), p. 8. For a compelling account of Arthur's dream vision from a psychoanalytic perspective, see Elizabeth J. Bellamy, 'Reading desire backwards: belatedness and Spenser's Arthur', *South Atlantic Quarterly* 88 (1989), pp. 789–809.

58. Karl Bottigheimer, *English Money and Irish Land: The 'Adventurers' in the Cromwellian Settlement of Ireland* (Oxford: Clarendon Press, 1971), p. 8; Vincent Carey, 'Gaelic reaction to plantation: the case of the O'More and O'Connor Lordships of Laois and Offaly, 1570–1603', (MA thesis, St Patrick's College, Maynooth, 1985), pp. 8–43; Edmund Curtis (ed.), 'The survey of Offaly in 1550', *Hermathena* 45 (1930), pp. 312–52; Robert Dunlop, 'The plantation of Leix and Offaly', *EHR* 6, 21 (1891), pp. 61–96; D. G. White, 'The Tudor plantations in Ireland, pre-1571' (PhD Thesis, University of Dublin, 1967), I, pp. 292–331.

59. Hamilton (ed.), *The Spenser Encyclopedia*, p. 478.

60. Donald Bruce, 'Spenser's Welsh', *Notes and Queries*, 230 [n.s. 32, 4] (1985), p. 466.

61. Brady, *The Chief Governors*, p. 300.

62. John Donne, 'The Funerall', in C. A. Patrides, *The Complete Poems of John Donne* (London: J. M. Dent, 1985), pp. 107–8.

63. Eva Gold, 'Spenser the borderer: boundary, property, identity in *A View of the Present State of Ireland* and Book 6 of *The Faerie Queene*', *Journal of the Rocky Mountain Medieval and Renaissance Association* 14 (1993), p. 110.

64. Gold, 'Spenser the borderer', p. 110.

65. Gold, 'Spenser the borderer', p. 111.

66. Gold, 'Spenser the borderer', p. 111.

67. Gold, 'Spenser the borderer', p. 112.

68. Gold, 'Spenser the borderer', p. 112.

69. Gold, 'Spenser the borderer', p. 112.

70. Ciarán Brady, 'The road to the *View*: on the decline of reform thought in Tudor Ireland', in Patricia Coughlan (ed.), *Spenser and Ireland: An Interdisciplinary Perspective* (Cork: Cork University Press, 1989), p. 33.

71. Richard A. McCabe, 'The fate of Irena: Spenser and political violence', in Patricia Coughlan (ed.), *Spenser and Ireland: An Interdisciplinary Perspective* (Cork: Cork University Press, 1989), p. 110.

72. McCabe, 'The fate of Irena', p. 118.

73. McCabe, 'The fate of Irena', p. 119.

74. McCabe, 'The fate of Irena', p. 117.

75. David J. Baker, '"Some quirk, some subtle evasion": legal subversion in Spenser's *A View of the Present State of Ireland*', *Spenser Studies* 6 (1986), p. 150.

76. Baker, '"Some quirk, some subtle evasion"', p. 150.

77. Baker, '"Some quirk, some subtle evasion"', p. 153.

78. Baker, '"Some quirk, some subtle evasion"', p. 154.

79. Cited in Margaret MacCurtain, 'The roots of Irish nationalism', in Robert Driscoll (ed.), *The Celtic Consciousness* (Edinburgh: Canongate, 1982), p. 377.

80. C. S. Lewis, *The Allegory of Love* (Oxford: Oxford University Press, 1966), pp. 336–7. See also Mary R. Bowman, '"she there as princess rained": Spenser's figure of Elizabeth', *Renaissance Quarterly* 43, 3 (1990), pp. 509–28. Bowman argues that in Britomart Spenser constructed a critical portrait of Elizabeth less acceptable than those

of Gloriana and Belphoebe alluded to in the 'Letter to Raleigh': 'There are many shadows of Elizabeth absent here, but Britomart is by far the most conspicuous' (p. 527).

CHAPTER 6: HOW CONTEMPORARIES READ SPENSER'S *VIEW*

* This is a slightly revised version of an essay that appeared in Brendan Bradshaw, Andrew Hadfield and Willy Maley (eds), *Representing Ireland: Literature and the Origins of Conflict, 1534–1660* (Cambridge: Cambridge University Press, 1993), pp. 191–208.

1. See Patricia Coughlan, '"Cheap and common animals": the English anatomy of Ireland in the seventeenth century', in Thomas Healy and Jonathan Sawday (eds), *Literature and the English Civil War* (Cambridge: Cambridge University Press, 1990), pp. 205–23, esp. pp. 206–7. For a list of the manuscripts of the *View* see Willy Maley, 'Edmund Spenser and Cultural Identity in Early Modern Ireland', PhD thesis (Cambridge, 1989), Appendix 2.

2. Terence Ranger, 'Richard Boyle and the Making of an Irish Fortune' *IHS* 10 (1957), pp. 257–97 at p. 297.

3. See entries in the *DNB* on Hanmer and Ware.

4. James Ware (ed.), *Two Histories of Ireland* (Dublin, 1633), p. iii.

5. J. T. Gilbert, *History of the Irish Confederation and the War in Ireland 1641–1643*, 7 vols (Dublin, 1882–91). I am grateful to Raymond Gillespie for directing me to this text.

6. Gilbert, *History of the Irish Confederation*, I, pp. xiv–xv.

7. See Geoffrey Keating, *The History of Ireland* (1633), ed. J. O'Mahoney (New York, 1886), and Thomas Stafford, *Pacata Hibernia, or, a history of the wars in Ireland during the reign of Queen Elizabeth* (1633), ed. Standish O'Grady, 2 vols (London, 1896).

8. A. J. Horwood, 'A common-place book of John Milton', *Camden Society* 6 (1878, revised edition), pp. 1–60; p. 35.

9. Ware, *Two Histories*, pp. 62–3.

10. See for example Ciarán Brady, 'Faction and the Origins of the Desmond Rebellion of 1579', *IHS* 22 (1981), pp. 289–312.

11. Willy Maley (ed.), 'The Supplication of the blood of the English, most lamentably murdred in Ireland, Cryeng out of the yearth for revenge (1598)', *Analecta Hibernica* 36 (1994), p. 65.

12. Ciarán Brady, 'Court, Castle, and Community: The Framework of Government in Tudor Ireland', in Ciarán Brady and Raymond Gillespie (eds), *Natives and newcomers: Essays on the Making of Irish Society, 1534–1641* (Dublin: Irish Academic Press, 1986), pp. 22–49.

13. Ware, *Two Histories*, p. 64.

14. John Milton, *Observations upon the articles of peace with the Irish Rebels, on the Letter of Ormond to Col. Jones, and the Representation of the Presbytery at Belfast* (London, 1649).

15. Horwood, 'A common-place book', p. 52.

16. See L. W. Henry, 'Contemporary sources for Essex's Lieutenancy in Ireland, 1599', *IHS* 11 (1958), pp. 8–17.
17. One thinks here immediately of Elizabeth's reaction to Grey's bestowing of lands and favours, and her disapproval of Essex's conferring of knighthoods upon his closest followers. Spenser benefited from the generosity of both Grey and Essex, becoming Clerk of the Council of Munster under Grey, and being nominated as sheriff of Cork in advance of Essex's Irish expedition. See R. B. Gottfried, 'Spenser's *View* and Essex', *PMLA* 52 (1937), pp. 645–51; M. Mac Lir, 'Spenser as High Sheriff of Cork County', *JCHAS* 7 (1901), pp. 249–50.
18. See Conrad Russell, 'The British Background to the Irish Rebellion of 1641', *Historical Research* 61 (1988), pp. 166–82; p. 169.
19. See Nicholas P. Canny, *From Reformation to Restoration: Ireland, 1534–1660* (Dublin: Helicon, 1987), pp. 188–204; Aidan Clarke, 'Ireland and the General Crisis', *P&P* 48 (1970): 79–99; H. F. Kearney, *Strafford in Ireland, 1633–41: A Study in Absolutism* (Manchester: Manchester University Press, 1959); Ranger, 'Richard Boyle'.
20. Nicholas P. Canny, 'Edmund Spenser and the Development of an Anglo-Irish Identity', *The Yearbook of English Studies: Colonial and Imperial Themes*, special number, 13 (1983), pp. 1–19 at p. 17.
21. Milton, *Observations*, p. 52.
22. Ware, *Two Histories*, p. 118.
23. Ware, *Two Histories*, p. 118.
24. See Canny, *From Reformation to Restoration*, pp. 188–204, and Kearney, *Strafford in Ireland*.
25. See R. B. Outhwaite, 'Dearth, the English Crown, and the "Crisis of the 1590s"', in Peter Clark (ed.), *The European Crisis of the 1590s* (London: Allen and Unwin, 1985), pp. 23–43.
26. Ware, *Two Histories*, pp. 84–5.
27. Ware, *Two Histories*, p. 85.
28. M. Mac Lir, 'Spenser as High Sheriff of Cork County', *JCHAS* (1901), pp. 249–50; p. 249.
29. See R. B. Gottfried, 'Irish Geography in Spenser's *View*', *ELH* 6, 2 (1939), pp. 114–37.
30. Ware, *Two Histories*, pp. 87–8.
31. K. M. Burton, *Milton's Prose Writings* (London, 1970), p. 329.
32. George Story, *An impartial History of the Wars of Ireland, with a Continuation thereof ... Together with some remarks upon the Present State of that Kingdom* (London, 1691–3), p. 325.
33. Brendan Bradshaw, 'Robe and Sword in the Conquest of Ireland', in C. Cross, D. Loades and J. J. Scarisbrick (eds), *Law and Government under the Tudors: Essays Presented to Sir Geoffrey Elton on his Retirement* (Cambridge: Cambridge University Press, 1988), pp. 139–62.
34. Milton, *Observations*, p. 47.
35. Milton, *Observations*, p. 49.
36. Temple, *The Irish Rebellion: or, An History of the Beginnings and first progresse of the General Rebellion raised within the kingdom of IRELAND, upon the three and twentieth day of October, in the year, 1641* (London, 1646), p. 6.

37. M. Y. Hughes, 'The Historical Setting of Milton's *Observations on the Articles of Peace, 1649*', *PMLA* 64 (1949), pp. 1049–73; p. 1050.

38. David J. Baker, '"Some Quirk, Some Subtle Evasion": Legal Subversion in Spenser's *A View of the Present State of Ireland*', *Spenser Studies* 6 (1986), pp. 147–63; p. 147; Hughes, 'Historical Setting', p. 1049.

39. Baker, '"Some Quirk"', p. 47; T. C. Barnard, 'Planters and Policies in Cromwellian Ireland', *P&P* 61 (1973), pp. 31–69; Jonathan Goldberg, *James I and the Politics of Literature: Jonson, Shakespeare, Donne and Their Contemporaries* (Baltimore and London: Johns Hopkins University Press, 1983), pp. 8–10.

40. Cited in David Norbrook, *Poets and Politics in the English Renaissance* (London: Routledge, 1984), p. 311.

41. Hughes, 'Historical Setting', pp. 1072–3.

42. Christopher Hill, 'Seventeenth-Century English Radicals and Ireland', in P. Corish (ed.), *Radicals, Rebels and Establishments, Historical Studies* 15 (Belfast: Appletree Press, 1985), pp. 33–49; p. 35.

43. Hill, 'Seventeenth-Century English Radicals', p. 37.

44. See Aidan Clarke, 'The Genesis of the Ulster Rising of 1641', in Peter Roebuck (ed.), *From Plantation to Partition: Essays in Honour of J. L. McCracken* (Belfast: Blackstaff, 1981); Sean Golden, 'Post-Traditional English Literature: A Polemic', *The Crane Bag Book of Irish Studies (1978–81)* (Dublin: Blackwater Press, 1983), pp. 427–38; p. 433; Lawrence Stone, *The Causes of the English Revolution, 1529–1642*, 6th edn (London: Routledge, 1984), pp. 137–9.

45. Burton, *Milton's Prose*, p. 329.

46. Cited in J. C., 'Biographical Sketches of Persons Remarkable in Local History', *JCHAS* 3, 29 (1894), p. 97. See also Pauline Henley, *Spenser in Ireland* (Cork: Cork University Press, 1928), pp. 206–7; Pat Coughlan, '"Cheap and common animals"', p. 221, n. 2.

47. Peter Walsh, *A Prospect of the State of Ireland from the year of the world 1750, to the year of Christ 1652* (London, 1682), p. C.Sig.1^{r-v}.

48. See entry on Walsh in *DNB*; Walsh, *A Prospect*, p. C.3.Sig. 1^r.

49. Richard Cox, *Hibernia Anglicana: or, The History of Ireland from the Conquest thereof by the English, To this Present Time*, 2 vols (London, 1689–90), 1, p. 6.

50. On the 'British Problem' in the early modern period, see Jane E. Dawson, 'Two kingdoms or three?: Ireland in Anglo-Scottish relations in the middle of the sixteenth century', in R. Mason (ed.), *Scotland and England, 1286–1815* (Edinburgh: John Donald, 1987), pp. 113–38; Steven G. Ellis, '"Not mere English": The British Perspective, 1400–1650', *History Today* 38, 12 (1988), pp. 41–8; Conrad Russell, 'The British Problem and the English Civil War', *History* 72 (1987), pp. 395–415; 'The British Background'; Steven G. Ellis and Sarah Barber (eds), *Conquest and Union: Fashioning a British State, 1485–1725* (London: Longman, 1995).

51. Lawrence Stone, *The Causes of the English Revolution, 1529–1642* (London and New York: Routledge, 1984), p. 138.

CHAPTER 7: THE *VIEW* FROM SCOTLAND

* This paper was first delivered to the Irish Studies section of the European Society for the Study of English (ESSE) 3rd Conference, in Glasgow on 10 September 1995, and revised for the 'Text and Conquest' Seminar at the Folger Shakespeare Institute in Washington on 27 October 1995. I want to thank participants at both events for their invaluable comments, but particularly Chris Morash and Hiram Morgan who invited me to speak on those illustrious occasions.

1. See, for example, Willy Maley, 'Rebels and Redshanks: Milton and the British Problem', *Irish Studies Review* 6 (1994), pp. 7–11; '"This Sceptred Isle": Shakespeare and the British Problem', forthcoming in John Joughin (ed.), *Shakespeare and National Culture* (Manchester: Manchester University Press); '"Another Britain?": Bacon's *Certain Considerations Touching the Plantation in Ireland* (1606)', *Prose Studies* 18, 1 (1995), pp. 1–18.

2. On the 'British Problem' see Jonathan Clark, 'English History's Forgotten Context: Scotland, Ireland, Wales', *The Historical Journal* 32 (1989), pp. 211–28; Conrad Russell, 'The British Problem and the English Civil War', *History* 72, 236 (1987), pp. 395–415; 'The British Background to the Irish Rebellion of 1641', *Historical Research*, 61, 145 (1988), pp. 166–82.

3. For an article that takes issue with the incorporation of Ireland into the 'British Problem', see Nicholas Canny, 'The Attempted Anglicisation of Ireland in the Seventeenth Century: An Exemplar of "British History"', in Ronald G. Asch (ed.), *Three Nations – A Common History England, Scotland, Ireland and British History, c.1600–1920* (Bochum: Universitäts verlag Dr N. Brockmeyer, 1993), pp. 49–82. For another view, see Steven G. Ellis, '"Not Mere English": The British Perspective, 1400–1650', *History Today* 38, 12 (1988), pp. 41–8.

4. David Stevenson, 'The Century of the Three Kingdoms', in *Scotland Revisited*, ed. Jenny Wormald (London: Collins & Brown, 1991), pp. 107–18. For an incisive treatment of an earlier period, see Jane E. Dawson, 'Two Kingdoms or Three?: Ireland in Anglo-Scottish Relations in the Middle of the Sixteenth Century', in *Scotland and England, 1286–1815*, ed. Roy Mason (John Donald, 1987), pp. 113–38.

5. I have charted the post-publication reception of the *View* in 'How Milton and Some Contemporaries Read Spenser's *View*', in *Representing Ireland: Literature and the Origins of Conflict, 1534–1660*, eds Brendan Bradshaw, Andrew Hadfield and Willy Maley (Cambridge: Cambridge University Press), pp. 191–208. All references to the *View*, given by page numbers in the text, are to the first published edition, Edmund Spenser, *A View of the State of Ireland* in *Two Histories of Ireland*, ed. James Ware (Dublin, 1633).

6. For instances of the genre, see John Arden, 'Rug-Headed Irish Kerns and British Poets', *New Statesman* (July 13, 1979), pp. 56–7, and, on the other side, as it were, Helen Watanabe-O'Kelly, 'Edmund Spenser and Ireland: A Defence', *Poetry Nation Review* 6 (1980), pp. 16–19.

7. On 'Anglo-Irish', 'Old English', and 'New English', and the interminable problem of terminology, see Toby Barnard, 'Planters and Policies in Cromwellian Ireland', *Past and Present* 61 (1973), n. 10; Karl Bottigheimer, 'Kingdom and Colony: Ireland in the Westward Enterprise, 1536–1660', in K. R. Andrews, N. P. Canny and P. E. Hair (eds), *The Westward Enterprise: English Activities in Ireland, the Atlantic and America, 1480–1650* (Liverpool: Liverpool University Press, 1978), p. 64; Ciarán Brady, 'Spenser's Irish crisis: humanism and experience in the 1590s', *Past and Present* 111 (1986), n. 21; 'Spenser's Irish Crisis: Reply to Canny', *Past and Present* 120 (1988), p. 212; Nicholas Canny, 'The Formation of the Old English Elite in Ireland', *18th O'Donnell Lecture* (Dublin, 1975), p. 2; 'Protestants, Planters and Apartheid in Early Modern Ireland', *IHS* 25, 98 (1986), p. 115; '"Spenser's Irish Crisis": A Comment', *Past and Present* 120 (1988), n. 9; Joseph Leerssen, *Mere Irish & Fíor-Ghael: Studies in the idea of Irish nationality, its development and literary expression prior to the nineteenth century* (Amsterdam and Philadelphia: Benjamens, 1986), n. 11, 12; and Colm Lennon, 'Richard Stanyhurst (1547–1618) and Old English Identity', *Irish Historical Studies* 21 (1978), pp. 121–43.

8. Roy Foster, 'Varieties of Irishness', in *Modern Ireland, 1600–1972* (Allen Lane: The Penguin Press, 1988), pp. 3–14. For a recent intervention that seeks to reinscribe Scotland within an Anglo-Irish framework, see W. J. McCormack's critique of the absence of Scotland from *The Field Day Anthology* in *From Burke to Beckett: ascendancy, tradition and betrayal in literary history* (Cork: Cork University Press, 1994), p. 445.

9. On this episode see Richard McCabe, 'The Masks of Duessa: Spenser, Mary Queen of Scots, and James VI', *English Literary Review* 17, 2 (1987), pp. 224–42; Donald V. Stump, 'The Two Deaths of Mary Stuart: Historical Allegory in Spenser's Book of Justice', *Spenser Studies* 9 (1988), pp. 81–105. John Hales wrote: 'How keenly these references were appreciated appears from the anxiety of the Scotch King to have the poet prosecuted for his picture of Duessa, in whom Mary Queen of Scots was generally recognised.' See John W. Hales, 'Edmund Spenser', in R. Morris (ed.), *The Works of Edmund Spenser: The Globe Edition* (London: Macmillan, 1910), p. lii. See also Michael O'Connell, 'Mary, Queen of Scots', in A. C. Hamilton (gen. ed.), *The Spenser Encyclopedia* (London and Toronto: Routledge, 1990), p. 458: 'After Queen Elizabeth, Mary Stuart is arguably the historical personage who bears most significance in *The Faerie Queene*.' Annabel Patterson describes the trial of Duessa as 'an episode central to the definition of Justice'. See Annabel Patterson, 'The Egalitarian Giant: Representations of Justice in History/Literature', in *Reading Between the Lines* (London: Routledge, 1993), p. 89.

Spenser had once before in print represented the Stuarts, in the fable of the Fox and the Kid in *The Shepheardes Calender*, where he depicted Esmé Stuart's success in Scotland. See Paul E. McLane, 'James VI in the *Shepheardes Calender*', *Huntington Library Quarterly* 16 (1953), pp. 273–85, and 'Aubigny and King James as Fox and Kid', in *A Study in Elizabethan Allegory* (Notre Dame, Indiana: Notre Dame University Press, 1961), pp. 77–91. Some of Spenser's most important patrons and intellectual influences had stood against Mary Queen of Scots. George Buchanan supported her execution and, as Richard McCabe reminds us, 'Grey had served as one of the Commissioners of the trial, and regarded Mary's execution as essential to the preservation of the Protestant state.' See Richard A. McCabe, 'The Fate of Irena: Spenser and Political Violence', in Patricia Coughlan (ed.), *Spenser and Ireland: An Interdisciplinary Perspective* (Cork: Cork University Press, 1989), p. 115. Probably the most incisive and theoretically sophisticated analysis of the role of Mary Stuart in Book V is that of Linda Gregerson, in *The Reformation of the Subject: Spenser, Milton and the English Protestant Epic* (Cambridge: Cambridge University Press, 1995), pp. 104–6.

10. On the arguments surrounding the alleged suppression of the *View* see David J. Baker, '"Some Quirk, Some Subtle Evasion": Legal Subversion in Spenser's *A View of the Present State of Ireland*', *Spenser Studies* 6 (1986), pp. 147–63; Jean Brink, 'Constructing the *View of the Present State of Ireland*', *Spenser Studies* 11 (1992), pp. 203–28; Andrew Hadfield, 'Was Spenser's *View of the Present State of Ireland* Censored? A Review of the Evidence', *Notes and Queries* 240, 4 (1994), pp. 459–63; Christopher Highley, 'Spenser's *View of Ireland*: Authorship, Censorship, and Publication', paper presented at 'Spenser at Kalamazoo' in 1994. I am grateful to the author for providing me with a typescript of this article.

11. See James Vink, 'Spenser's "Easterland" as the Columban Church of ancient Ireland', *Éire-Ireland* 25, 3 (1990), p. 105. According to Vink: 'Ireland's "Redshank" Picts formed a single cultural unit with the Scots in South Scotland, and the Picts in Northumberland, in the sixth century' (p. 102).

12. Irenius, having dispensed with the Irish claim to Spanish provenance, comments: 'But the *Irish* doe herein no otherwise, then our vaine *Englishemen* doe in the Tale of *Brutus*, whom they devise to have first conquered and inhabited this Land, it being as impossible to proove, that there was ever any such *Brutus* of *England*, as it is, that there was any such *Gathelus* of *Spaine*' (p. 27). It is true, as Patricia Coughlan points out, that Spenser is not unique in claiming that the Irish are of Scythian descent, but Spenser is unique in meshing this with a nascent Scottishness and linking it to the contemporary threat from Scotland. See Patricia Coughlan, '"Some secret scourge which shall by her come unto England": Ireland and Incivility in Spenser', in Patricia Coughlan (ed.), *Spenser and Ireland: An Interdisciplinary Perspective* (Cork: Cork University Press, 1989), p. 63.

13. Richard Stanyhurst, 'The Description of Ireland', in Raphael Holinshed (ed.), *The Chronicles of England, Scotland, Ireland and Wales* (London, 1586) vol. 2, p. 52.

14. John Major, *Historia Majoris Britanniae tam Angliae quam Scotiae* (Paris, 1921), ed. and trans. Archibald Constable, *John Major's History of Greater Britain*, Scottish History Society, 1st ser., no. 10 (Edinburgh, 1892).

15. Willy Maley, 'Britannia Major: Writing and Unionist Identity', in Tracey Hill and William Hughes (eds), *Contemporary Writing and National Identity* (Bath College of Higher Education: Sulis Press, 1995), pp. 46–53.

16. On the Tyrone Rebellion, see Nicholas Canny, 'Hugh O'Neill, Earl of Tyrone, and the Changing Face of Gaelic Ulster', *Studia Hibernica* 10

(1970), pp. 7–35. For the broader context and implications, see Hiram Morgan, 'The End of Gaelic Ulster: a thematic interpretation of events between 1534 and 1610', *Irish Historical Studies* 26, 101 (1988), pp. 8–32. Richard McCabe is in no doubt that Spenser's determination to bring Ulster under control is the crux of the strategic section of the *View*: 'In effect what he recommends is the siege of the province', while G. A. Hayes-McCoy noted that 'the North was the part of Ireland which the English knew the least'. See Richard A. McCabe, 'The Fate of Irena: Spenser and Political Violence', in Coughlan (ed.), *Spenser and Ireland*, p. 117; G. A. Hayes-McCoy, Introduction to *Ulster and other Irish maps c. 1600* (Dublin: Irish Manuscripts Commission, 1964), cited in John Breen, 'The Empirical Eye: Edmund Spenser's *A View of the Present State of Ireland*', *The Irish Review* (1995), p. 50. Sir William Herbert, one of the principal undertakers in the Munster plantation, had spoken at the beginning of the 1590s of 'foreign aggression and evils which proceed from elsewhere, namely the ravages, furies and arms of the Scots', and hoped that in the future 'the province of Ulster will be most like the province of the North of England'. See Arthur Keaveney and John A. Madden (eds), *Sir William Herbert: Croftus Sive de Hibernia Liber* (Dublin: Irish Manuscripts Commission, 1992), pp. 93, 95.

17. Jenny Wormald, 'The Creation of Britain: Multiple Kingdoms or Core and Colonies?', *Transactions of the Royal Historical Society* 6, 2 (1992), p. 185.

18. Steve Bruce, 'The Ulster Connection', in Graham Walker and Tom Gallagher (eds), *Sermons and Battle Hymns: Protestant Popular Culture in Modern Scotland* (Edinburgh: Edinburgh University Press, 1990), pp. 231–55, esp. pp. 231–2. For an intriguing analysis of the Ulster Rising in the context of the 'British Problem', see Michael Perceval-Maxwell, 'Ulster 1641 in the Context of Political Developments in the Three Kingdoms', in *Ulster 1641: Aspects of the Rising*, ed. Brian Mac Cuarta (Belfast: Institute of Irish Studies, The Queen's University of Belfast, 1993), pp. 93–106.

19. Alasdair Gray, *Why Scots Should Rule Scotland* (Edinburgh: Canongate, 1992), p. 30.

20. Maley, '"Another Britain?": Bacon's *Certain Considerations Touching the Plantation in Ireland* (1606)'.

21. I heard Sabina Sharkey give a paper at Warwick entitled 'Ireland: A Border Perspective' in September 1995, in which she drew attention to the function of the border as constitutive of sectarianism.

22. Bob Purdie, 'The Lessons of Ireland for the SNP', in Tom Gallagher (ed.), *Nationalism in the Nineties* (Edinburgh: Polygon, 1991), p. 66; pp. 72–3.

23. On the anti-European bias of the so-called 'Atlantic Archipelago', see Keith G. Robbins, *Insular Outsider? 'British History' and European Integration: The Stenton Lecture 1989* (Reading: University of Reading, 1990).

24. Ciarán Brady, 'The Road to the *View*: On the Decline of Reform Thought in Tudor Ireland', in Coughlan (ed.), *Spenser and Ireland*, p. 42. Anne Fogarty is one of the few literary critics to touch on the appearance of Scotland in the *View*, noting that Eudoxus 'expresses amazement at

Irenius's cross-comparisons of Ireland and Scotland'. See Anne Fogarty, 'The Colonization of Language: Narrative Strategy in *A View of the Present State of Ireland* and *The Faerie Queene*, Book VI', in Coughlan (ed.), *Spenser and Ireland*, p. 80. It is more than a 'cross-comparison'. Their overlapping and cross-checking within a general theory of the anachronistic interaction of antiquity and contemporaneity draw a more complex figure. The fact that Eudoxus is surprised should alert us to the fact that something crucial is happening in the discourse at this juncture. Paradoxically, despite Eudoxus's alarm and Irenius's subsequent elaboration and emphasis, critics of Spenser have remained, on the whole, impervious to Scotland. Even Andrew Hadfield, in an excellent article on origin-myths in the *View*, plays down the Scottish connection: See 'Briton and Scythian: Tudor representations of Irish origins', *Irish Historical Studies* 28, 112 (1993), pp. 390–408. Of course, in this essay I am playing down the 'British' dimension, or playing it up, depending upon one's perspective.

25. David J. Baker, '"Some Quirk, Some Subtle Evasion": Legal Subversion in Spenser's *A View of the Present State of Ireland*', *Spenser Studies* 6 (1986), p. 151.

26. David J. Baker, '"Some Quirk, Some Subtle Evasion": Legal Subversion in Spenser's *A View of the Present State of Ireland*', *Spenser Studies* 6 (1986), p. 162.

27. Brendan Bradshaw, 'Robe and sword in the conquest of Ireland', in C. Cross, D. Loades and J. J. Scarisbrick (eds), *Law and Government under the Tudors: Essays presented to Sir Geoffrey Elton on his retirement* (Cambridge: Cambridge University Press, 1988), p. 153.

28. Ciarán Brady, 'Spenser's Irish Crisis: Humanism and Experience in the 1590s', *Past and Present* 111 (1986), p. 45.

29. Nicholas Canny, 'Edmund Spenser and the Development of an Anglo-Irish Identity', *The Yearbook of English Studies* 13 (1983), p. 11.

30. Clare Carroll, 'The construction of gender and the cultural and political Other in *The Faerie Queene* and *A View of the Present State of Ireland*: the critics, the context, and the case of Radigund', *Criticism* 32, 2 (1990), p. 176.

31. Frank F. Covington, 'Spenser's use of Irish history in the *Veue of the Present State of Ireland*', *University of Texas Bulletin* 2411 (1924), pp. 27–8. On the Scottish patriotic sentiment of this period see Diane Watt, 'Nationalism in Barbour's *Bruce*', *Parergon* n.s. 12, 1 (1994), pp. 89–107.

32. James Vink, 'Spenser's "Easterland" as the Columban Church of ancient Ireland', *Éire-Ireland* 25, 3 (1990), p. 104.

33. Vink, 'Spenser's "Easterland"', p. 105. In Buchanan's *Rerum Scoticarum Historia* he speaks of the three nations that impinged upon Ireland – the Britons, the Picts and the Scots. See F. F. Covington, 'Another view of Spenser's linguistics', *SP* 19, 2 (1922), p. 245.

34. R. B. Gottfried, 'Irish Geography in Spenser's *View*', *ELH* 6, 2 (1939), p. 120.

35. Rudolf Gottfried, 'Irish Geography in Spenser's *View*', *ELH* 6, 2 (1939), p. 119.

36. R. B. Gottfried, 'Irish Geography in Spenser's *View*', *ELH* 6, 2 (1939), p. 120.

37. See M. D. O'Sullivan, 'Barnabe Googe: Provost-Marshal of Connaught, 1582–1585', *JGAHS* 18, 1&2 (1938), p. 1. Helena Shire points out that: 'When Spenser set foot in Ireland only one-twentieth of that island was firmly under English rule and occupation.' See Helena Shire, *A Preface to Spenser* (London: Longman, 1978; 1981), p. 59.

38. Clare Carroll, 'The construction of gender and the cultural and political Other in *The Faerie Queene* and *A View of the Present State of Ireland*: the critics, the context, and the case of Radigund', *Criticism* 32, 2 (1990), p. 177.

39. Carroll, 'The construction of gender', p. 178.

40. F. F. Covington, 'Another view of Spenser's linguistics', *SP* 19, 2 (1922), p. 247. Frank Covington was right to upbraid Draper for failing to see that Spenser was making a joke, not simply a feeble one, but one borrowed from Stanyhurst.

41. Rudolf B. Gottfried, 'Spenser and Stanyhurst', *TLS* 35 (October 31, 1936), p. 887.

42. J. W. Draper, 'Spenser's linguistics in *The Present State of Ireland*', *Modern Philology* 17, 8 (1919), p. 116.

43. Draper, 'Spenser's linguistics', p. 118.

44. Frank F. Covington, 'Spenser's use of Irish history in the *Veue of the Present State of Ireland*', *University of Texas Bulletin* 2411 (1924), p. 12.

45. Covington, 'Spenser's use of Irish history', p. 14.

46. Covington, 'Spenser's use of Irish history', p. 14.

47. Covington, 'Spenser's use of Irish history', p. 16.

48. Covington, 'Spenser's use of Irish history', p. 21.

49. *Holinshed's Chronicles of England, Scotland, and Ireland* (London, 1807), I, p. 10. Cited in Draper, 'Spenser's linguistics', p. 128.

50. Roland M. Smith, 'Spenser, Holinshed, and the *Leabhar Gabhála*', 43, 4 (1944), p. 396.

51. Rudolf B. Gottfried, 'Spenser as an Historian in Prose', *Transactions of the Wisconsin Academy of Sciences, Arts and Letters* 30 (1937), p. 328.

52. Maria Edgeworth, *Castle Rackrent*, ed. George Watson (Oxford and New York: Oxford University Press, 1995), pp. 7–8.

53. Mary Parmenter, 'Spenser's "Twelve Eglogues Proportionable to the Twelve Monethes"', *ELH* 3 (1936), p. 205; Paul E. McLane, 'Aubigny and King James as Fox and Kid', in *Spenser's 'Shepheardes Calender'*, pp. 77–91. See also James E. Phillips, 'George Buchanan and the Sidney Circle', *Huntington Library Quarterly* 12 (1948), pp. 23–55.

54. Brady, 'Spenser's Irish crisis', p. 18.

55. *Cal. S. P. Scot.*, 12, pp. 288, 352–4.

56. *Cal. S. P. Scot.*, 12, 291, pp. 357–62.

57. McCabe, 'The Masks of Duessa', p. 242.

58. Graham Hough, 'Book V: Justice', in *A Preface to The Faerie Queene* (London: Duckworth, 1962; 1983), p. 198.

59. Hough, 'Book V: Justice', p. 199.

60. *Cal. S. P. Scot.*, 13, 126. 6, pp. 167–8.

61. David J. Baker, '"Some quirk, some subtle evasion": legal subversion in Spenser's *A View of the Present State of Ireland'*, *Spenser Studies* 6 (1986), p. 147; W. L. Renwick (ed.), *A View of the Present State of Ireland* (Oxford: Clarendon Press, 1970), p. vii. Many critics persist in seeing this edition as a 'reprint' of Renwick's 1934 Scholartis Press edition, but it is much less than that. It is an edition with modernized spelling that has lost a lot in the translation, specifically Spenser's delightful punning and verbal dexterity.

62. Jonathan Goldberg, 'Authorities', in *James I and the Politics of Literature: Jonson, Shakespeare, Donne, and Their Contemporaries* (Baltimore and London: The Johns Hopkins University Press, 1983), pp. 8–9.

63. Baker, '"Some quirk, some subtle evasion"', p. 154. See also Brian P. Levack, 'Law and ideology: the Civil Law and theories of Absolutism in Elizabethan and Jacobean England', in Heather Dubrow and Richard Strier (eds), *The Historical Renaissance: New Essays on Tudor and Stuart Literature and Culture* (Chicago and London: Chicago University Press, 1988), pp. 220–41; Hans S. Pawlisch, *Sir John Davies and the Conquest of Ireland: A Study in Legal Imperialism* (Cambridge: Cambridge University Press, 1985).

64. Steven G. Ellis, *Tudor Ireland: Crown, Community and the Conflict of Cultures, 1470–1603* (London: Longman, 1985), pp. 292, 314–20; David Norbrook, *Poetry and Politics in the English Renaissance* (London: Routledge, 1984), pp. 16, 173.

65. See Robert Dunlop, 'Sixteenth-century schemes for the plantation of Ulster', *SHR* 22, nos 85–7 (1924–5), pp. 51–60, 115–26, 199–212. See also D. G. White, 'The Tudor plantations in Ireland, pre-1571', (PhD thesis, University of Dublin, 1967), pp. 421–2.

66. J. Small (ed.), *The Image of Irelande, with A Discoverie of Woodkarne*, by John Derricke (London, 1581; Edinburgh, 1883), p. 89.

67. J. O'Donovan, 'Original letters in the Irish and Latin languages, by Shane O'Neill, Prince of Tyrone, and Proclamation of High Treason against him by Queen Elizabeth', *UJA* 5 (1857), p. 273.

68. Francis Bacon, 'Certain considerations touching the plantations in Ireland (1606)', in *Francis Bacon: Works*, 5 vols (London, 1778), I, p. 192.

69. See J. E. Phillips, 'George Buchanan and the Sidney Circle', *HLQ* 12, 25 (1948), p. 27. See also Ian D. MacFarlane, *Buchanan* (London: Duckworth, 1981).

70. Vink, 'Spenser's "Easterland"', p. 101.

71. Vink, 'Spenser's "Easterland"', pp. 101–2.

72. Vink, 'Spenser's "Easterland"', p. 103.

73. Cited in H. Wood (ed.), *The Chronicle of Ireland, 1584–1608, by J. Perrot* (Dublin: Irish Manuscripts Commission, 1933), p. 44.

74. Wood (ed.), *The Chronicle of Ireland*, p. 44.

75. Ellis, *Tudor Ireland*, pp. 230–1.

76. See Hales, 'Edmund Spenser', p. xxxii. Hales says this cannot be Edmund, but why not? We know that a James Spenser later served as Master for Musters in Munster, and that this Spenser addressed King James on 24 July 1610. See BL Royal Ms. 18A.19.275.

CHAPTER 8: SPENCERSHIP: A JUDICIAL REVIEW

1. Jean R. Brink, 'Constructing the *View of the Present State of Ireland*', *Spenser Studies* 11 (1994), pp. 203–28.
2. Nicholas Canny, 'Introduction: Spenser and the Reform of Ireland', in Patricia Coughlan (ed.), *Spenser and Ireland: An Interdisciplinary Perspective* (Cork: Cork University Press, 1989), p. 11. Brendan Bradshaw writes: 'Offered for publication in 1596 – but, significantly, declined a licence.' See Bradshaw, 'Robe and sword in the conquest of Ireland', in C. Cross, D. Loades and J. J. Scarisbrick (eds), *Law and Government under the Tudors: Essays presented to Sir Geoffrey Elton on his retirement* (Cambridge: Cambridge University Press, 1988), p. 154. Ciarán Brady contends that 'Spenser's work, on being submitted to the Master Stationer in 1598, was refused registration and blacked by the government. Apparently it was even then, as it has been since, a source of some embarrassment.' See Brady, 'Spenser's Irish Crisis: Humanism and Experience in the 1590s', *Past and Present* 111 (1986), p. 25. Critics have been pontificating about the *View* for centuries, and without the hint of a blush. The incitement to discourse has fought shy of embarrassment.
3. Ciarán Brady, 'The road to the *View*: on the decline of reform thought in Tudor Ireland', in Coughlan (ed.), *Spenser and Ireland*, p. 41.
4. John M. Breen, 'Imagining voices in *A View of the Present State of Ireland*: a discussion of recent studies concerning Edmund Spenser's dialogue', *Connotations* 4, 1–2 (1994/95), p. 119.
5. Jonathan Goldberg, 'Authorities', in *James I and the Politics of Literature: Jonson, Shakespeare, Donne, and Their Contemporaries* (Baltimore and London: The Johns Hopkins University Press, 1983), pp. 8–9.
6. Goldberg, 'Authorities', p. 9.
7. Elizabeth Porges Watson, 'Spenser's life and times', in *Spenser: Selected Writings* (London: Routledge, 1992), p. 16. Donald Bruce also claims that the *View* was suppressed because Irenius espoused the opinions on Ireland chiefly of Lord Grey, discredited in 1582. See Bruce, 'Spenser's Irenius and the nature of dialogue', *N&Q* n.s. 39, 3 (1992), p. 357.
8. Brady, 'The Road to the *View*', pp. 41–2.
9. Tracey Hill, 'Humanism and homicide: Spenser's *A View of the Present State of Ireland*', *Irish Studies Review* 4 (1993), p. 4.
10. Thomas Healy, 'Civilisation and its discontents: the case of Edmund Spenser', in *New Latitudes: Theory and English Renaissance Literature* (London: Edward Arnold, 1992), p. 101.
11. Kenneth Gross, 'Mythmaking in Hibernia (*A View of the Present State of Ireland*)', in *Spenserian Poetics: Idolatry, Iconoclasm, and Magic* (Ithaca: Cornell University Press, 1985), p. 81.
12. Gross, 'Mythmaking in Hibernia', p. 85. Incidentally, Gross, citing Renwick, gives the wrong date for the entry of the *View* in the Stationers' Register – 20 January 1596 is of course the date at which Books IV–VI of *The Faerie Queene* were entered (Gross, 'Mythmaking in Hibernia',

p. 85, n. 5). It was of course another two years before the alleged suppression of the *View*.

13. Constantia Maxwell, 'Edmund Spenser: The poet in exile (1580–1598)', in *The Stranger in Ireland: From the Reign of Elizabeth to the Great Famine* (London, 1954), p. 31. Some contemporaries believed that the text had been published at the time of writing. Nicholas Canny refers to a mid-seventeenth century text that recommends Spenser's *View*. Canny quotes from the paper *Perfect Diurnall* 150, June 1652, p. 1928: 'he that desire to advance the plantation of Ireland can hardly find better hints than are in Mr. Ed. Spenser his *View of the State of Ireland*, published almost three score years ago, 1596'. Cited in Nicholas Canny, 'Edmund Spenser and the Development of an Anglo-Irish Identity', *The Yearbook of English Studies* 13 (1983), p. 18. On Ware and Irish antiquarianism, see M. Herity, 'Rathmullach, Ware and MacFirbisigh', *UJA* 33 (1970), pp. 49–53. See also Margaret MacCurtain, 'The Roots of Irish Nationalism', in Robert O'Driscoll (ed.), *The Celtic Consciousness* (Edinburgh: Canongate, 1982), pp. 379–80.

14. Brady, 'The Road to the *View*', p. 43.)

15. Raymond Jenkins, 'Spenser: the uncertain years 1584–1589', *PMLA* 53 (1938), p. 362.

16. David J. Baker, '"Some Quirk, Some Subtle Evasion": Legal Subversion in Spenser's *A View of the Present State of Ireland*', *Spenser Studies* 6 (1986), p. 147.

17. Baker, '"Some Quirk, Some Subtle Evasion"', p. 149.

18. Brink, 'Constructing the *View*', p. 203. Subsequent references to Brink's essay will be given by page number in the text.

19. See David Lee Miller, 'Authorship, anonymity, and *The Shepheardes Calender*', *MLQ* 40, 3 (1979), pp. 219–36.

20. See 'Dialogue between Peregryne and Sylvanus, c.1598', *State Papers, Ireland*, 63/203/119, ff. 283–357 (London: Public Record Office); Willy Maley (ed.), anon., *The Supplication of the blood of the English, most lamentably murdred in Ireland, Cryeng out of the Yearth for Revenge (1598)*, introduced and transcribed, *Analecta Hibernica* 36 (1994), pp. 3–91.

21. R. B. Gottfried, 'Spenser's *View* and Essex', *PMLA* 52, 3 (1937), p. 647.

22. R. B. Gottfried, 'Spenser's *View* and Essex', *PMLA* 52, 3 (1937), p. 646.

23. Gottfried, 'Spenser's *View* and Essex', p. 646.

24. On this episode see Richard McCabe, 'The Masks of Duessa: Spenser, Mary Queen of Scots, and James VI', *English Literary Review* 17, 2 (1987), pp. 224–42; Donald S. Stump, 'The two deaths of Mary Stuart: Historical Allegory in Spenser's Book of Justice', *Spenser Studies* 9 (1988), pp. 81–105. See also Michael O'Connell, 'Mary, Queen of Scots', in A. C. Hamilton (gen. ed.), *The Spenser Encyclopedia* (London and Toronto: Routledge, 1990), p. 458: 'After Queen Elizabeth, Mary Stuart is arguably the historical personage who bears most significance in *The Faerie Queene*.' Annabel Patterson describes the trial of Duessa as 'an episode central to the definition of Justice'. See Annabel Patterson, 'The Egalitarian Giant: Representations of Justice in History/Literature', in *Reading Between the Lines* (London: Routledge, 1993), p. 89. Spenser had once before in print represented the Stuarts, in the fable of the Fox and

the Kid in *The Shepheardes Calender*, where he depicted Esmé Stuart's success in Scotland. See Paul E. McLane, 'James VI in the *Shepheardes Calender*', *Huntington Library Quarterly* 16 (1953), pp. 273–85. Although in a letter to Leicester James had written 'how fonde and inconstant I were if I shulde preferre my mother to the title', the sacrifice of Queen for King that he made would have been jeopardized by a poet still harping on mothers when the son was banking on a British kingdom. Cited in Goldberg, *James I and the Politics of Literature*, p. 245, n. 15. James looked on Elizabeth as a surrogate mother, calling her 'madame and mother', and referring to himself 'as zour [sic] natural sone [sic] and conpatriot' (Goldberg, *James I and the Politics of Literature*, p. 245, n. 16). Anthony Riley argues that, since the *View* is more arse-kicking than arse-licking, Marx must have had *The Faerie Queene* in mind when he called Spenser Elizabeth's arse-kissing poet: 'Since Spenser's *Vewe* challenges, rather more than apologizes for, official policy, Marx might better be referring to *The Faerie Queene*, which is dedicated to Elizabeth in hope of her patronage.' See Riley, 'Marx & Spenser', in Hamilton (gen. ed.), *The Spenser Encyclopedia*, p. 457. Yet it was ironically *The Faerie Queene* that first felt the ire of a monarch, albeit a future one from an English perspective.

25. Goldberg, 'Authorities', p. 1.
26. See Roland M. Smith, 'Irish names in *The Faerie Queene*', *MLN* 61, 1 (1946), pp. 30–1.
27. Annabel Patterson, 'The Egalitarian Giant: Representations of Justice in History/Literature', in *Reading Between the Lines* (London: Routledge, 1993), p. 113.
28. John W. Hales, 'Edmund Spenser', in R. Morris (ed.), *The Works of Edmund Spenser: The Globe Edition* (London: Macmillan, 1910), p. li.
29. Hales, 'Edmund Spenser', p. lii.
30. R. Morris (ed.), *The Works of Edmund Spenser: The Globe Edition* (London: Macmillan, 1910), p. iii. The author of a late seventeenth-century discourse, *The Present State of Ireland* (1673), complains that there has been no tract under that heading 'since his Majesties happy Restauration', pointing out that:

> this our age affords many Treatises entituled The Present State of England, France, Italy, Holland, Venice, Muscovy, &c. yet not anything of that Nature hath been hitherto presented to publick view in relation to the State of Ireland, though it be one of the chiefest members of the British Empire; as if either there was no such thing in Nature; Or at least that the Affairs thereof afforded not anything worthy of Note. (p. A^2)

31. Andrew Hadfield, 'Was Spenser's *View of the Present State of Ireland* censored? A review of the evidence', *Notes & Queries* n.s. 41, 4 (1994), p. 460. Andrew Hadfield develops the arguments in this essay in a piece entitled, 'Certainties and uncertainties: by way of response to Jean Brink', forthcoming in *Spenser Studies* 12, pp. 197–202. I am grateful to Dr Hadfield for providing me with a copy of this text at the proof stage.

32. Hadfield, 'Was Spenser's *View of the Present State of Ireland* censored?', p. 460. D. B. Quinn writes: 'It is significant that Ware, in publishing *Vewe* for the first time in 1633 (the abortive attempt to have it published in 1598 was hopeless from the start as no English official would sanction it) was able to say that many of his recommendations had been implemented in some form or another; but nevertheless he deleted some 50 items as objectionable to men of all groups in Ireland in his time.' See Quinn, '*A Vewe of the Present State of Ireland*', in Hamilton (gen. ed.), *The Spenser Encyclopedia*, p. 714. But what is left untouched? Critics have been more concerned with what the *View* does not say than what it says, and more preoccupied with unpublished manuscripts and elusive copy-texts than with the published version. The real act of censorship has taken the form of a refusal to read.

33. Hadfield, 'Was Spenser's *View of the Present State of Ireland* censored?', p. 460, n. 10.

34. Brady, 'Spenser's Irish Crisis', pp. 25–6.

35. Patricia Coughlan, '"Cheap and common animals": the English anatomy of Ireland in the seventeenth century', in Thomas Healy and Jonathan Sawday (eds), *Literature and the English Civil War* (Cambridge: Cambridge University Press, 1990), p. 208.

36. Hadfield, 'Was Spenser's *View of the Present State of Ireland* censored?', p. 460.

37. Hadfield, 'Was Spenser's *View of the Present State of Ireland* censored?', p. 461.

38. Hadfield, 'Was Spenser's *View of the Present State of Ireland* censored?', p. 462.

39. Hadfield, 'Was Spenser's *View of the Present State of Ireland* censored?', p. 462.

40. Judith H. Anderson, 'The Antiquities of Fairyland and Ireland', *JEGP* 86, 2 (1987), p. 202.

41. Anne Fogarty, 'The colonization of language: narrative strategy in *A View of the Present State of Ireland* and *The Faerie Queene*, Book VI', in Coughlan (ed.), *Spenser and Ireland*, p. 79.

42. Coughlan, '"Cheap and common animals"', p. 208.

43. Jacques Derrida, *The Truth in Painting*, trans. Geoff Bennington and Ian McLeod (Chicago: Chicago University Press, 1987), pp. 326–7.

44. Hadfield, 'Was Spenser's *View of the Present State of Ireland* censored?', p. 463. See Richard Beacon, *Solon his follie* (Oxford, 1594), 'Dedication', p. 4: 'all nations shall rightly honour you with the ladies of Rome, which sometimes offered their jewels to be solde for the furtherance of public services; for huge be the charges already imployed by your Majestie, for bringing to passe so great things tending to the sound and universall reformation of this your Realme of Ireland, as in the acte of subsidie more at large may appeare'.

45. W. B. Yeats, 'The Cutting of an Agate: Edmund Spenser', in *Essays and Introductions* (London: Macmillan, 1961), p. 363.

46. See Katherine Wilson, *Incomplete Fictions: The Formation of English Renaissance Dialogue* (Washington, DC: Catholic University Press, 1985). Linda Gregerson contends one of the 'inoculatory strategies' of

Protestant epic 'announces the poem's artificial status and disrupts the illusion of wholeness'. See Linda Gregerson, *The Reformation of the Subject: Spenser, Milton, and the English Protestant epic* (Cambridge: Cambridge University Press, 1995), pp. 3–4.

47. Breen, 'Imagining Voices in *A View of the Present State of Ireland*', p. 126.
48. Richard A. McCabe, 'The fate of Irena: Spenser and political violence', in Patricia Coughlan (ed.), *Spenser and Ireland: An Interdisciplinary Perspective* (Cork: Cork University Press, 1989), p. 109.
49. McCabe, 'The fate of Irena', p. 109. McCabe insists that he seeks 'neither to condemn nor exonerate Spenser's political philosophy but to examine the complex process whereby the blunt recommendations of the prose were transformed into the idealised vision of the poem, the process whereby political violence became a moral imperative within a fundamentally providential world-view' (p. 110). I must confess I find the prose no less sharp than the poetry, cloudily enwrapped as the latter is, and that I find the poetry more violent if anything than the prose. *The Faerie Queene* is a corpse-strewn epic. To oppose or juxtapose 'the blunt recommendations of the prose' with 'the idealised vision of the poem' is, despite protestations to the contrary, both to condemn and exonerate.
50. See Michel Foucault, 'Preface' to Gilles Deleuze and Félix Guattari, *Anti-Oedipus: Capitalism and Schizophrenia*, trans. Robert Hurley, Mark Seem and Helen R. Lane (London: The Athlone Press, 1984), p. xiii.
51. Fogarty, 'The colonization of language', p. 86. In the Argument to Book I of *Paradise Lost* Milton echoes Spenser's poetic dictum from the 'Letter to Raleigh' – 'a Poet thrusteth into the middest' – when he says 'the Poem hasts into the midst of things'.
52. Anne Fogarty, 'The Colonization of Language: Narrative Strategy in *A View of the Present State of Ireland* and *The Faerie Queene*, Book VI', in Coughlan (ed.), *Spenser and Ireland*, pp. 86–7.
53. Andrew Hadfield, 'Spenser, Ireland, and sixteenth-century political theory', *Modern Language Review* 9, 1 (1994), p. 2.
54. Helena Shire, *A Preface to Spenser* (London: Longman, 1978; 1981), p. 60.
55. Gross, 'Mythmaking in Hibernia', pp. 80–1.
56. Nicholas Canny, 'Ireland, the historical context', in A. C. Hamilton (gen. ed.), *The Spenser Encyclopedia* (London and Toronto: Routledge, 1990), p. 405.
57. Andrew Hadfield, '"Who knowes not Colin Clout?" The permanent exile of Edmund Spenser', in *Literature, Politics and National Identity: Reformation to Renaissance* (Cambridge: Cambridge University Press, 1994), p. 201.
58. Roland Smith, 'Review of *Variorum* edition of the View', *JEGP* 49, 3 (1950), p. 405.
59. Roland Smith, 'Review of *Variorum* edition of the View', *JEGP* 49, 3 (1950), p. 416.
60. Canny, 'Introduction: Spenser and Reform in Ireland', p. 11.

61. Nicholas Canny, 'Introduction: Spenser and Reform in Ireland', in Patricia Coughlan (ed.), *Spenser and Ireland: An Interdisciplinary Perspective* (Cork: Cork University Press, 1989), pp. 11–12.
62. Willy Maley, *A Spenser Chronology* (London: Macmillan, 1994), pp. 80–1.
63. Rudolf B. Gottfried, 'The debt of Fynes Moryson to Spenser's *View*', *Philological Quarterly* 17, 3 (1938), p. 298.
64. Rudolf B. Gottfried, 'The debt of Fynes Moryson to Spenser's *View*', *Philological Quarterly* 17, 3 (1938), p. 307.
65. Stephen Booth, *The Book Called Holinshed's Chronicles* (San Francisco: The Book Club of California, 1968), p. 72, cited in Annabel Patterson, 'Censorship and the 1587 "Holinshed's" Chronicles', in Paul Hyland and Neil Sammells (eds), *Writing and Censorship in Britain* (London and New York: Routledge, 1992), p. 23. Speaking of Holinshed, one text that does not figure in discussions of the *View*, including Brink's, is Richard Stanyhurst's contribution to the *Chronicles*, the 'Description of Ireland'. Yet this must be a central text in any discussion of Spenser and censorship of the *View*, since it was read by Spenser and since it was subject to state intervention. See my 'Spenser's *View* and Stanyhurst's *Description*', forthcoming in *N&Q* (June, 1996).
66. I am thinking for example of a recent exchange between John Arden and Conor Cruise O'Brien which foregrounds some of the problems implicit in approaches to 'Spenser and Ireland' that are neither theoretically informed nor historically grounded. The exchange exposed the degree of cultural investment in canonical authors in terms of oppositional discourses, as an aside on Spenser elicited a yelp of protest from an ardent Spenserian. See John Arden, 'Rug-Headed Irish Kerns and British Poets', *New Statesman* (13 July 1979), pp. 56–7; Conor Cruise O'Brien, 'Shakespeare: not guilty', *New Statesman* (27 July 1979), p. 130; John Arden, 'Shakespeare guilty', *New Statesman* (10 August 1979), p. 199; Helen Watanabe-O'Kelly, 'Edmund Spenser and Ireland: a defence', *Poetry Nation Review* 6 (1980), pp. 16–19. The whole debate, if it deserves that term, is very much caught up in the language of 'guilt' and 'defence'.
67. Maley, *A Spenser Chronology*, p. 75.
68. John T. Gilbert, *History of the Irish Confederation, and The War in Ireland, 1641–1643* (Dublin: M. H. Gill, 1882), p. xiii.
69. Cited in John T. Gilbert, *History of the Irish Confederation, and The War in Ireland, 1641–1643* (Dublin: M. H. Gill, 1882), p. xiv.
70. See J. C., 'Biographical Sketches of Persons Remarkable in Local History', *JCHAS* 3, 29 (1894), p. 97.
71. J. C., 'Biographical Sketches of Persons Remarkable in Local History', *JCHAS* 3, 29 (1894), p. 99.
72. Nicholas Canny and Andrew Carpenter (eds), 'The early planters: Spenser and his contemporaries', in Seamus Deane (ed.), *The Field Day Anthology of Irish Writing* (Derry: Field Day, 1991), I, p. 171.
73. Ray Heffner, 'Spenser's *View of Ireland*: some observations', *Modern Language Quarterly* 3, 4 (1942), p. 510.
74. Heffner, 'Spenser's *View of Ireland*', pp. 510–11.

75. Roland M. Smith, 'More Irish words in Spenser', *MLN* 59, 7 (1944), p. 477.
76. Roland M. Smith, 'Spenser's scholarly script and "right writing"', in D. C. Allen, *Studies in Honor of T. W. Baldwin* (Urbana, Illinois: University of Illinois Press, 1958), pp. 96–7. Brink's case is not based upon a linguistic analysis, or comparative study, such as that of Smith.
77. Christopher Highley warns of the dangers of premature exoneration in 'Spenser's *View of Ireland*: Authorship, Censorship, and Publication', a paper presented at Kalamazoo in 1994. I am grateful to the author for providing me with a typescript of this article. Of course, the converse of an act of oblivion issuing as a result of doubt being cast on Spenser's authorship of the *View* is that Spenser remains the solitary scapegoat for English and British activities in Ireland. I find neither option particularly desirable.
78. Ciarán Brady, '*A Brief Note of Ireland*', in A. C. Hamilton (gen. ed.), *The Spenser Encyclopedia* (London and Toronto: Routledge, 1990), p. 111.
79. Brady, '*A Brief Note of Ireland*', p. 111.
80. Brady, '*A Brief Note of Ireland*', p. 112.
81. Ray Heffner, 'Review of Renwick's 1934 edition of the *View*', *Modern Language Notes* 52, 1 (1937), p. 58.
82. For example, Paul Gaston writes: 'His castle was razed, his fields spoiled, his unpublished manuscripts burned.' See Paul L. Gaston, 'Spenser's order, Spenser's Ireland: Competing fantasies', in Jan Hokenson and H. D. Pearce, *Forms of the Fantastic* (New York: Greenwood, 1986), p. 123.
83. The original grant issued on 26 October 1590 reads: 'To hold for ever, in fee farm, by the name of "Hap Hazard" by fealty, in common socage.' Cited in J. G. White, *Historical and Topographical Notes, etc., on Buttevant, Castletown Roche, Doneraile, Mallow, And Places in their Vicinity*, 5 vols (1905–16), III *Cork* (1913), p. 264.

Select Bibliography:
Spenser and Ireland

MANUSCRIPTS

'Dialogue between Peregryne and Sylvanus, c.1598', *State Papers, Ireland*, 63/203/119, ff. 283–357, London: Public Record Office.

THESES

Baker, David J. (1992), '"Who Talks of my Nation?": Colonialist Representation in Shakespeare and Spenser', unpublished PhD thesis, Johns Hopkins University.

Baumgartner, Virginia (1972), 'Irish Elements in Spenser's *Faerie Queene*', Columbia University, New York, unpublished PhD thesis.

Cooper, L. T. (1913), 'Spenser's Veue of the Present State of Ireland: An Introduction with Notes on the first 55 pages in Grosart's Edition', Cornell University, unpublished MA thesis.

Covington, F. F. (1924), 'Spenser in Ireland', Yale University, unpublished PhD thesis.

Gottfried, R. B. (1935), 'A Vewe of the Presente State of Ireland', Yale University, unpublished PhD thesis.

Hadfield, Andrew (1988), 'The English Conception of Ireland c.1540–c.1600, with special reference to the Works of Edmund Spenser', New University of Ulster at Coleraine, unpublished PhD thesis.

Highley, Christopher (1992), 'Shakespeare, Spenser, and Elizabethan Ireland', unpublished PhD thesis, Stanford University.

McGuire, James K. (1958), 'Spenser's *View of Ireland* and Sixteenth Century Gaelic Civilization', Fordham University, unpublished PhD thesis.

McLean, George E. (1986), 'Spenser's Territorial History: Book V of *The Faerie Queene* and *A View of the Present State of Ireland*', The University of Arizona, unpublished PhD thesis.

Magill, Andrew J. (1967), 'Spenser and Ireland: A Synthesis and Revaluation of Twentieth Century Scholarship', University of Texas at Austin, unpublished PhD thesis.

Maley, Willy (1989), 'Edmund Spenser and Cultural Identity in Early Modern Ireland', University of Cambridge, unpublished PhD thesis.

Martin, William C. (1925), 'Edmund Spenser, *A View of the Present State of Ireland*; An Annotated Edition', Cornell University, unpublished PhD thesis.

Michie, Sara (1935), 'Celtic Myth and Spenserian Romance', University of Virginia, unpublished PhD thesis.

Pailet, Leonard Marvin (1983), 'Schemes and Tropes as Organizational Devices in Sixteenth and Seventeenth Century English Literature: Edmund Spenser, Fulke Greville, and Thomas Nashe', unpublished PhD thesis, Ann Arbor, Michigan.

EDITIONS OF *A VIEW OF THE PRESENT STATE OF IRELAND*

Spenser, Edmund (1633), *A View of the State of Ireland*, in James Ware, ed., *Two Histories of Ireland*, Dublin, pp. 1–127.
—— (1763), *A View of the State of Ireland as it was in the reign of Queen Elizabeth. Written by way of a Dialogue between Eudoxus and Ireneus: To which is prefix'd the Author's Life, and an Index added to the Work*, Dublin.
—— (1809), *A View of the Present State of Ireland*, in *Ancient Irish Histories*, ed. James Ware. 2 vols, Dublin, 1, pp. 1–266.
—— (1869; 1910), *A View of the Present State of Ireland*, ed. R. Morris, in *The Works of Edmund Spenser: The Globe Edition*, Macmillan: London, pp. 609–83.
—— (1890), *A View of the Present State of Ireland*, in H. Morley, ed., *Ireland under Elizabeth and James I, described by Edmund Spenser, by Sir John Davies ... and by Fynes Moryson*, London.
—— (1934), *A View of the Present State of Ireland*, ed. W. L. Renwick, London: Scholartis Press. Reissued 1970, with modernized spelling, Oxford: Clarendon Press.
—— (1949), *A View of the Present State of Ireland*, ed. R. B. Gottfried, *Variorum* edition, Baltimore: Johns Hopkins University Press.

SECONDARY WORKS

Anderson, Judith H. (1987), 'The Antiquities of Fairyland and Ireland', *Journal of English and Germanic Philology*, 86, pp. 199–214.
Anon., 'Pedigree of the Poet Spencer's Family' (1906), *Journal of the Cork Historical and Archaeological Society* 12, facing page 197.
Arden, J. (1979), 'Rug-Headed Irish Kerns and British Poets', *New Statesman* (July 13), pp. 56–7.
Avery, Bruce (1990), 'Mapping the Irish Other: Spenser's *A View of the Present State of Ireland*', *ELH* 57, 2, pp. 263–79.
Baker, David J. (1986), '"Some Quirk, Some Subtle Evasion": Legal Subversion in Spenser's *A View of the Present State of Ireland*', *Spenser Studies* 6, pp. 147–63.
—— (1993), 'Off the map: charting uncertainty in Renaissance Ireland', in Bradshaw *et al* (eds), *Representing Ireland*, pp. 76–92.
Bennett, Josephine Waters (1937), 'Did Spenser Starve?', *Modern Language Notes* 52, 6, pp. 400–1.
Bradshaw, Brendan (1987), 'Edmund Spenser on Justice and Mercy', *Historical Studies* 16, pp. 76–89.
—— (1988), 'Robe and Sword in the Conquest of Ireland', in *Law and Government under the Tudors: Essays presented to Sir Geoffrey Elton on his*

retirement, eds C. Cross, D. Loades and J. J. Scarisbrick, Cambridge: Cambridge University Press, pp. 139–62.

Brady, Ciarán (1986), 'Spenser's Irish Crisis: Humanism and Experience in the 1590s', *Past and Present* 111, pp. 17–49.

—— (1988), 'Spenser's Irish Crisis: Reply to Canny', *Past and Present* 120, pp. 210–15.

—— (1989), 'The Road to the View: On the Decline of Reform Thought in Tudor Ireland', in *Spenser and Ireland: An Interdisciplinary Perspective*, ed. Patricia Coughlan, Cork: Cork University Press, pp. 25–45.

—— (1990), '*A Brief Note of Ireland*', in A. C. Hamilton (ed.), *The Spenser Encyclopedia*, pp. 111–12.

—— (1990), 'Grey, Arthur, fourteenth Baron of Wilton (1536–93)', in A. C. Hamilton (ed.), *The Spenser Encyclopedia*, pp. 341–2.

Breen, John (1994–5), 'Imagining Voices in *A View of the Present State of Ireland*: A Discussion of Recent Studies Concerning Edmund Spenser's Dialogue', *Connotations* 4, 1–2, pp. 119–32.

—— (1995), 'The Influence of Edmund Spenser's *View* on Fynes Moryson's *Itinerary*', *Notes and Queries* 42, 3, pp. 363–4.

—— (1995), 'The Empirical Eye: Edmund Spenser's *A View of the Present State of Ireland*', *Irish Review* 16 (1994), pp. 44–52.

Brink, Jean (1992), 'Constructing the *View of the Present State of Ireland*', *Spenser Studies* 11, pp. 203–28.

—— (1994), 'Documenting Edmund Spenser: A new life study', *American Notes and Queries* n.s. 7 (October), pp. 201–8.

Bruce, Donald (1992), 'Spenser's Irenius and the nature of Dialogue', *N&Q* 39 [237], 3, pp. 355–7.

—— (1995), 'Edmund Spenser and the Irish War', *Contemporary Review* 266, pp. 129–38.

Buck, P. M. (1904), 'New Facts Concerning the Life of Edmund Spenser', *Modern Language Notes*, 19, pp. 237–8.

Canny, Nicholas P. (1983), 'Edmund Spenser and the Development of an Anglo-Irish Identity', *The Yearbook of English Studies: Colonial and Imperial Themes*, 13, pp. 1–19.

—— (1987) 'Identity Formation in Ireland: The Emergence of the Anglo-Irish', in *Colonial Identity in the Atlantic World, 1500–1800*, eds Nicholas Canny and A. Pagden. Princeton, New Jersey: Princeton University Press, pp. 159–212.

—— (1988), '"Spenser's Irish Crisis": A Comment', *Past and Present* 120, pp. 201–9.

—— (1989), 'Introduction: Spenser and the Reform of Ireland', in *Spenser and Ireland: An Interdisciplinary Perspective*, ed. Patricia Coughlan, Cork: Cork University Press, pp. 9–24.

—— (1990), 'Ireland, the historical context', in A. C. Hamilton (ed.), *The Spenser Encyclopedia*, pp. 404–7.

—— and Andrew Carpenter (eds) (1991), 'The Early Planters: Spenser and his Contemporaries', in Seamus Deane (ed.), *The Field Day Anthology of Irish Writing*, 3 vols, Derry: Field Day Publications, pp. 171–234.

—— (forthcoming), 'Poetry as Politics: A View of the Present State of *The Faerie Queene*', in Hiram Morgan (ed.), *Text and Conquest*.

Carey, Vincent P. (1994), 'Collaborator *and* Survivor?: Gerald the eleventh Earl of Kildare and Tudor Ireland', *History Ireland* 2, 2, pp. 13–17.

Carpenter, F. I. (1922), 'Desiderata in the Study of Spenser', *Studies in Philology* 19, 2, pp. 238–43.

—— (1922), 'Spenser in Ireland', *Modern Philology* 19, pp. 405–19.

—— (1923), *A Reference Guide to Edmund Spenser*, Chicago: Chicago University Press.

Carroll, Clare (1990), 'The Construction of Gender and the Cultural and Political Other in *The Faerie Queene* 5 and *A View of the Present State of Ireland*: The Critics, the Context, and the Case of Radigund', *Criticism* 32, 2, pp. 163–91.

Cavanagh, Sheila T. (1986), '"Such Was Irena's Countenance": Ireland in Spenser's Prose and Poetry', *Texas Studies in Language and Literature* 28, pp. 24–50.

—— (1993), '"The fatal destiny of that land": Elizabethan views of Ireland', in Bradshaw *et al* (eds), *Representing Ireland*, pp. 116–31.

—— (1994), '"That Savage Land": Ireland in Spenser's Legend of Justice', in David Lee Miller and Alexander Dunlop (eds), *Approaches to Teaching Spenser's 'Faerie Queene'*, New York: Modern Language Association, pp. 143–52.

Chaudhuri, Supriya (1990), 'Grill', in A. C. Hamilton (ed.), *The Spenser Encyclopedia*, p. 342.

Coleman, J. (1894), 'Biographical Sketches of Persons Remarkable in Local History: X. Edmund Spenser', *JCHAS* 3, 29, pp. 89–100.

—— (1895), 'The Poet Spenser's Wife', *JCHAS*, 2nd ser., 1 (1895), pp. 131–3.

—— (1908), 'Memorials of Edmund Spenser, the Poet, and his Descendants in the County Cork, from the Public Records of Ireland', *JCHAS* 4, 78, pp. 39–43.

Coughlan, Patricia (1989), '"Some Secret Scourge which shall by her come unto England": Ireland and Incivility in Spenser', in *Spenser and Ireland: An Interdisciplinary Perspective*, ed. Patricia Coughlan, Cork: Cork University Press, pp. 46–74.

—— (1990), '"Cheap and common animals": the English anatomy of Ireland in the seventeenth century', in Thomas Healy and Jonathan Sawday (eds), *Literature and the English Civil War*, Cambridge: Cambridge University Press, pp. 205–23.

Covington, F. F. (1921), 'Elizabethan Notions of Ireland', *Texas Review* 6 (1921), pp. 222–46.

—— (1922), 'Another View of Spenser's Linguistics', *Studies in Philology* 19, pp. 244–8.

—— (1924), 'Spenser's Use of Irish History in the *Veue of the Present State of Ireland*', *University of Texas Bulletin*, 2411: *Studies in English* 4 (1924), pp. 5–38.

Crino, Anna M. (1968), 'La Relazione Barducci-Ubaldini Sull'Impresa D'Irlanda (1579–1581)', *English Miscellany* 19, pp. 339–67. I am grateful to Dr Warren Boutcher for translating parts of this essay.

Crowley, Seamus (1985), 'Some of Spenser's Doneraile Neighbours', *The North Cork Writers Journal* 1, pp. 71–5.

Day, John T. (1990), 'dialogue, prose', in A. C. Hamilton (ed.), *The Spenser Encyclopedia*, p. 217.

Draper, J. W. (1919), 'Spenser's Linguistics in *The Present State of Ireland*', *Modern Philology* 17, pp. 111–26.

—— (1926), 'More Light on Spenser's Linguistics', *Modern Language Notes*, 41, pp. 127–8.

Falkiner, C. Litton (1909), 'Spenser in Ireland', in *Essays Relating to Ireland: Biographical, Historical, and Topographical*, London, pp. 3–31.

Fogarty, Anne (1989), 'The Colonization of Language: Narrative Strategies in *A View of the Present State of Ireland* and *The Faerie Queene*, Book VI', in *Spenser and Ireland: An Interdisciplinary Perspective*, ed. Patricia Coughlan, Cork: Cork University Press, pp. 75–108.

Fogarty, Anne (1995), in Timothy P. Foley, Lionel Pilkington, Sean Ryder and Elizabeth Tilley (eds), *Gender and Colonialism*, Galway: Galway University Press, pp. 23–34.

Fowler, Alastair (1989), 'Spenser and war', in *War, Literature and the Arts in Sixteenth-Century Europe*, eds J. R. Mulryne and M. Shewing, Basingstoke: Macmillan, pp. 147–64.

Fowler, Elizabeth (1995), 'The Failure of Moral Philosophy in the Work of Edmund Spenser', *Representations* 51, pp. 47–76.

Fukuda, Shohachi (1990), 'Bregog, Mulla', in A. C. Hamilton (ed.), *The Spenser Encyclopedia*, p. 110.

Fumerton, Patricia (1986), 'Exchanging Gifts: The Elizabethan Currency of Children and Poetry', *ELH* 53, pp. 241–78.

Gaston, Paul L. (1986), 'Spenser's Order, Spenser's Ireland: Competing Fantasies', in Jan Hokenson and Howard D. Pearce (eds), *Forms of the Fantastic*, New York: Greenwood, pp. 121–7.

Gold, Eva (1993), 'Spenser the Borderer: Boundary, Property, Identity in *A View of the Present State of Ireland* and Book 6 of *The Faerie Queene*', *Journal of the Rocky Mountain Medieval and Renaissance Association* 14, pp. 98–113.

Gottfried, R. B. (1936), 'Spenser's Ireland Dialogue', *Times Literary Supplement* 35 (8 February), p. 116.

—— (1936), 'Spenser and Stanyhurst', *Times Literary Supplement*, 35 (31 October), p. 887.

—— (1937), 'The Date of Spenser's *View*', *Modern Language Notes* 52, pp. 176–80.

—— (1937), 'Spenser as an Historian in Prose', *Transactions of the Wisconsin Academy of Sciences, Arts, and Letters* 30, pp. 317–29.

—— 'Spenser's View and Essex', *PMLA*, 52, pp. 645–51.

—— (1938), 'The Debt of Fynes Moryson to Spenser's View', *Philological Quarterly* 17, pp. 297–307.

—— (1939), 'Irish Geography in Spenser's View', *English Literary History* 6, pp. 114–137.

—— (1943), 'The Early Development of the Section on Ireland in Camden's Britannia', *English Literary History*, 10, pp. 17–30.

—— (1949), (ed.) *The Works of Edmund Spenser: A Variorum Edition*, 11 vols (1932–49), Baltimore: Johns Hopkins University Press, 9, *The Prose Works*.

Graham, Rigby (1975), *Edmund Spenser's Kilcolman*, Leicester: Brewhouse Private Press.

Gray, M. M. (1930), 'The Influence of Spenser's Irish Experiences on *The Faerie Queene*', *Review of English Studies* 6, pp. 413–28.

Greenblatt, Stephen J. (1980), 'To Fashion a Gentleman: Spenser and the Destruction of the Bower of Bliss', in *Renaissance Self-Fashioning: From More to Shakespeare*, Chicago: Chicago University Press, pp. 157–92.

Greenlaw, E. A. (1912), 'Spenser and British Imperialism', *Modern Philology* 9, pp. 1–24.

—— (1930), 'Review of Pauline Henley, *Spenser in Ireland*', *Modern Language Notes* 45, pp. 320–3.

Grennan, Eamonn (1982), 'Language and Politics: A Note on Some Metaphors in Spenser's *A View of the Present State of Ireland*', *Spenser Studies* 3, pp. 99–110.

Gross, Kenneth (1985), 'Mythmaking in Hibernia (*A View of the Present State of Ireland*)', in *Spenserian Poetics: Idolatry, Iconoclasm, and Magic*, Ithaca and London: Cornell University Press, pp. 78–109.

Hadfield, Andrew (1988a), 'The Spectre of Positivism?: Sixteenth-Century Irish Historiography', *Text and Context* 3, pp. 10–16.

—— (1988b), 'Spenser's *A View of the Present State of Ireland*: Some Notes Towards a Materialist Analysis of Discourse', in *Anglo-Irish and Irish Literature: Aspects of Language and Culture*, 2 vols, eds B. Bramsback and M. Croghan, Stockholm: Uppsala, 2, pp. 265–72.

—— (1993a), 'English Colonialism and National Identity in Early Modern Ireland', *Éire-Ireland* 27, 1, pp. 69–86.

—— (1993b), 'The Course of Justice: Spenser, Ireland and Political Discourse', *Studia Neophilologica* 65, pp. 187–96.

—— (1993c), 'Briton and Scythian: Tudor representations of Irish origins', *Irish Historical Studies* 28, 112, pp. 390–408.

—— (1994a), 'Spenser, Ireland, and Sixteenth-Century Political Theory', *The Modern Language Review* 89, 1, pp. 1–18.

—— (1994b), 'Was Spenser's *View of the Present State of Ireland* Censored? A Review of the Evidence', *Notes and Queries* 240, 4, pp. 459–63.

—— (1994c), '"Who knowes not Colin Clout?": The permanent exile of Edmund Spenser', in *Literature, Politics and National Identity: Reformation to Renaissance*, Cambridge: Cambridge University Press, pp. 170–201.

—— (1994/95), 'Who is Speaking in Spenser's *A View of the Present State of Ireland*? A Response to John Breen', *Connotations* 4.1–2 (1994/95), pp. 119–32.

—— (1996a), 'The "sacred hunger of ambitious minds": Spenser's savage religion', in Donna B. Hamilton and Richard Strier (eds), *Religion, Literature, and Politics in Post-Reformation England, 1540–1688*, Cambridge: Cambridge University Press, pp. 27–45.

—— (1996b), 'The Trials of Jove: Spenser's Irish Allegory and the Mastery of the Irish', *Bullán* 4 (1996), pp. 1–15.

—— (forthcoming), 'Certainties and uncertainties: by way of response to Jean Brink', *Spenser Studies* 12, pp. 197–202. I am grateful to Dr Hadfield for providing me with a copy of this text at the proof stage.

—— (ed.) (forthcoming), 'Introduction', *Edmund Spenser: A Critical Reader*, London: Longman, 1996, pp. 1–22.

—— (forthcoming), 'From English to British Literature: John Lyly's *Euphues* and Edmund Spenser's *The Faerie Queene*', in Brendan Bradshaw and Peter Roberts (eds), *British Identity and British Consciousness in the Making of the United Kingdom, 1533–1707*, Cambridge: Cambridge University Press.

Hales, John W. (1910), 'Edmund Spenser', in R. Morris (ed.), *The Works of Edmund Spenser: The Globe Edition*, London: Macmillan, pp. xi–lv.

Healy, Thomas (1992), 'Civilisation and Its Discontents: The Case of Edmund Spenser', in *New Latitudes: Theory and English Renaissance Literature*, London: Edward Arnold, pp. 84–109.

Heffner, Ray (1931), 'Spenser's Acquisition of Kilcolman', *Modern Language Notes* 46, pp. 493–98.

—— (1936), 'Essex and Book Five of *The Faerie Queene*', *ELH*, 3, pp. 67–82.

—— (1937), 'Review of W. L. Renwick's edition of *A View of the Present State of Ireland* (London, 1934)', *Modern Language Notes* 52, 1, pp. 57–8.

—— (1942), 'Spenser's *View of Ireland*: Some Observations', *Modern Language Quarterly* 3, pp. 507–15.

Henley, Pauline (1928), *Spenser in Ireland*, Cork: Cork University Press.

—— (1936), 'Spenser's "Stony Aubrian"', *Times Literary Supplement* 35 (28 November), p. 996.

Highley, Christopher (1994), 'Spenser's *View of Ireland*: Authorship, Censorship, and Publication', paper presented at Kalamazoo. I am grateful to the author for providing me with a typescript of this article.

—— (forthcoming), 'Spenser and the Bards', *Spenser Studies*. I am grateful to the author for providing me with a typescript of this article.

Hill, Tracey (1993), 'Humanism and Homicide: Spenser's *A View of the Present State of Ireland*', *Irish Studies Review* 4, pp. 2–4.

Hinton, Edward M. (1935), 'Edmund Spenser', in *Ireland Through Tudor Eyes*, Philadelphia: University of Pennsylvania Press, pp. 43–6.

Hough, Graham (1983), 'Book V: Justice', *A Preface to 'The Faerie Queene'*, London: Duckworth, pp. 191–200.

Hulbert, Viola B. (1937), 'Spenser's Relation to Certain Documents on Ireland', *Modern Philology* 34 (1937), pp. 345–53.

Hull, Vernam (1941), 'Edmund Spenser's Mona-Shul', *PMLA* 56, pp. 578–9.

Jardine, Lisa (1993), 'Encountering Ireland: Gabriel Harvey, Edmund Spenser and English colonial ventures', in Bradshaw *et al* (eds), *Representing Ireland*, Cambridge: Cambridge University Press, pp. 60–75.

Jenkins, Raymond (1932), 'Spenser and the Clerkship in Munster', *PMLA* 47, pp. 109–21.

—— (1932), 'Spenser's Hand', *TLS* 31 (7 January), p. 12.

—— (1933), 'Spenser at Smerwick', *TLS* 32 (11 May), p. 331.

—— (1935), '*Newes out of Munster*, a document in Spenser's hand', *Studies in Philology* 32, pp. 125–30.

—— (1937), 'Spenser with Lord Grey in Ireland', *PMLA* 52 (1937), pp. 338–53.

—— (1938), 'Spenser: The Uncertain Years 1584–1589', *PMLA* 53, pp. 350–62.

—— (1952), 'Spenser and Ireland', in *That Soveraine Light: Essays in Honor of Edmund Spenser 1552–1952*, eds W. R. Meuller and D. C. Allen, Baltimore: Johns Hopkins University Press, pp. 51–62.

Johnson, D. Newman (1990), 'Kilcolman Castle', in A. C. Hamilton (ed.), *The Spenser Encyclopedia*, pp. 417–22.

Jones, Ann Rosalind and Peter Stallybrass (1992), 'Dismantling Irena: the sexualising of Ireland in early modern England', in Andrew Parker *et al* (eds), *Nationalisms and Sexualities*, London: Routledge, pp. 157–71.

Jones, H. S. V. (1919), 'Spenser's Defense of Lord Grey', *University of Illinois Studies in Language and Literature* 5, pp. 7–75.
—— (1930), 'A View of the Present State Of Ireland', in *A Spenser Handbook*, New York: Cornell University Press, pp. 377–87.
Jones, W. (1901), 'Doneraile and Vicinity', *JCHAS* 7, pp. 238–42.
Joyce, P. W. (1878), 'Spenser's Irish rivers', *Fraser's Magazine* 97, pp. 315–33.
—— (1911), 'Spenser's Irish Rivers', in *The Wonders of Ireland*, Dublin, pp. 72–114.
Judson, Alexander C. (1933), *Spenser in Southern Ireland*, Bloomington, Indiana: Indiana University Press.
—— (1944), 'Two Spenser Leases', *Modern Language Quarterly* 50, pp. 143–7.
—— (1945), *The Works of Edmund Spenser: A Variorum Edition*, 11 vols, Baltimore, 1932–49, 11, *The Life of Edmund Spenser*.
—— (1947), 'Spenser and the Munster Officials', *Studies in Philology* 44, pp. 157–73.
Keach, William (1990), 'Arlo Hill', in A. C. Hamilton (ed.), *The Spenser Encyclopedia*, p. 60.
Keightley, Thomas (1869), 'Irish Rivers Named in *The Faerie Queene*', *Notes and Queries* 4 (28 August), pp. 169–70.
Klein, Bernhard (1995), '"And quickly make that, which was nothing at all": English National Identity and the Mapping of Ireland', in *Nationalismus und Subjektivität, Mitteilungen Beiheft* 2, Johann Wolfgang Goethe-Universität Zentrum zur Erforschung der Frühen Neuzeit: Frankfurt am Main, pp. 200–26.
Kliger, Samuel (1950), 'Spenser's Irish Tract and Tribal Democracy', *South Atlantic Quarterly* 49, pp. 490–7.
Koller, Kathleen (1934), 'Spenser and Raleigh', *English Literary History* 1 (1934), pp. 37–60.
Lewis, C. S. (1931), 'Spenser's Irish Experiences and *The Faerie Queene*', *Review of English Studies* 7, pp. 83–5.
Lupton, Julia (1990), 'Home-making in Ireland: Virgil's Eclogue I and Book VI of *The Faerie Queene*', *Spenser Studies* 8, pp. 119–45.
—— (1993), 'Mapping mutability: or, Spenser's Irish plot', in Bradshaw *et al* (eds), *Representing Ireland*, Cambridge: Cambridge University Press, pp. 93–115.
Lysaght, Sidney (1882), 'Kilcolman Castle', *The Antiquary* 5, pp. 153–6.
George MacBeth (1992), *The Testament of Spencer*, London: Andre Deutsch.
McCabe, Richard A. (1989), 'The Fate of Irena: Spenser and Political Violence', in *Spenser and Ireland: An Interdisciplinary Perspective*, ed. Patricia Coughlan, Cork: Cork University Press, pp. 109–25.
MacCurtain, Margaret (1982), 'The Roots of Irish Nationalism', in Robert O'Driscoll (ed.), *The Celtic Consciousness*, Edinburgh: Canongate, pp. 371–82.
McLane, Paul E. (1959), 'Was Spenser in Ireland in Early November 1579?', *Notes and Queries* 204, pp. 99–101.
Mac Lir, M. (1901), 'Spenser as High Sheriff of Cork County', *JCHAS* 7, pp. 249–50.
Maley, Willy (1991), 'Spenser and Ireland: A Select Bibliography', *Spenser Studies* 9, pp. 227–42.

—— (1992), 'Review of A. C. Hamilton, gen. ed., *The Spenser Encyclopedia*', *Textual Practice* 6, 3, pp. 543–9.

—— (1993), 'How Milton and some contemporaries read Spenser's *View*', in Bradshaw *et al* (eds). *Representing Ireland*, pp. 191–208.

—— (1994), *A Spenser Chronology*, London: Macmillan.

—— (1994), 'Rebels and Redshanks: Milton and the British Problem', *Irish Studies Review* 6, pp. 7–11.

—— (1994), 'Spenser's Irish English: Language and Identity in Early Modern Ireland', *Studies in Philology* 91, 4, pp. 417–31.

—— (1995), 'Review of Robert Welch, *The Kilcolman Notebook*, (Brandon Press: Dingle, Co. Kerry, 1994)', *Spenser Newsletter* 26, 1, pp. 20–1.

—— (1995), '"The Land of Ire": Frühe englische Darstellungen Irlands', in Anne Fuchs and Theo Harden (eds), *Reisen im Diskurs: Modelle der literarischen Fremderfahrung von den Pilgerberichten bis zur Postmoderne* (Heidelberg: Universitätsverlag C. Winter, 1995), pp. 393–403.

Manning, John (1988), 'Spenser and the long-haired Egyptians', *Notes and Queries* 35, pp. 40–1.

Marjarum, E. W. (1940), 'Wordsworth's View of the State of Ireland', *PMLA* 55, pp. 608–11.

Martin, William C. (1932), 'The Date and Purpose of Spenser's Veue', *PMLA* 47 (1932), pp. 137–43.

Maxwell, Constantia (1954), 'Edmund Spenser: The Poet in Exile (1580–1598)', in *The Stranger in Ireland: From the Reign of Elizabeth to the Great Famine*, London: Jonathan Cape, pp. 20–37.

Moore, Courtenay (1904), 'Spenser's Knowledge of the Neighbourhood of Mitchelstown', *JCHAS* 10, pp. 31–3.

—— (1913), 'The Bregoge', *JCHAS* 19, pp. 40–2.

Moore, Marianne (1981), 'Spenser's Ireland', in *The Complete Poems of Marianne Moore*, New York, pp. 112–13.

Morley, Henry (ed.) (1890), *Ireland under Elizabeth and James I, described by Edmund Spenser, by Sir John Davies ... and by Fynes Moryson*, London.

Morris, R. (ed.) (1910), *A View of the Present State of Ireland*, in *The Works of Edmund Spenser: The Globe Edition*, London: Macmillan, pp. 609–83.

Ní Chuilleanáin, Eiléan (1990), 'Ireland, the cultural context', in A. C. Hamilton (ed.), *The Spenser Encyclopedia*, pp. 403–4.

Norbrook, David (1984), '*The Faerie Queene* and Elizabethan Politics', in *Poetry and Politics in the English Renaissance*, London: Routledge, pp. 109–56.

O'Connell, Michael (1990), '*The Faerie Queene*, Book V', in A. C. Hamilton (ed.), *The Spenser Encyclopedia*, pp. 280–3.

O'Donovan, J. (ed.) (1858), 'Errors of Edmund Spenser: Irish Surnames', *Ulster Journal of Archaeology* 6, pp. 135–44.

Ong, Walter J. (1942), 'Spenser's View and the Tradition of the "Wild" Irish', *Modern Language Quarterly* 3, pp. 561–71.

O'Rahilly, T. A. (1916), 'Identification of the Hitherto Unknown River "Aubrian", of Spenser Fame', *JCHAS* 22, pp. 49–56.

Parkin-Speer, Diane (1992), 'Allegorical Legal Trials in Spenser's *The Faerie Queene*', *Sixteenth Century Journal* 23, 3, pp. 494–505.

Patterson, Annabel (1992), 'The Egalitarian Giant: Representations of Justice in History/Literature', *Journal of British Studies* 31, pp. 97–132.

——— (1993), 'The Egalitarian Giant: Representations of Justice in History/Literature', in *Reading between the lines*, London: Routledge, pp. 80–116.

Plomer, H. R. (1923), 'Edmund Spenser's Handwriting', *Modern Philology* 21, pp. 201–7.

Pollen, J. H. (1903), 'The Irish Expedition of 1579', *The Month* 101, pp. 69–85.

The Present State of Ireland Together with Some Remarks upon the Ancient State Thereof (1673), London.

Quinn, David Beers (1990), '*A vewe of the Present State of Ireland*', in A. C. Hamilton (ed.), *The Spenser Encyclopedia*, pp. 713–15.

Renwick, W. L. (1929), 'Spenser's Galathea and Naera', *TLS* 28 (14 March), pp. 206–7.

——— (ed.) (1934), *A View of the Present State of Ireland, by Edmund Spenser*, London: Scholartis Press.

——— (ed.) (1970), *A View of the Present State of Ireland, by Edmund Spenser*, Oxford: Clarendon Press.

Riley, Anthony W., and the editors (1990), 'Marx & Spenser', in A. C. Hamilton (ed.), *The Spenser Encyclopedia*, pp. 457–8.

Salces, Juan Emilio Tazón (1988), 'Some Ideas on Spenser and the Irish Question', *Revista Canaria de Estudios Ingleses* 16 (April), pp. 105–19.

Shepherd, Simon (1989), 'Politics', in *Spenser*, New York and London: Harvester Wheatsheaf, pp. 4–55.

Smith, Roland M. (1935), 'Spenser's Irish River Stories', *PMLA* 50, 4, pp. 1047–56.

——— (1935), 'Una and Duessa', *PMLA* 50, pp. 917–19.

——— (1942), 'Spenser's Tale of the Two Sons of Milesio', *Modern Language Quarterly* 3, pp. 547–57.

——— (1943), 'The Irish Background of Spenser's View', *Journal of English and Germanic Philology* 42, pp. 499–515.

——— (1944a), 'More Irish Words in Spenser', *Modern Language Notes* 59, pp. 472–7.

——— (1944b), 'Spenser, Holinshed, and the *Leabhar Gabhala*', *Journal of English and Germanic Philology* 43, pp. 390–401.

——— (1944c), 'Spenser's "Stony Aubrian"', *Modern Language Notes* 59, pp. 1–5.

——— (1946a), 'A further note on Una and Duessa', *PMLA* 61 (1946), pp. 592–6.

——— (1946b), 'Irish Names in The Faerie Queene', *Modern Language Notes* 61, pp. 27–38.

——— (1950), 'A Review of R. B. Gottfried's edition of *The Prose Works of Edmund Spenser* (Johns Hopkins University Press: Baltimore, 1949)', *Journal of English and Germanic Philology* 49, pp. 405–16.

——— (1955), 'Origines Arthurianae: The Two Crosses of Spenser's Red Cross Knight', *Journal of English and Germanic Philology* 54, pp. 670–83.

——— (1958), 'Spenser's Scholarly Script and "Right Writing"', in *Studies in Honor of T. W. Baldwin*, ed. D. C. Allen, Urbana, Illinois: University of Illinois Press, pp. 66–111.

'Spenser in Ireland: Review of Pauline Henley, *Spenser in Ireland* (Cork: Cork University Press, 1928)' (1928), *TLS* 27 (7 June), p. 422.

Steinberg, Clarence (1971), 'Atin, Pyrochles, Cymochles: On Irish Emblems in The Faerie Queene', *Neuphilologische Mitteilungen* 72, pp. 749–61.

—— (1989), 'Politics, Literature, and Colonization: A View of Ireland in the Sixteenth Century', in C. C. Barfoot and Theo D'haen (eds), *The Clash of Ireland: Literary Contrasts and Connections*, Amsterdam and Atlanta: Rodopi Press, pp. 23–36.

Vink, James (1990), 'Spenser's "Easterland" as the Columban Church of Ancient Ireland', *Éire-Ireland* 25, 3, pp. 96–106.

Watson, Elizabeth Porges (1992), 'Introduction', *Spenser: Selected Writings*, London: Routledge, pp. 1–30.

Watson, Sarah Ruth (1950), 'A note on Spenser's uses of the word "Lee"', *N&Q* 185, pp. 448–9.

Watanabe-O'Kelly, Helen (1980), 'Edmund Spenser and Ireland: A Defence', *Poetry Nation Review* 6, pp. 16–19.

Welch, Robert (1994), *The Kilcolman Notebook*, Dingle, Co. Kerry: Brandon Press.

Welply, W. H. (1933), 'Spenser in Ireland', *Times Literary Supplement* 32 (18 May), p. 348.

—— (1940), 'Edmund Spenser's Brother-in-law, John Travers', *Notes and Queries* 179, pp. 70–8, 92–7, 112–15.

West, Michael (1988), 'Spenser's Art of War: Chivalric Allegory, Military Technology, and the Elizabethan Mock-Heroic Sensibility', *Renaissance Quarterly* 41, 4, pp. 654–704.

Westerweel, Bart (1989), 'Astrophel and Ulster: Sidney's Ireland', in C. C. Barfoot and Theo D'haen (eds), *The Clash of Ireland: Literary Contrasts and Connections*, Amsterdam and Atlanta: Rodopi Press, pp. 5–22.

Wilson, F. P. (1926), 'Spenser and Ireland', *Review of English Studies* 2, 8, pp. 456–7.

Wright, Thomas E. (1990), 'Bryskett, Lodowick', in A. C. Hamilton (ed.), *The Spenser Encyclopedia*, London: Routledge, p. 119.

Yeats, W. B. (1961), 'The Cutting of an Agate: Edmund Spenser', in *Essays and Introductions*, London: Macmillan, pp. 356–83.

Index